A Therapist's Guide to Child Development

A Therapist's Guide to Child Development gives therapists and counselors the basics they need to understand their clients in the context of development and to explain that development to parents. The chapters take the reader through the various physical, social, and identity developments occurring at each age, explaining how each stage of development is closely linked to mental health and how that is revealed in therapy. This ideal guide for students, as well as early and experienced professionals, will also give readers the tools with which to communicate successfully with the child's guardians or teachers, including easy-to-read handouts that detail what kind of behaviors are not cause for concern and those behaviors that indicate it may be time to seek help. As an aid to practitioners, this book matches developmental ages with appropriate, evidence-based mental health interventions.

Dee C. Ray, PhD, is a distinguished teaching professor in the counseling program and director of the Child and Family Resource Clinic at the University of North Texas. She is the author of *Advanced Play Therapy* (Routledge, 2011), coauthor of *Group Play Therapy* (with Daniel Sweeney and Jennifer Baggerly, Routledge, 2014), and the editor of the *Journal of Child and Adolescent Counseling*.

A Therapist's Guide to Child Development

The Extraordinarily Normal Years

Edited by
Dee C. Ray

 Routledge
Taylor & Francis Group

NEW YORK AND LONDON

First published 2016
by Routledge
711 Third Avenue, New York, NY 10017

and by Routledge
2 Park Square, Milton Park, Abingdon, Oxon, OX14 4RN

Routledge is an imprint of the Taylor & Francis Group, an informa business

Library of Congress Cataloging-in-Publication Data
A therapist's guide to child development : the extraordinarily normal years / edited by Dee C. Ray.
pages cm
Includes bibliographical references and index.
1. Child psychology. 2. Child psychotherapy. 3. Child development.
I. Ray, Dee C.
BF721.T4554 2015
155.4—dc23
2015016520

ISBN: 978-1-138-82896-4 (hbk)
ISBN: 978-1-138-82897-1 (pbk)
ISBN: 978-1-315-73795-9 (ebk)

Typeset in Garamond MT & Futura BT
by Swales & Willis Ltd, Exeter, Devon, UK

This book is dedicated to the students and graduates of the
University of North Texas.
They inspire me to grow every day.

Contents

Contributors

Sinem Akay, PhD, is an adjunct professor at Sam Houston State University, and a professional counselor and intern supervisor at Children's Safe Harbor. She researches and writes in areas related to anxiety and maladaptive perfectionism, as well as publications related to promising treatment approaches for maladaptive perfectionism in children. Sinem also has a particular interest in working with children and teenagers with posttraumatic stress disorder (PTSD).

Jenifer W. Balch, PhD, is a senior lecturer in the counseling program at the University of North Texas. She is a licensed professional counselor-supervisor in the state of Texas and a registered play therapist-supervisor, with extensive experience of counseling children and families. She serves on the executive board of the North Texas Chapter of the Texas Association for Play Therapy, and has researched, published, and presented on various topics involving children. Jenifer has published research in the area of autism and play therapy.

Dalena L. Dillman Taylor, PhD, is an assistant professor at the University of Central Florida, and the coordinator for both clinical experiences and the play therapy certificate program. Her research interests include the effectiveness of Adlerian play therapy, child counseling in schools, and inclusion of the family in counseling children. Dalena has published in the areas of ethics, developmental practice, and play therapy with children.

Liz Ener, MA, PhD, is an adjunct professor at the University of North Texas, a licensed professional counselor in Texas, and a registered play therapist. She earned her Master's degree in professional counseling from Texas State University and her PhD in counseling from the University of North Texas, where she specialized in play therapy. Her primary interests include play therapy, clinical assessment, and bereavement. Liz has extensive clinical experience of working with children, adolescents, adults, families, and groups in a variety of settings, including community agencies and schools.

Kimberly M. Jayne, PhD, LPC, NCC, RPT, is an assistant professor of counselor education and the school counseling program coordinator at Portland State University. She has extensive experience of working with children, adolescents, and their families in both clinical and school settings. Kimberly actively researches developmentally responsive counseling interventions for children and adolescents, and has authored numerous articles and book chapters. She also provides counseling services through her own private practice and in collaboration with local public schools.

Kasie R. Lee, PhD, LPC, LMHC, NCC, RPT, is an assistant professor in the counseling program at Arkansas State University. She received her Master's degree in human development counseling from Vanderbilt University and her PhD in play therapy from the University of North Texas. Her dissertation, "Child-centered play therapy parent services: A Q-methodical investigation," was one of the first research studies to investigate the needs of parents in child-centered play therapy. Kasie is a registered play therapist and an active member of the Association for Play Therapy, and has published in the *International Journal of Play Therapy*. Her clinical and scholarly interests include play therapy with young children and caregivers, and the training and supervision of play therapists.

Emily Michero, MEd, is a licensed professional counselor-supervisor, and has more than a decade of clinical experience working with children and adolescents. She currently maintains a private practice in Fort Worth, Texas, specializing in play therapy and adolescent counseling. She has experience of child and adolescent clients in settings including inpatient hospitals, intensive outpatient clinics, schools, college clinics, and private practice. Emily is also a doctoral candidate at the University of North Texas, with research interests including ethics in counseling, interpersonal neurobiology and counseling, and the client–counselor relationship.

Deborah Ojiambo, PhD, NCC, is a lecturer in the Department of Mental Health, School of Psychology, at Makerere University. Her research interests include school counseling, counselor supervision, and play therapy, especially with children and adolescents traumatized by chronic armed conflict. She is a pioneer play therapist in Uganda, and is passionate about training child and family counselors to provide therapy to the large number of Ugandan children orphaned by war, disease, and other disasters. Deborah is a recipient of local and national research awards for her research with children.

Katie Purswell, PhD, LPC, NCC, RPT, is an assistant professor at the University of Scranton. In addition to her work as a child counselor, she has developed a graduate-level play therapy course, and authored manuscripts in the field of play therapy and play therapy supervision. Katie presents regularly at state and national counseling conferences.

Dee C. Ray, PhD, is a distinguished teaching professor in the counseling program and director of the Child and Family Resource Clinic at the University of North Texas. She is the author of *Advanced Play Therapy* (Routledge, 2011), coauthor of *Group Play Therapy* (with Daniel Sweeney and Jennifer Baggerly, Routledge, 2014), and the editor of the *Journal of Child and Adolescent Counseling*.

Julia E. Smith, MS, is a licensed professional counselor, psychotherapist, and adjunct professor at the University of North Texas, where she teaches undergraduate counseling students and provides clinical supervision for counselors in training. She is also presently a doctoral candidate researching trauma and interpersonal neurobiology. Julia has experience working with adolescents and adults in a variety of settings, including private practice, agencies, and university and community clinics. In addition to teaching and research, she currently maintains a private practice in Fort Worth, Texas, where she provides counseling for adolescents, adults, couples, and families. Her clinical specialties include eating disorders and addictions, interpersonal neurobiology, mind–body therapies, transpersonal counseling, and traumatic stress.

Hayley L. Stulmaker, PhD, is an assistant professor at Sam Houston State University. She researches, presents, and publishes in areas related to play therapy and understanding facilitative processes. In addition to her teaching and research responsibilities, she has worked in a variety of clinical settings, including community agencies, schools, and private practice. She continues to work with children, adolescents, and families within a private practice setting.

LaKaavia Taylor, MEd, is a doctoral student at the University of North Texas. Her research interest is play therapy, with a specific focus on African American children. LaKaavia has received advanced training and clinical experiences in individual and group play therapy. She has presented at numerous national and state conferences on a wide range of topics concerning effective child counseling and treatment practices. LaKaavia provides counseling services to children, adolescents, and adults at the Child and Family Resource Clinic (CFRC), where she is the assistant director of assessment services. In her position at the CFRC, LaKaavia provides supervision and training for doctoral students in the administration and interpretation of psychoeducational assessments.

Brittany J. Wilson, MA, University of North Texas; Child and Family Resource Clinic. Brittany Wilson is currently a doctoral candidate at the University of North Texas, where she specializes in play therapy and clinical supervision, working with children exhibiting disruptive behaviors. She currently serves as the assistant director of clinical services at a local counseling clinic, where she provides intensive weekly group and individual supervision to Master's level internship students and consultation to doctoral level counseling interns. Brittany has extensive clinical experience of working with children, adolescents, and adults.

Part I

1

An Overview of Child Development

Dee C. Ray

AN OVERVIEW OF CHILD DEVELOPMENT

In the world of mental health, most therapists would agree that each child is extraordinary; each child is unique; each child follows an individual path of meaning-making and interaction. Each child deserves to be regarded as an individual with his or her own ways of thinking and his or her own ways of being. Just as does any adult, a child will create and construct a personal reality from relationships, interactions, and events in his or her life. The child will then operate on the basis of this phenomenological perception. These views of children are primary to therapeutic work. In order to facilitate expression, growth, and change, a therapist must see the world through the individual child's eyes.

Yet the phenomenological world sits in the context of the real world. In this real world, children follow fairly typical stages of development. For more than 100 years, researchers have followed the maturational paths of children and concluded that they follow a predictable trajectory of cognitive, physical, and emotional development (NAEYC, 2009). Although there is no way to predict how each child will construct his or her personal reality, there is strong agreement that children will progress sequentially through developmental stages – and often at predictable time periods. If therapists seek to understand each child's world, they will benefit from understanding the world of children; in so doing, the therapist experiences the child as a unique individual traversing through expected chronological and naturally occurring changes. Each child is *extraordinarily normal.*

The Problem with "Normal"

> My son can't sit still. He's always moving. Is that normal?
> My daughter seems scared of everything. Is that normal?

"Is that normal?" I believe that this may be the question we are asked most frequently as therapists. Parents want to know that their children are progressing at a good pace, that they have a sense of belonging, and that they will ultimately be successful in adulthood. "Is that normal?" is the question used to evaluate a child's movement toward these goals. The therapist's answer to this question affects the parental view of the child: what the parent expects from the child and how the parent will respond to the child. "Is that normal?" is loaded with multiple meanings for parents, including "Will she be okay?," "Should I be worried?," "How will he fit in with others?," and "What should I be doing to ensure that she'll be normal?"

As therapists who are knowledgeable regarding the limitations of the word "normal," we will often shy away from answering this question. We would like to help the parent to see that each child is unique and worthy. Each child is growing at his or her own pace, on his or her own individualized path. We want parents to embrace their children as persons who do not strive to be normal, but strive to be fulfilled, contributory, and in relationships with others. As we continue to enlighten parents regarding the distinctive value of *not* being normal, we can also use research and a century of child development observations to help parents to understand the continuum of typical behavior for children at different ages. Therapists can guide parents to develop further understanding of their children in the context of chronological and developmental age. We can help parents to set reasonable expectations for their children and to avoid the pitfalls of rushing a child through childhood.

As therapists, we are also faced with the trials of the word "normal." Not only does Western culture emphasize the importance of being normal, but also the field of mental health goes to great lengths to identify and categorize what is "abnormal" or what qualifies as a disorder (APA, 2013). Therapists are charged as arbiters of normal, providing criteria, reports, and labels with which to distinguish the normal from the abnormal. If a therapist embraces this role within mental health, it is incumbent on the therapist to know and understand thoroughly what is normal among everyday children. Therapists' knowledge of normal is sometimes limited because they are encircled by children who are struggling. Therapists often make the mistake of labeling a child "abnormal" when the child responds to an abnormal event in a very developmentally appropriate way. In these cases, it is the event that is abnormal, not the child or the child's reaction. A therapist's knowledge of typically expected developmental stages safeguards children against being inappropriately labeled. Even the most normal of children, by virtue of being human, will encounter obstacles, challenges, and emotional struggles throughout childhood. The therapist's knowledge of development informs his or her choice and execution of intervention. And this knowledge is best gathered through literature on child development. Understanding the cognitive, physical, and emotional lives of children at various ages provides a roadmap for therapists to select appropriate and effective mental health interventions.

The Basic Principles of Development

Children develop best in an environment of physical and emotional safety It is commonly known that infants will suffer cognitively and physically if not given food, shelter, and at least minimal relational nurturing. Brain activity will be negatively affected and physical growth can often be inhibited by a lack of proper environment. Although this is widely accepted knowledge regarding infants, there is less awareness of the need for safety in young and middle childhood. Physical and emotional abuse or neglect slows the developmental process by focusing children on attaining what is needed for survival. If food is limited or physical safety is threatened, many children will rigidly hold to their current understanding of the world and will often fail to expand their ways of thinking or to take in new information. When children are emotionally unsafe when expressing new cognitive abilities, they will limit their expression and use of such abilities. If caretakers respond in harmful or negative ways to a child's initiative, that child's repeated experiences of failure will discourage his or her further attempts. However, when children are physically nurtured and emotionally safe, new information or experiences are seen as opportunities for interaction or exploration and will spur further growth.

Higher is not better   Although most developmental theories are presented as stage theories in which humans progress from one stage to the next, developmentalists stress the importance of not valuing later stages more than earlier stages. Each stage of development serves a purpose or concentrates on a necessary task – a purpose or task that is essential to meaning-making and self-construction. No one stage is better than another; they are all integral to development. A young child who appears opportunistic and reward-driven is becoming initiated into a world of rules within which there are consequences for actions. This is an essential experience, leading to an understanding of how the world works and, from that understanding, to finding a sense of self in that world.

Development cannot be rushed, but it can be slowed   Development is not a race. In current Western culture, we often applaud children who appear to display advanced development and advocate intervention for those who do not move as quickly (Ray, 2011). Children move at their own pace, when they are developmentally ready to do so. Although we know through observational research that we can estimate the ages at which children might reach certain stages, these estimates are crude and may not fit the experience of many children. Stage sequences are fairly predictable, but pace is not. If a child is not progressing at the rate of his or her peers, a therapist may look for barriers or, possibly, simply differences in personality. Children will meet interventions designed to force development with anxiety, self-doubt, and often overt resistance. Different developmental paths do not equal pathology. Burman (2008, p. 22) wrote: "The normal child, the ideal type, distilled from the comparative scores of age-graded populations, is therefore a fiction or myth. No individual or real child lies at its basis". Hence there is no one normal way in which to develop; rather, there is a long continuum, and most children fit at some point on the continuum, moving along it at an individualized pace.

Although development cannot be rushed, it can be slowed. As mentioned in relation to the need for physical and emotional safety, a child's development will be limited if he or she experiences certain events or environments. Trauma events are likely to slow development, to initiate regressed development, or in some cases to interrupt development altogether. Slower and regressed development is a developmentally appropriate response to trauma. It is typically the way in which children respond to trauma and it allows for recovery from, and integration of, new experiences. More problematic, however, is a child's withdrawal from interaction or exploration: This response is likely to result in the interruption of development entirely, limiting the child's ability to garner necessary support to work through the trauma experience. Loss – especially repeated loss – is also likely to slow development, because a child is spending internal resources on maintaining homeostasis and thus has little energy for growth experiences.

Development is not defined by skills   Natural development tends to be holistic, in that a child's mind and body move forward at relatively the same speed. As a child's body and physical ability grow, cognitive understanding becomes more abstract and emotional life becomes more complex. However, if a child is required and/or expected to accomplish tasks in a certain domain, it is possible that he or she will be able to develop the requisite skills. In current Western culture, children are exposed to developmentally inappropriate tasks before they are ready, such as academic or social tasks. For example, a 4-year-old may be required to write with an adult-like pencil grip or may be required to write specific words: requirements that are not appropriately matched to the typical 4-year-old. The 4-year-old may be able to hold the pencil or to write out certain words – but these are skills that should not be confused with the child's overall developmental age and readiness for other tasks. Moreover, while the child may successfully produce the desired outcome, the expectation that he or she will do so may increase the child's anxiety or damage his or her sense of self should the task be imposed before the child is developmentally ready. Another example might be expecting that those 8-, 9-, or 10-year-olds with social media skills and knowledge will be prepared to deal with the emotional impact of interacting over social media. There are emotional risks inherent to pushing children to demonstrate certain skills before they are holistically ready. Impelling children, actively or simply through exposure and expectation, to accomplish outcomes that are beyond their developmental capacity is likely to have deleterious consequences on their self-concept and overall emotional well-being.

DEVELOPMENTAL MODELS

Keeping these basic principles in mind, individual developmental models can be helpful in providing a framework of development in the context of maturation ("stage to age"). Therapists will recognize the traditional developmental models employed in this book to help to describe each age of childhood. In each chapter, the author emphasizes specific concepts or stages from appropriate developmental models, aiming to produce enhanced understanding of a child at that age. The core developmental models were developed over the course of the last century and many of these models therefore originated many years ago. The authors in this book consequently use current literature to support the ongoing relevance of these developmental models today. As a reminder of the essentials of each developmental model, full descriptions of the theories used most frequently throughout this book follow.

Maturational-Developmental Theory

Arnold Gesell was one of the earliest developmental theorists to conduct extensive observations of children from birth to adolescence. He identified a cycle of development and established norms for each age in areas of motor, adaptive, language, and personal-social behaviors. Gesell noted that child development followed a cyclical pattern marked by periods of equilibrium and disequilbrium. *Equilibrium* stages are characterized by calm, compliance, and confidence, while children in *disequilibrium* stages may be explosive, fearful, and self-involved (Gesell Institute, 2011). Recent research conducted by the Gesell Institute has confirmed that Gesell's original findings continue to be applicable to children today.

Table 1.1 outlines the Gesell cycle of development, including definitions for each stage.

Although Gesell identified and established norms for children at each age, he emphasized the child's individual pace and pattern of growth. Typically developing children will progress through the cycle stages, yet they may be unique in their timing of stages – and not all children will arrive at the stages within the specified ages. Each child can be expected to cycle through periods of time during which they feel a sense of belonging in their own bodies and world, and periods during which they feel "out of sorts," or "at odds" with themselves and others. While these stages can therefore be seen as mediated by a child's temperament, personality, and environment, the maturational-developmental model provides a roadmap for therapists to better understand the intricate changes that take place over time within each child.

Erikson's Psychosocial Identity Theory

Erik Erikson expanded Sigmund Freud's psychoanalytic perspective of development as driven by psychosexual instincts. Erikson's theory is identified as "psychodynamic" because it is based on the premise that humans are motivated to develop socially and in relation to their personal

Table 1.1
Gesell Developmental Cycle

Ages (yrs)			Cycle	Stage	Description
2	5	10	Equilibrium	Smooth	Calm; little difficulty within self or with environment
2½	5½–6	11	Disequilibrium	Breakup	Disturbed; troubled; at odds with self and environment
3	6½	12	Equilibrium	Sorting out	Good social awareness and physical development; balanced in relationships
3½	7	13	Disequilibrium	Inwardizing	Drawing in of outer world to be digested; marked sensitivity; excessive withdrawal
4	8	14	Equilibrium	Expansion	Outgoing behavior; constant movement; engages in high-risk behaviors
4½	9	15	Disequilibrium	Neurotic fitting together	Marked by worry; less outgoing; bothered
5	10	16	Equilibrium	Smooth	Calm; little difficulty with self or outside world

Source: Gesell Institute (2011)

environments. Erikson defined eight stages across the lifespan, four of which occur prior to adolescence. A person's identity or personality is created throughout all stages and is not fixed within one period of development. In each stage, there is a specific psychosocial or emotional challenge that the person must meet. Each stage is predicated on the resolution of the crisis that occurred during the previous stage. As a child encounters each stage and as there is successful resolution to the crisis, he or she assigns new meaning to all of the previously encountered stages, as well as to future stages. Ray (2011, p. 22) concluded that "unresolved tasks lead to future unresolved tasks and set a trajectory of cumulative failure. Hence, the earlier there is task failure, the more likely the child is to present clinically due to accumulated task failures".

Because this book focuses specifically on childhood, Table 1.2 offers a stage description of Erikson's theory up to adolescence.

Loevinger's Ego Development

Jane Loevinger described the "ego" as the internal structure that organizes and gives meaning to experiences of the person. She further explained that personality develops by acquiring successive freedoms, initially from personal impulses, followed by conventions and social pressures. The theory of ego development is holistic, and each stage encompasses the feelings, thoughts, and behaviors of a person. Each stage represents a person's worldview: how he or she sees himself or herself in relation to others and to his or her community. Loevinger hesitated to assign age categories to ego development stages, noting that a person – child or adult – could theoretically operate from any stage. However, developmental researchers have applied ego development to specific ages based on typical descriptors of children at different ages.

Table 1.2

Erikson's Psychosocial Identity Childhood Stages of Development

Age (yrs)	Stage	Description
Birth–1	Trust vs. mistrust	Infant learns to trust or mistrust environment, mostly through primary caretaker relationship.
		As basic nurturing needs are met, trust is developed.
		Resulting psychosocial strength: Hope
1–3s	Autonomy vs. shame and doubt	Toddler gains self-control and sense of separateness from caregivers.
		Resulting psychosocial strength: Will
3–5	Initiative vs. guilt	Child initiates action for the sake of action: a need to try, but not to accomplish.
		Resulting psychosocial strength: Sense of purpose
6–11/12	Industry vs. inferiority	Child has a need to master activities: to demonstrate competency.
		Resulting psychosocial strength: Sense of competence

Source: Erikson (1963)

Table 1.3 presents those ego development stages most correlated with childhood – but the cited age ranges should be reviewed with caution as a result of the significant variability of individual growth in Loevinger's model.

Piaget's Cognitive Theory

Jean Piaget is known as one of the leading cognitive developmental theorists and is credited with initiating the study of child development within the discipline of psychology.

Table 1.3

Loevinger's Ego Development Stages: Limited to Childhood

Age (yrs)	Stage	Description
Birth–2	Symbiotic	Infant fulfills primary needs; emotional fusion with primary caretaker
3–5	Impulsive	Child ruled by physical and emotional impulsivity; egocentric; immediate gratification
6–10	Self-protective	Child structures behavior to gain rewards and avoid punishment; opportunistic; growing in ability to understand and follow rules
10–15	Conformist	Child conforms to group norms; individual welfare is related to group; little tolerance for ambiguity

Source: Loevinger (1976)

Table 1.4

Piaget's Cognitive Development Stages

Age (yrs)	Stage	Description
Birth–2	Sensorimotor	Primary goal is to establish object permanence; ability to physically manipulate objects through senses informs infant about world
2–7	Preoperational	Ability to represent objects through symbols, including language; strong attachment to symbols; increased desire to play
7–11	Concrete operations	Ability to manipulate symbols (e.g. language, materials) and ideas; strong tie to logic and concrete ways of thinking; rules apply to all
11–Adult	Formal operations	Onset of abstract reasoning/conceptualization abilities; new awareness and understanding of complex emotions

Source: Piaget (1932/1965)

Piaget concluded from his research that children actively construct reality out of interactions with the environment and hence "learn by doing." He also proposed that children are predisposed toward organizing their thoughts and finding ways in which to adapt when they are faced with new circumstances or information. Although children think qualitatively differently from adults, unable to think, reason, and judge in the same way as adults do (Elkind, 2007), they progress through stages during the course of their development that lead to adult patterns of thinking. Most people will reach the highest identified level of Piaget's cognitive development theory, yet the pace and timing of their early development will be dependent on their experiences.

Table 1.4 outlines Piaget's theory of cognitive development.

Kohlberg's Moral Development

Lawrence Kohlberg was heavily influenced by Piaget's work on cognitive development and researched the application of cognitive thought to moral reasoning. In Kohlberg's theory, a child moves from moral decision-making based on external factors toward rationale based on internal processes, often in relation to multiple factors. Moral development relies on the cognitive development of a person arising from his or her need to consider diverse factors when making moral decisions. Kohlberg's theory includes three levels, consisting of six stages overall. Kohlberg was one of the few developmental theorists to purport that higher stages of moral development are "better" because higher stages involve more complex and integrated cognitive processes that serve the greater good. However, he was clear that persons at higher levels of moral development are not more worthy as humans, but only morally superior thinkers.

Table 1.5 presents Kohlberg's theory, along with ages and descriptors.

Vygotsky's Cognitive Development Theory

Lev Vygotsky has become well known over the last few decades and has arguably been as influential as Piaget regarding his contributions to understanding early cognitive development. Vygotsky did not offer a stage theory of development, but his extensive research offered a greater understanding of the developmental processes that occur in early childhood. Vygotsky noted play as a central component to development:

Table 1.5

Kohlberg's Moral Development Levels and Stages

Age	Level	Stage	Description
Infancy	Preconventional	1 – Punishment and obedience orientation	Egocentric; does not consider interests of others; actions considered physically; avoidance of punishment; recognition of superior power of authorities
Preschool		2 – Individualism, purpose, and exchange	Concrete, individualistic perspective; serves own needs; follows rules only when in best interest of self
School age	Conventional	3 – Mutual interpersonal expectations, relationships, and interpersonal conformity	Perspective of individual in relation to others; aware of shared feelings and beliefs; group takes precedence over individual interests; desire to maintain rules that support "good" behavior
		4 – Social system and conscience	Differentiates societal point of view from interpersonal agreement; takes perspective of system that defines rules; laws to be upheld; doing "right" contributes to society
Adolescence to adult	Postconventional	5 – Social contract, or utility, and individual rights	Aware that people hold a variety of values and opinions; feeling contractual commitment to family, friends, and work; considers moral and legal points of view; recognizes conflicts in perspectives
Adulthood		6 – Universal ethical principles	Follows self-chosen ethical principles; recognizes equality of human rights; acts according to principles when in conflict with rules or laws

Source: Kohlberg (1987)

It seems that every advance from one age stage to another is connected with an abrupt change in motives and incentives to act. What is of the greatest interest to the infant has almost ceased to interest the toddler. This maturing of new needs and new motives for action is, of course, the dominant factor, especially as it is impossible to ignore the fact that a child satisfies certain needs and incentives in play, and without understanding the special character of these incentives we cannot imagine the uniqueness of that type of activity which we call play.

– Vygotsky (1966, p. 7)

Vygotsky described play as liberating children from the constraints of reality and allowing them to move into the world of ideas, which is necessary for cognitive development. As part of emotional development, Vygotsky recognized that a child invents play when he or she can no longer make reality fit with desires or tendencies, usually around the age of 3. Additionally, Vygotsky coined the concept of the "zone of proximal development," defined as a dynamic that occurs in play through which the child acts older than his or her average age and thus is able to reach a higher level of development without the restriction of reality. A child in the zone of proximal development can be helped by an experienced peer or wiser adult to gain greater understanding or to acquire skills.

Greenspan's Emotional Development

Stanley Greenspan built upon the theories of Erikson and Piaget, but discovered, through his own research, the significance of children's emotional lives within the context of maturation (Greenspan, 1993, 1997). Greenspan's theory integrates physical maturation, cognitive patterns, and social and communication interactions, as well as emotional understanding. He identified four areas (that is, "milestones") through which all children needed to maneuver for emotional growth: self-regulation, relationships, reality and fantasy, and communication. In each stage of a child's development, he or she must master the challenges related to the milestone. If he or she is unsuccessful in a milestone area, intervention may be indicated to help the child to develop the required mastery.

Table 1.6 outlines the ages and milestones identified in Greenspan's theory.

USING THIS BOOK

The chapters in this book rely heavily on applying these leading developmental theories to child development. Each chapter captures the holistic and complex nature of a child at a particular age. Chapter authors use information from traditional experts on development, such as Piaget, Erikson, and Kohlberg, but also integrate new information on brain development, sexual identity, racial/ethnic identity, and growing up in the age of technology. The goal of the developmental information offered in each chapter is to provide the reader with a comprehensive picture of a child at the specific age, as constructed from current literature. Each chapter is written to stand alone, meaning that the reader can refer to an individual chapter and gain a detailed understanding of a child at that age. However, every chapter builds on the knowledge offered in the previous chapter to place each age in context within the full spectrum of growing older. Each chapter author is a therapist experienced with the age group explored in the chapter. Based on age tasks and worldviews, some chapters emphasize aspects of development more heavily than others. Hence if a reader follows the age chapters from birth to 12 years old, the connections between the ages become obvious, as do the building blocks of one age that support the worldview of another.

Most books on development present childhood in groupings, such as early, middle, and late childhood, or preschool and school age. This book divides the chapters by each year of development. Dramatic changes in physical, cognitive, and emotional development take place monthly during infancy, every six months in early childhood, and yearly in middle childhood. Although many resources exist to help professionals and parents to understand the extraordinary growth during the first two years of life, detailed accounts of expected developmental shifts in early and middle childhood are difficult to find. In fact, many authors often group the ages from 6 to 10 years, perhaps influenced by Freud's conceptualization of the latency stage in which it is claimed that drives are suppressed. Yet between the ages 6 and 7, 7 and 8, 8 and 9, and so forth, great differences in abilities, attitudes, and perspectives are evident. Therapists will benefit from knowledge of the specific nature of each age and what that year will entail for the child. In this volume, we therefore approach infancy by grouping the ages from birth to 2 into one chapter that summarizes the intensity of growth for that time period and sets the stage for early childhood. Chapter authors for early childhood, ages 3–6, emphasize differences demonstrated by children at the six-month mark during each of those years. Chapter authors for ages 7–12 concentrate on the unique nature and perspective of the child during each individual year.

Table 1.6

Greenspan's Emotional Development Stages

Age (yrs)	Stage	Milestones	Goals
Birth–5	"First five"	Self-regulation	Calm; regulated; impulse-control; attentive
		Relationships	Relates warmly to parents, peers, and adults
		Reality and fantasy	Participates and enjoys fantasy play; can distinguish make-believe from fantasy
		Communication	Demonstrates desires and intentions through gestures; intuitively responds to others' gestures; organizes words and communicates two or more words at a time
5–7	"World is my oyster"	Self-regulation	Carries out self-care and self-regulatory functions (e.g. calming down, focusing) with minimal support
		Relationships	Enjoys and feels secure in parental relationship; able to take interest in parents or peers; plays independently from parents; asserts will with peers
		Reality and fantasy	Tries to get expectations met, but learns to deal with frustration of reality
		Communication and emotional thinking	Allows fears and worries to coexist with expectations; understands reason for reality limits
8–10	"World is other kids"	Self-regulation	Ability to concentrate for longer periods of time; carries out most self-care activities without support
		Relationships	Participates fully in peer groups and is aware of role in group; mostly concerned with friends; maintains nurturing relationships with parents
		Reality and fantasy	Enjoys fantasy, but follows rules
		Communication and emotional thinking	Organizes ideas into communication; prioritizes emotions and groups them into categories; faces competition and disappointment without avoidance or overreaction
11–12	"World inside me"	Self-regulation	Concentrates for long periods of time; carries out self-care
		Relationships	Enjoys one or a few intimate friends; less dependent on position in group; takes interest in parents or adults as role models, but establishes independence from them
		Reality and fantasy	Enjoys daydreams and reflection; able to understand and use rules flexibly
		Communication and emotional thinking	Observes and evaluates personal communication; understands and empathizes with others; holds and communicates two competing feelings

Source: Greenspan (1993)

The final chapter of this book provides the mental health professional with condensed handout versions of the information offered for each age. The handouts are intended for dissemination to those parents and teachers who may benefit from a reminder of developmentally appropriate expectations.

REFERENCES

American Psychiatric Association (APA). (2013). *Diagnostic and statistical manual of mental disorders: DSM-5* (5th ed.). Arlington, VA: APA.

Burman, E. (2008). *Deconstructing developmental psychology* (2nd ed.). London: Routledge.

Elkind, D. (2007). *The hurried child: Growing up too fast too soon* (3rd ed.). Cambridge, MA: Perseus.

Erikson, E. (1963). *Childhood and society.* New York, NY: Norton.

Gesell Institute of Child Development. (2011). *Gesell developmental observation: Revised examiner's manual.* New Haven, CT: Gesell Institute.

Greenspan, S. (1993). *Playground politics: Understanding the emotional life of your school-age child.* Reading, MA: Addison-Wesley.

Greenspan, S. (1997). *The growth of the mind — and the endangered origins of intelligence.* Reading, MA: Perseus.

Kohlberg, L. (1987). *Child psychology and childhood education: A cognitive-developmental view.* White Plains, NY: Longman.

Loevinger, J. (1976). *Ego development.* San Francisco, CA: Jossey-Bass.

National Association for the Education of Young Children (NAEYC). (2009). *Developmentally appropriate practice in early childhood programs serving children from birth through age 8.* Retrieved from http://www.naeyc.org/files/naeyc/file/positions/PSDAP.pdf [accessed March 2, 2015].

Piaget, J. (1932/1965). *The moral judgment of the child* (M. Gabain, trans.). New York, NY: Free Press.

Ray, D. (2011). *Advanced play therapy: Essential conditions, knowledge, and skills for child practice.* New York, NY: Routledge.

Vygotsky, L. (1966). Play and its role in the mental development of the child. *Voprosy psikhologii, 12*(6), 62–76.

2

DEVELOPMENTALLY APPROPRIATE INTERVENTIONS

Dee C. Ray

Given that knowledge of child development increases the therapist's understanding of each child, this same knowledge is also relevant to decision-making regarding developmentally appropriate interventions. When a therapist grasps the developmental framework from which each child is working, counseling interventions can be tailored to the child's developmental needs and worldview. Throughout this book, chapter authors select counseling approaches that are likely to be effective owing to the developmental match between modality and child. Early interventions begin with a focus on the parent–child relationship, move through a focus on therapist–child relationship with nonverbal communication, and then reach more individualized or group approaches that emphasize growing cognitive and emotional complexity. Recognizing that children will respond more favorably to interventions that target their developmental age is fundamental to effective child therapy.

THE SEQUENCE OF DEVELOPMENTALLY EFFECTIVE THERAPY

Over the developmental span of childhood, elements of counseling approaches become crucial therapeutic factors that impact on outcome. Specifically, three elements should be considered when selecting a therapeutic approach for children at different ages: the primacy of relationships, the primacy of language, and cognitive operations. The priority order of these elements of consideration when choosing appropriate interventions changes depending upon the child's developmental and chronological age.

Relationships

Effective interventions for early childhood – specifically, birth through 3 years old – are rooted in the parent–child or caregiver–child relationship. Children in this age group are most affected by their relationships with their primary caregivers and hence intervention should be focused on these relationships. By involving parents in intervention, the therapist sets a course for improving the parent–child relationship in later years. Additionally, typical fears of separation from caregivers or introduction to strangers limit the positive impact of working alone with a therapist. As a child reaches the age at which an individualized sense of self is emerging, yet he or she is still profoundly influenced by adult relationships (that is, 4–8 years old), a relationship with a therapist who is caring, understanding, and accepting becomes a crucial healing factor for a child facing difficult circumstances or contexts. Children in this age group are typically responsive to relationships in which they feel valued and understood, and use these relationships to work through challenges and to modify behaviors. The therapeutic relationship itself becomes the healing factor in change. And as they reach middle childhood (that is, 8–12 years old), relationships with peers become influential in shaping children's perceptions of themselves and others. Children in middle childhood often use peer relationships to try out new behaviors and ways of seeing themselves; hence group interventions become much more effective at this age.

Language

Play is the natural language of children (Axline, 1947; Landreth, 2012; Piaget, 1932/1965; Ray, 2011; Vygotsky, 1966). Theorists and therapists agree that children have difficulty expressing their thoughts and emotions verbally, but appear to feel comfortable and expressive when provided with safety, time, and space in which to play. Developmentally, young children are drawn to symbols for expression: a component of learning verbal language. Toys provide these symbols and consequently young children will seek to express themselves through these symbols. Children also learn by doing – by interacting with their environments and with the people within those environments. The abilities to manipulate concrete materials and to interact with people are essential to a child's maturational competency, including mastery over emotional and behavioral challenges. Young children aged 2–7 express their internal worlds almost exclusively through play owing to their lack of language mastery, especially when conveying abstract constructs such as emotions. Free play is particularly beneficial in therapy, because it allows young children to initiate work in areas of need that they may themselves identify, but which may be unknown to the therapist. Older children gain greater language and expressive skills, yet are still in the process of integrating their verbal and nonverbal abilities, indicating a continued need for play in order to express themselves fully. In this way, play is therefore a central element of effective child therapy: Young children require play as a primary form of communication between therapist and child, while older children appear to need play components to strengthen the effectiveness of counseling interventions. Because of the central role of play in child expression, chapter authors in this book lean heavily on play therapy interventions, emphasizing play approaches as developmentally matched to children's natural language.

Cognitive operations

The cognitive ability of children determines the level at which they can engage in, and benefit from, certain forms of therapy. Children who see the world in terms of what they can touch and feel, and who have little ability to construct a world internally outside of the felt senses, are likely to be limited in more cognitively or verbally oriented therapies. Yet they will respond to interventions through which they can actively interact with their environments or receive felt consequences for their actions. This is the reason why both play and behavioral interventions are effective at younger ages. As children gain the ability to think logically, they may respond more positively to interventions that stress the importance of logic or concreteness (that is, interventions that add a cognitive component to play). Because emotions are abstract constructs, children with concrete operational thinking may struggle with interventions that ask for the expression or mental manipulation of emotional content. As older children become more abstract in their thinking (that is, as they engage in "formal operations"), they will be likely to respond to talk therapies such as cognitive and psychodynamic approaches.

INTERVENTIONS

To decrease duplication in chapters, chapter authors present interventions that appear well matched to each age, yet discuss the rationale(s) for the match, or possible modifications to the approach, only for that age. In the following section of this chapter, we present a description of the main interventions mentioned in the chapters and also list resources to guide therapists who may be seeking more knowledge or training for that approach.

Child-Centered Play Therapy (CCPT)

Child-centered play therapy (CCPT) is perhaps the most researched and oldest therapy for children, with research dating back to the 1940s (e.g. Axline, 1947). It is the approach most used among play therapists in working with children (Lambert et al., 2005). There are multiple volumes of literature dedicated to educating therapists on the principles and strategies used in CCPT (Axline, 1947; Cochran, Nordling, & Cochran, 2010; Landreth, 2012; Ray, 2011; VanFleet, Sywulak, & Sniscak, 2010). Ample research over the last 70 years has provided empirical evidence for the effectiveness of CCPT, including multiple and rigorous controlled studies conducted in the last decade. Meta-analyses and systematic reviews demonstrate that children participating in CCPT make statistically significant gains in emotional and behavioral issues when compared to nonparticipating peers (see Bratton, Ray, Rhine, & Jones, 2005; LeBlanc & Ritchie, 2001; Lin & Bratton, 2015; Ray, Armstrong, Balkin, & Jaynes, 2015).

Child-centered play therapy is rooted in person-centered theory (Rogers, 1951, 1957), while using play as the primary form of communication between therapist and child. Landreth (2012, p. 11) defined CCPT as:

> a dynamic interpersonal relationship between a child (or person of any age) and a therapist trained in play therapy procedures who provides selected play materials and facilitates the development of a safe relationship for the child (or person of any age) to fully express and explore self (feelings, thoughts, experiences, and behaviors) through play, the child's natural medium of communication, for optimal growth and development.

Following the conditions for effective person-centered therapy (Rogers, 1957), CCPT requires that:

1 the child and therapist are in psychological contact,
2 the child is in a state of vulnerability or incongruence,
3 the therapist is congruent in the relationship,
4 the therapist experiences unconditional positive regard for the child,
5 the therapist experiences empathic understanding of the child and communicates this understanding to the child, and
6 the child is able to receive the communication of unconditional positive regard and empathic understanding. (Ray, 2011).

If all conditions are met, therapy will result in positive change for the child. Person-centered theoretical constructs are made manifest in play sessions by allowing the child to lead and direct his or her own play, providing numerous materials for expression and facilitating an environment of permissiveness within reasonable limits. Through their relationship with the therapist, and the facilitation of a safe and expressive environment, children develop greater self-responsibility, self-acceptance, self-concept, self-trust, self-control, and self-direction, resulting in more self-enhancing behaviors (Landreth, 2012).

Child-centered play therapy is conducted in a playroom furnished with a variety of carefully selected toys, designed to promote the expression of a wide range of feelings (Ray & Landreth, 2015). Categories of play materials include real-life toys to help children to play out realistic life scenes, acting-out/aggressive toys to allow them to express more intense emotions, and creative expression/emotional release materials to offer children the opportunity for unstructured expression (Landreth, 2012). Playroom materials typically include toys, craft materials, paints and an easel, a puppet theater, a sandbox, and child-sized furniture (Ray, 2011).

For further learning about CCPT, please see the following resources:

- Center for Play Therapy, University of North Texas. (n.d.). Home page. Retrieved from http://cpt.unt.edu/
- Cochran, N. Nordling, W., & Cochran, J. (2010). *Child-centered play therapy: A practical guide to developing therapeutic relationships with children.* Hoboken, NJ: Wiley.
- Landreth, G. (2012). *Play therapy: The art of the relationship* (3rd ed.). New York, NY: Routledge.

- National Institute for Relationship Enhancement and Center for Couples, Families, and Children. (n.d.). Child-centered play therapy. Retrieved from http://www.nire.org/professional-training-supervision-and-certification-programs/child-centered-play-therapy/
- Ray, D. (2011). *Advanced play therapy: Essential conditions, knowledge, and skills for child practice*. New York, NY: Routledge.
- VanFleet, R., Sywulak, A., & Sniscak, C. (2010). *Child-centered play therapy*. New York, NY: Guilford Press.

Filial Therapy/Child–Parent Relationship Therapy (CPRT)

Bernard and Louise Guerney developed the filial model of therapy as a parent-focused intervention grounded in CCPT (Guerney & Ryan, 2013). Based on the premise that parents were not pathological, but often lacked the relationship skills with which to parent their children, the Guerneys proposed a model of therapy that taught parents basic CCPT skills to use with their children in home play sessions. Filial therapy is thus a blended intervention in which education, group process, and play sessions are used to help parents to build emotionally enhancing relationships with their children. Parents learn interpersonal skills through didactic instruction, process through their learning in a support group format for parents, and practice skills in home play sessions with their children, which are supervised by a trained filial therapist. Typically designed for parents of children between the ages of 2 and 12, filial therapy can be modified to fit the needs of infants and adolescents.

Landreth and Bratton (2006) adapted the original filial model to a ten-week intervention that is referred to as "child–parent relationship therapy" (CPRT) (Landreth & Bratton, 2006). The CPRT model is manualized, and presents a practical, time-limited intervention that has demonstrable appeal to therapists and parents.

The terms "filial therapy" and "CPRT" are often used interchangeably because they represent the same general intervention. However, CPRT is the specific intervention more commonly found in the research literature as a result of the structured nature of the program. Evidence from filial/CPRT research indicates reductions in children's behavioral problems, decreases in parental stress, and increases in parental empathy toward their children (Bratton, Opiola, & Dafoe, 2015; Lin & Bratton, 2015). Therapists who facilitate filial therapy are trained in both CCPT and filial therapy/CPRT.

For further learning about filial therapy and CPRT, please see the following resources:

- Bratton, S., Landreth, G., Kellam, T., & Blackard, S. (2006). *Child–parent relationship therapy (CPRT) treatment manual: A ten-session filial therapy model for training parents*. New York, NY: Routledge.
- Center for Play Therapy, University of North Texas. (n.d.). Home page. Retrieved from http://cpt.unt.edu/
- Guerney, L., & Ryan, V. (2013). *Group filial therapy: The complete guide to teaching parents to play therapeutically with their children*. London: Jessica Kingsley.
- Landreth, G., & Bratton, S. (2006). *Child–parent relationship therapy (CPRT): A ten-session filial therapy model*. New York, NY: Routledge.
- National Institute for Relationship Enhancement and Center for Couples, Families, and Children. (n.d.). Child-centered play therapy. Retrieved from http://www.nire.org/professional-training-supervision-and-certification-programs/child-centered-play-therapy/
- VanFleet, R. (2013). *Filial therapy: Strengthening parent-child relationships through play* (3rd ed.). Sarasota, FL: Professional Resource Press.
- VanFleet, R., Sywulak, A., & Sniscak, C. (2010). *Child-centered play therapy*. New York: Guilford Press.

Relationship Enhancement for Learner and Teacher (RELATe)/Child–Teacher Relationship Training (CTRT)/Play-Based Teacher Consultation (PBTC)/Kinder Training Teacher–child relationship interventions have also been derived from the filial model. These programs seek to help teachers to build positive relationships with students by practicing skills in play sessions and generalizing responses to the classroom. These programs have been subjected to experimental design studies and have demonstrated promising results in relation to teacher

interpersonal skills and classroom behavioral problems. The implementation of these models requires a therapist trained in both CCPT and CPRT, who is also familiar with the school setting.

For further learning about teacher–child filial models, please see the following resources:

- Carlson, S. (2012). *A play-based teaching consultation (PBTC) program: Strengthening relationships between elementary school teachers and students*. Saarbrücken: Lambert Academic.
- Helker, W. P., & Ray, D. (2009). Impact of child–teacher relationship training on teachers' and aides' use of relationship building skills and the effects on student classroom behavior. *International Journal of Play Therapy*, 18(2), 70–83.
- Morrison, M., & Helker, W. (2010). Child–teacher relationship training. In A. Drewes & C. Schaefer (Eds.), *School-based play therapy* (2nd ed., pp. 181–195). Hoboken, NJ: Wiley.
- Ray, D., Muro, J., & Schumann, B. (2004). Implementing play therapy in the schools: Lessons learned. *International Journal of Play Therapy*, 13(1), 79–100.
- White, J., & Wynne, L. (2009). Kinder training: An Adlerian-based model to enhance teacher–student relationships. In A. Drewes (Ed.), *Blending play therapy with cognitive behavioral therapy: Evidence-based and other effective treatments and techniques* (pp. 281–296). Hoboken, NJ: Wiley.

Adlerian Play Therapy (AdPT)

Adlerian play therapy is the application of individual psychology, developed by Alfred Adler (Mosak & Maniacci, 2008), to play therapy (Kottman, 2003). Play is used as the primary form of communication between therapist and child. Kottman (2009, p. 244) suggested seven goals for Adlerian play therapy, including helping the child to:

- gain an awareness of, and insight into, his or her lifestyle;
- alter faulty self-defeating apperceptions and move from private logic to common sense;
- move toward positive goals of behavior;
- replace negative strategies for belonging and gaining significance with positive strategies;
- increase his or her social interest;
- learn new ways of coping with feelings of inferiority; and
- optimize creativity, and begin to use his or her assets to develop self-enhancing decisions about attitudes, feelings, and behaviors (Kottman, 2009).

Theoretical constructs integral to AdPT include "Crucial 'C's", personality priorities, and mistaken beliefs, all of which help a therapist to better understand a child's lifestyle – that is, the child's personal perception of his or her world and place in it (Kottman & Ashby, 2015).

The "Crucial 'C's" are those of the child's assets that should be developed to ensure an adaptive lifestyle, including:

- connection (a sense of belonging in relationships),
- capability (a sense of competence),
- counting (a sense of mattering and feeling valued), and
- courage (a hopeful belief in a positive outcome when taking on life's challenges).

Kottman and Ashby (2015, p. 36) defined "personality priority" as "the organizational principle for people's pattern of behavior and their reactions to interpersonal situations" (Kottman & Ashby, 2015). There are four identified personality priorities, including:

- pleasing (gaining a sense of belonging by means of pleasing others),
- comfort (seeking pleasure and avoiding stress),
- control (gaining a sense of belonging through controlling self or others), and
- superiority (striving for perfection and achievement).

"Mistaken beliefs" are cognitive distortions that entail beliefs about ourselves and others, which typically lead to discouragement and self-defeating behaviors. The AdPT therapist seeks to understand a child through these constructs, often using play as the primary communication tool.

Considering the child and the child's system as the actual client, the AdPT therapist facilitates the therapy process through four phases (Kottman & Ashby, 2015).

1 In the first phase, the therapist seeks to build an egalitarian relationship with the child and the child's caregivers. The relationship with the child is often initiated by means of a nondirective play environment in which the child can feel safe and free to express himself or herself, similarly to CCPT.
2 In the second phase, the therapist explores the child's lifestyle. Such exploration can be conducted through nondirective or directive play techniques.
3 During the third phase, the therapist helps the child to gain insight into his or her own lifestyle and the lifestyle of his or her caregivers, as well as facilitates insight for caregivers into the child's lifestyle. The therapist will use active and direct techniques to help children to recognize maladaptive patterns and mistaken beliefs (Kottman & Ashby, 2015).
4 In the final phase, the therapist provides reorientation or re-education, aiming to teach skills while also offering encouragement during a nondirective play component.

Although AdPT is widely used with children, there is only limited – albeit promising – evidence of its effectiveness (see Meany-Walen, Bratton, & Kottman, 2014).

For further learning about AdPT, please see the following resources:

- Encouragement Zone, The. (n.d.). Home page. Retrieved from http://www.encouragementzone. com/index.html
- Kottman, T. (2003). *Partners in play: An Adlerian approach to play therapy* (2nd ed.). Alexandria, VA: American Counseling Association.
- Kottman, T. (n.d.). *Adlerian play therapy* (Video file). Retrieved from http://www.psychotherapy.net/ video/adlerian-play-therapy

Gestalt Play Therapy

Gestalt play therapy is based on the central premise that the organism (that is, the child) is in relationship with the environment. A child seeks self-regulation by satisfying his or her needs through interaction with his or her environment or people within it. This pursuit of self-regulation initiates all behaviors (Blom, 2006). Interaction of the child with the environment is called "contact" and is the core of experience that develops the self – a key concept in Gestalt theory (Carroll, 2009). In Gestalt play therapy, the therapist seeks to help children to restore healthy self-regulation, to become aware of internal and external experiences, and to be able to use the environment to get their needs met (Carroll, 2009). Blom (2006) proposed that the goal of play therapy is to make children more aware of their own processes. When a child experiences higher levels of awareness, he or she will see a greater number of behavioral choices designed to meet his or her needs. The role of the Gestalt play therapist is to facilitate awareness through multiple methods, which are most typically play-based. Oaklander (1988, pp. 192–193) wrote:

So it is up to me to provide the means by which we will open doors and window to their inner worlds. I need to provide methods for children to express their feelings, to get what they are keeping guarded inside out into the open, so that together we can deal with this material.

Gestalt play therapy views the child as a holistic organism; hence the therapist observes and responds to all aspects of a child. Blom (2006, pp. 68–70) suggested 13 areas in which a therapist assesses and determines intervention:

1 therapeutic relationship,
2 contact and contact skills,
3 contact boundary disturbances,
4 interest,
5 body posture,
6 humor,

7   resistance,
8   emotional expression,
9   cognitive aspects,
10 creativity,
11 sense of self,
12 social skills, and
13 process (Blom, 2006).

Play techniques are used to assess and provide intervention for all aspects that cause disturbance in the child. Because Gestalt play therapy is derived from Gestalt therapy, there are intricate constructs necessary for understanding the intervention; the therapist therefore requires specific Gestalt training. Empirical research has offered promising, if limited, evidence to support the use of Gestalt play therapy (Ray, 2015).

For further learning on Gestalt play therapy, please see the following resources:

- Blom, R. (2006). *The handbook of Gestalt play therapy: Practical guidelines for child therapists.* London: Jessica Kingsley.
- Oaklander, V. (1988). *Windows to our children.* Highland, NY: Gestalt Journal Press.
- Oaklander, V. (2006). *Hidden treasure: A map to the child's inner self.* London: Karnac Books.
- Oaklander, V. (n.d.). *Gestalt therapy with children* (Video file). Retrieved from http://www.psycho-therapy.net/video/oaklander-gestalt-child-therapy
- Violet Solomon Oaklander Foundation. (n.d.). Home page. Retrieved from http://www.vsof.org/index.html
- West Coast Institute for Gestalt Play Therapy. (n.d.). Home page. Retrieved from http://www.feliciacarroll.com/

Jungian Play Therapy

Jungian play therapy focuses on the unconscious processes that occur within the child during the therapeutic intervention. Douglas (2008, pp. 103–104) suggested that personality rests upon the psyche, which is made up of conscious and unconscious components that are tied to the collective unconscious, "underlying patterns of images, thoughts, behaviors, and experiences". Allan (1998) proposed that the healthy person experiences a fluid, yet regulated, connection between the conscious and the unconscious. Jungian theory is known as one of the more difficult theories to enact as a result of the deep level of its basic constructs, such as the collective unconscious, the role of ego and self, and archetypes. These unconscious processes enacted in the child's environment lead to behaviors or symptoms that may interrupt healing and integration. The playroom is one environment that presents a collection of archetypal images found in the collective unconscious (Lilly, 2015). Play materials represent symbols and metaphors from the unconscious that engage the child in healing play when provided within a safe environment.

The Jungian play therapist provides such a safe environment for the child through the playroom and use of the self as therapist. It is through this relationship that a child will cease to be overwhelmed by unconscious material met within an unsafe environment and be able to move toward the healing process. Providing this environment may require nondirective methods of facilitating play, placing the therapist in the role of observer. However, directive techniques are also helpful to the healing process. Allan (1997, p. 105) believed the goal of Jungian play therapy to be the activation of the individuation process, which he defined as "helping the child to develop his or her unique identity, to overcome or come to terms with his or her losses or traumas while accepting and adapting to the healthy demands of family, school, and society at large". Green (2009) suggested that experiential techniques such as drawings, drama, or sand play would benefit the exploration of symbols in art interpretation and analysis of transference. Through these techniques, Jungian play therapists seek to help children to acknowledge unconscious components, to integrate them into conscious components, and to activate the self-healing mechanism available to them (Ray, 2011). Although there is anecdotal case support for the use of Jungian play therapy, there are no empirical studies available at time of writing to demonstrate its effectiveness.

For further learning on Jungian play therapy, please see the following resources:

- Allan, J. (1998). *Inscapes of the child's world: Jungian counseling in schools and clinics.* Dallas, TX: Spring.
- Allan, J. (n.d.). *Jungian analytic play therapy: Analytical session and interview* (DVD). Denton, TX: University of North Texas Center for Play Therapy.
- Green, E. (2013). *Jungian play therapy and sandplay with children: Myth, mandala, and meaning* (Video file). Retrieved from https://www.academicvideostore.com/video/jungian-play-therapy-and-sandplay-children-myth-mandala-and-meaning
- Green, E. (2014). *The handbook of Jungian play therapy with children and adolescents.* Baltimore, MD: Johns Hopkins Press.
- Green, E. (2015). Soulplay. Retrieved from http://drericgreen.com/home

Cognitive Behavioral Play Therapy (CBPT)

Cognitive behavioral play therapy (CBPT), rooted in cognitive theory (Beck & Weishaar, 2008), is a brief, structured, directive, and problem-oriented intervention facilitated within the context of a trusting relationship between child and therapist (Knell, 2009). Cognitive theory proposes that personality is shaped by interaction between innate characteristics and environment, emphasizing the role of learning in human behavior and adaptation. Each person is susceptible to cognitive vulnerabilities that lead to psychological maladjustment (Beck & Weishaar, 2008). Psychological distress and behavioral problems may be attributed to biological, developmental, or environmental factors, yet cognitive distortions appear prevalent in maladjustment. Recognizing the limitation of a traditional Cognitive or cognitive behavioral therapy (CBT) approach in working with young children, Knell (2009) suggested that empirically based techniques supported in CBT research can be integrated into activity that is developmentally appropriate. Hence CBPT is indirectly supported by a large research base of CBT techniques found throughout mental health literature.

Cognitive behavioral play therapy focuses on specific problems in a child's life and works toward solutions for these problems, goals being directed toward reducing symptoms and increasing functioning (Cavett, 2015). Features of CBPT include the establishment of goals, the selection of play activities, education, and the use of praise and interpretations (Knell, 2009). The role of the therapist in CBPT is to educate the child – and possibly caregivers – and to facilitate activities that lead the child toward better strategies for functioning (Cavett, 2015). The role of the therapist requires a directive approach in which he or she selects play materials and activities to lead the child toward better problem-solving and adjustment.

The techniques of CBPT are divided into cognitive and behavioral techniques depending on the goals of therapy. Cognitive behavioral play therapists seek to provide play activities that will help to shift a child's negative thoughts toward positive or neutral ones, and then provide opportunities for learning and practice of new coping skills (Knell & Dasari, 2011). Although CBT has shown to be effective with older children and adolescents, lesser evidence exists to support its use with young children. Knell and Dasari (2011) suggested that, through the mediating process of play in CBPT, effectiveness can be enhanced with young children, but no experimental studies specifically focusing on CBPT have been conducted to date at time of writing.

For further learning on CBPT, please see the following resources:

- Drewes, A. (2009). *Blending play therapy with cognitive behavioral therapy: Evidence-based and other effective treatments and techniques.* Hoboken, NJ, Wiley.
- Knell, S. (1993). *Cognitive-behavioral play therapy.* Northvale, NJ: Jason Aronson.
- Russ, S., & Niec, L. (2011). *Play in clinical practice: Evidence-based approaches.* New York, NY: Guilford.
- Therapy with a Twist. (2015). Home page. Retrieved from http://www.therapywithatwist.com/professional-training/play-therapy-training/

For further information and training on all play therapy approaches, please see the Association for Play Therapy (APT), online at http://www.a4pt.org

Parent–Child Interaction Therapy (PCIT)

While parent–child interaction therapy (PCIT) was originally designed as an intervention for disruptive behaviors in preschoolers (Brinkmeyer & Eyberg, 2003), it has since been adapted to a broad range of children struggling with symptomatic behaviors. Parent–child interaction therapy is a parent–child intervention the goal of which is to improve the parent–child relationship and the behavior management skills of the parent. The therapy consists of two phases: child-directed interaction (CDI), and parent-directed interaction (PDI). During CDI, the parent is directed to follow the child's lead in play sessions and is coached by the therapist to use specified interpersonal skills. During PDI, the parent gives the child directions, and is coached in using interpersonal skills to gain compliance and decrease inappropriate behaviors. Parent–child interaction therapy is considered to be an evidence-based treatment, and is supported by multiple empirical studies demonstrating its effectiveness in improving parent and child functioning, as well as the parent–child relationship (Niec, Gering & Abbenante, 2011).

For further learning on PCIT, please see the following resources:

- Bodiford McNeil, C., & Hembree-Kigin, T. (2011). *Parent–child interaction therapy* (2nd ed.). New York, NY: Springer.
- Parent–Child Interaction Therapy International. (2011). Home page. Retrieved from http://www.pcit.org/
- UC Davis Children's Hospital Parent–Child Interaction Therapy Training Center. (2015). Home page. Retrieved from http://pcit.ucdavis.edu/

The Incredible Years (IY)

The "Incredible Years" (IY) series consists of three group training programs for parents, teachers, and children – specifically for children who demonstrate behavioral problems and fall between the ages of 2 and 12 (Webster-Stratton & Reid, 2010). In the parent program, IY teaches parents the skills with which to improve children's social competence and emotional regulation, while decreasing behavioral problems. The parent programs are divided into three developmentally targeted age groups, including young, middle, and older children. These programs typically last three to five months.

The teacher program provides a curriculum for teachers that help them to improve classroom management and to encourage the social-emotional development of children.

The child program can be delivered in small groups or the classroom, and includes teaching children interpersonal skills, empathy, and how to be academically successful.

Incredible Years offers a certification program for group leaders that involves group training, self-study, and group leadership review. In a meta-analysis of 50 outcome studies on IY, Menting, de Castro and Matthys (2013) concluded that it was a successful intervention in terms of decreasing childhood problems.

For further learning on IY, please see the following resources:

- Incredible Years, The. (2013). Home page. Retrieved from http://incredibleyears.com/
- Incredible Years, The. (n.d.). Youtube channel (Video files). Retrieved from https://www.youtube.com/user/TheIncredibleYears
- Webster-Stratton, C. (2006). *The Incredible Years: A trouble shooting guide for parents of children aged 2–8 years*. Seattle, WA: Incredible Years.

Child–Parent Psychotherapy (CPP)

Child–parent psychotherapy (CPP) was designed specifically for children between birth and the age of 6, who have experienced a trauma event, including abuse, loss, accident, or disaster (Lieberman & Van Horn, 2008). Child–parent psychotherapy focuses on how the trauma is integrated into the parent–child relationship, with particular attention paid to the family's background, culture, and spiritual beliefs. The goal of CPP is to help to return the child to normal developmental functioning by means of intervening with the parent–child dyad to provide safety and attachment, and to normalize developmentally appropriate responses to trauma for the parent. The therapist educates and guides the parent to respond therapeutically to the child, often using play as a communication tool. Child–parent psychotherapy is a long-term treatment, typically spanning approximately 50 parent–child sessions. Child–parent psychotherapists participate in a training and case supervision model over a period of 18 months. The intervention has been shown to be effective across multiple cultures and research demonstrates positive outcomes evidenced through several randomized controlled trials (RCTs).

For further learning on CPP, please see the following resources:

- Child Trauma Research Program. (n.d.). Home page. Retrieved from http://childtrauma.ucsf.edu/
- Lieberman, A. F., & Van Horn, P. (2004). *Don't hit my mommy: A manual for child–parent psychotherapy with young witnesses of family violence.* Washington, DC: Zero to Three Press
- Lieberman, A. F. & Van Horn, P. (2008). *Psychotherapy with infants and young children: Repairing the effects of stress and trauma on early attachment.* New York, NY: Guilford.

Positive Discipline/Systematic Training for Effective Parenting (STEP)

Positive discipline and systematic training for effective parenting (STEP) are parent-focused programs rooted in Adlerian psychology. Both programs educate parents, typically in a group format, on the skills necessary to help children to become more productive and capable. Positive discipline and STEP are targeted toward parents of typically developing children, but offer skills and knowledge that help to prevent behavioral problems in children. Focusing on Adlerian constructs applied to parenting, both programs teach skills related to understanding a child's motivations and behaviors, encouragement, the application of consequences, active listening, and the implementation of family meetings designed to involve children in decision-making. Positive discipline and STEP provide videos, books, and activities directed toward different developmental ages of children. Additionally, they both offer programs designed to teach effective interpersonal skills to teachers. The STEP model has been extensively reviewed in the literature in more than 70 empirical studies and has been found to be an evidence-based intervention. Positive discipline has concentrated on practice and application, thereby providing anecdotal evidence, but no empirical support.

For further learning on positive discipline or STEP, please see the following resources:

- Dinkmeyer, D., McKay, G., & Dinkmeyer, D. (2007). *The parent's handbook: Systematic training for effective parenting.* Coral Springs, FL: STEP.
- Dinkmeyer, D., McKay, G., Dinkmeyer, J., Dinkmeyer, D., & McKay, J. (2008). *Parenting young children: Systematic training for effective parenting.* Coral Springs, FL: STEP.
- Nelsen, J. (2006). *Positive discipline.* New York, NY: Ballantine.
- Nelsen, J., Erwin, C., & Duffy, R. (2007). *Positive discipline: The first three years – Infant to toddler.* New York, NY: Three Rivers.
- Nelsen, J., Erwin, C., & Duffy, R. (2007). *Positive discipline for preschoolers.* New York, NY: Three Rivers.
- Nelsen, J., Lott, L., & Glenn, H. S. (2013). *Positive discipline in the classroom.* New York, NY: Three Rivers.
- Positive Discipline. (2015). Home page. Retrieved from http://www.positivediscipline.com/
- STEP Publishers. (2015). Home page. Retrieved from http://www.steppublishers.com/

CONCLUSIONS

In this chapter, we sought to provide the rationales behind, and examples of, developmentally appropriate mental health interventions for children. Play therapy is an especially applicable intervention because it uses the primary and natural language of children: play. Yet different play therapy approaches emphasize constructs related to theory and thereby demonstrate relevance at different developmental periods of childhood. Other counseling and educational interventions can also be helpful at certain developmental stages. In the following chapters, authors will suggest the use of numerous interventions aimed at meeting a child's needs at a particular age and stage. Although this chapter addressed interventions that are cited multiple times across ages, other interventions that may be specific to a single age or stage may be introduced in the relevant chapters.

REFERENCES

Allan, J. (1997). Jungian play psychotherapy. In K. O'Connor & L. Braverman (Eds.), *Play therapy: A comparative presentation* (2nd ed., pp. 100–130). New York, NY: Wiley.

Allan, J. (1998). *Inscapes of the child's world: Jungian counseling in schools and clinics.* Dallas, TX: Spring.

Axline, V. (1947). *Play therapy.* New York, NY: Ballantine.

Beck, A., & Weishaar, M. (2008). Cognitive therapy. In R. Corsini & D. Wedding (Eds.), *Current psychotherapies* (8th ed., pp. 263–294). Belmont, CA: Thomson.

Blom, R. (2006). *The handbook of Gestalt play therapy: Practical guidelines for child therapists.* London: Jessica Kingsley.

Bratton, S., Opiola, K., & Dafoe, E. (2015). Child–parent relationship therapy: A 10-session filial therapy model. In D. Crenshaw & A. Stewart (Eds.), *Play therapy: A comprehensive guide to theory and practice* (pp. 129–140). New York, NY: Guilford.

Bratton, S., Ray, D., Rhine, T., & Jones, L. (2005). The efficacy of play therapy with children: A meta-analytic review of treatment outcome. *Professional Psychology: Research and Practice, 36*(4), 376–390.

Brinkmeyer, M., & Eyberg, S. (2003). Parent–child interaction therapy for oppositional children. In A. Kazdin & J. Weisz (Eds.), *Evidence-based psychotherapies for children and adolescents* (pp. 204–223). New York, NY: Guilford.

Carroll, F. (2009). Gestalt play therapy. In K. O'Connor & L. Braverman (Eds.), *Play therapy theory and practice: Comparing theories and techniques* (2nd ed., pp. 283–314). Hoboken, NJ: Wiley.

Cavett, A. (2015). Cognitive-behavioral play therapy. In D. Crenshaw & A. Stewart (Eds.), *Play therapy: A comprehensive guide to theory and practice* (pp. 83–98). New York, NY: Guilford.

Cochran, N., Nordling, W., & Cochran, J. (2010). *Child-centered play therapy: A practical guide to developing therapeutic relationships with children.* Hoboken, NJ: Wiley.

Douglas, C. (2008). Analytical psychotherapy. In R. Corsini and D. Wedding (Eds.), *Current psychotherapies* (8th ed., pp. 113–147). Belmont, CA: Thomson.

Green, E. (2009). Jungian analytical play therapy. In K. O'Connor & L. Braverman (Eds.), *Play therapy theory and practice: Comparing theories and techniques* (2nd ed., pp. 83–121). Hoboken, NJ: Wiley.

Guerney, L., & Ryan, V. (2013). *Group filial therapy: The complete guide to teaching parents to play therapeutically with their children.* London: Jessica Kingsley.

Knell, S. (2009). Cognitive-behavioral play therapy. In K. O'Connor & L. Braverman (Eds.), *Play therapy theory and practice: Comparing theories and techniques* (2nd ed., pp. 203–236). Hoboken, NJ: Wiley.

Knell, S., & Dasari, M. (2011). Cognitive-behavioral play therapy. In S. Russ & L. Niec (Eds.), *Play in clinical practice: Evidence-based approaches* (pp. 236–263). New York, NY: Guilford.

Kottman, T. (2003). *Partners in play: An Adlerian approach to play therapy* (2nd ed.). Alexandria, VA: American Counseling Association.

Kottman, T. (2009). Adlerian play therapy. In K. O'Connor & L. Braverman (Eds.), *Play therapy theory and practice: Comparing theories and techniques* (2nd ed., pp. 237–282). Hoboken, NJ: Wiley.

Kottman, T., & Ashby, J. (2015). Adlerian play therapy. In D. Crenshaw & A. Stewart (Eds.), *Play therapy: A comprehensive guide to theory and practice* (pp. 32–47). New York, NY: Guilford.

Lambert, S., LeBlanc, M., Mullen, J., Ray, D., Baggerly, J., White, J., & Kaplan, D. (2005). Learning more about those who play in session: The national play therapy in counseling practices project. *Journal of Counseling & Development, 85*(1), 42–46.

Landreth, G. (2012). *Play therapy: The art of the relationship* (3rd ed.). New York, NY: Routledge.

Landreth, G., & Bratton, S. (2006). *Child–parent relationship therapy (CPRT): A ten-session filial therapy model.* New York, NY: Routledge.

LeBlanc, M., & Ritchie, M. (2001). A meta-analysis of play therapy outcomes. *Counseling Psychology Quarterly, 14*(2), 149–163.

Lieberman, A. F. & Van Horn, P. (2008). *Psychotherapy with infants and young children: Repairing the effects of stress and trauma on early attachment.* New York, NY: Guilford.

Lilly, J. P. (2015). Jungian analytical play therapy. In D. Crenshaw & A. Stewart (Eds.), *Play therapy: A comprehensive guide to theory and practice* (pp. 48–65). New York, NY: Guilford.

Lin, D., & Bratton, S. (2015). A meta-analytic review of child-centered play therapy approaches. *Journal of Counseling & Development, 93*(1), 45–58.

Meany-Walen, K., Bratton, S., & Kottman, T. (2014). Effects of Adlerian play therapy on reducing students' disruptive behaviors. *Journal of Counseling and Development, 92*(1), 47–56.

Menting, A. T. A., de Castro, B. O., & Matthys, W. (2013). Effectiveness of the Incredible Years parent training to modify disruptive and pro-social child behavior: A meta-analytic review. *Clinical Psychology Review, 33*(8), 901–913.

Mosak, H., & Maniacci, M. (2008). Adlerian psychotherapy. In R. Corsini and D. Wedding (Eds.), *Current psychotherapies* (8th ed., pp. 67–112). Belmont, CA: Thomson.

Niec, L., Gering, C., & Abbenante, E. (2011). Parent–child interaction therapy. In S. Russ & L. Niec (Eds.), *Play in clinical practice: Evidence-based approaches* (pp. 149–167). New York, NY: Guilford.

Oaklander, V. (1988). *Windows to our children.* Highland, NY: Gestalt Journal Press.

Piaget, J. (1932/1965). *The moral judgment of the child* (M. Gabain, trans.). New York, NY: Free Press.

Ray, D. (2011). *Advanced play therapy: Essential conditions, knowledge, and skills for child practice.* New York, NY: Routledge.

Ray, D. (2015). Research in play therapy: Empirical support for practice. In D. Crenshaw & A. Stewart (Eds.), *Play therapy: A comprehensive guide to theory and practice* (pp. 467–482). New York, NY: Guilford.

Ray, D., & Landreth, G. (2015). Child-centered play therapy. In D. Crenshaw & A. Stewart (Eds.), *Play therapy: A comprehensive guide to theory and practice* (pp. 3–16). New York, NY: Guilford.

Ray, D., Armstrong, S., Balkin, R., & Jayne, K. (2015). Child-centered play therapy in the schools: Review and meta-analysis. *Psychology in the Schools, 52*(2), 107–123.

Rogers, C. (1951). *Client-centered therapy: Its current practice, implications and theory.* Boston, MA: Houghton Mifflin.

Rogers, C. (1957). The necessary and sufficient conditions of therapeutic personality change. *Journal of Consulting Psychology, 21*(2), 95–103.

VanFleet, R., Sywulak, A., & Sniscak, C. (2010). *Child-centered play therapy.* New York, NY: Guilford Press.

Vygotsky, L. (1966). Play and its role in the mental development of the child. *Voprosy psikhologii, 12*(6), 62–76.

Webster-Stratton, C., & Reid, M. (2010). The Incredible Years parents, teachers, and children training series: A multifaceted treatment approach for young children with conduct disorders. In A. Kazdin & J. Weisz (Eds.), *Evidence-based psychotherapies for children and adolescents* (2nd ed., pp. 194–210). New York, NY: Guilford.

Part II

3

THE EXTRAORDINARY BEGINNING YEARS

Birth to 2 Years Old

Liz Ener

As a newborn, Elliott delights in his mother's embrace and often falls peacefully asleep in his parent's arms. At 2 months, Elliott is sleeping three or four hours a night and is beginning to try to pick up his head to study brightly colored objects. At 6 months old, Elliott likes rhythmic activities, such as being bounced, jiggled, or swayed gently. He also likes to play with soft, squeaky toys, which Elliott's parents often find him putting in his mouth.

Now a toddler, Elliott loves to be a helper, for example helping his mother put away the laundry; however, he can often get into trouble when left alone: His mother has often found him emptying the dresser drawers instead of helping to put laundry away. Elliott's parents have found that he demonstrates a newfound interest in reading – especially books that have a lot of repetition, such as those by Dr. Seuss. Elliott's parents often read to him, during which time he loves to talk about the pictures in the books. Elliott, now well into his second year, enjoys dressing up and imitating others, for example putting on his mother's high-heel shoes and walking around the house. Elliott additionally likes to be around other children, but he does not really play well with them. Sometimes, he gets mad at his friends, and will even push and shove them when they take his toys. Elliott always feels bad after he hurts his friends and will often try to make up with them by giving them big hugs.

A child's development is complex and unique to his or her experiences; however, development occurs within certain sequences. The first two years in a child's life signify the most rapid period of his or her development (Berger, 2011). During these initial years, the rate and pace at which infants, toddlers, and 2-year-olds grow and develop surpass those of any other developmental period for children. Thus the age and developmental span of infants, toddlers, and 2-year-olds encompasses an expansive and technical period of development.

Infants enjoy using their senses and developing motor skills with which to explore their world (Marotz & Allen, 2012). As newborns, their primary manner of communication is to cry in an effort to gain the attention of adults. As they near the age of 1, infants are beginning to ready themselves to walk and talk. Toddlers are full of energy and curiosity. Pruning their motor abilities allows infants to physically explore the world around them. Two-year-olds wear their hearts on their sleeves and often exhibit various outbursts of emotionality, including laughter and anger (Marotz & Allen, 2012).

A number of developmental theorists have studied human development, but Arnold Gesell, an American pediatrician, was the first to systematically examine development across the lifespan (Gesell Institute, 2011; Thelen & Adolph, 1992). Studying the progression of a number of developmental capacities throughout the lifespan, including physical, cognitive, social, and emotional development, Gesell generated a maturational development model based on observations and documentations of the patterns of typically developing children (Gesell Institute, 2011).

Through his work, he found that children progress through similar, predictable sequences; he found too, however, that the pace, or rate, at which children progress through these sequences varies (Thelen & Adolph, 1992). Gesell noted that growth tends to oscillate back and forth between stages of *equilibrium*, during which children tend to be agreeable and confident, and stages of *disequilibrium*, during which children tend to be explosive and self-absorbed (Gesell Institute, 2011). Gesell likened this oscillation to that of an upward spiral, with each full-circle turn signifying a definable stage. Six of these definable stages make up one full cycle, and these stages occur more rapidly in the initial years of life and slow down as a child matures. He termed the stages "smooth," "breaking-up," "sorting out," "inwardizing," "expansion," and "neurotic" (Gesell Institute, 2011). More information regarding the progression of these stages for children from birth to age 2 can be found in Table 3.1.

By the time a child reaches 3 years of age, he or she has typically progressed through three complete cycles (Gesell Institute, 2011). Each of these cycles are characterized by uniqueness and individuality. The first cycle, which occurs between birth to 3 weeks old, is geared toward perpetuating and regulating life-sustaining functions (Gesell Institute, 2011). Children within the second cycle, which occurs between 1 month and about 10 months old, tend to be in the discovery period during which they begin to find and explore their senses. Additionally, children within the second cycle tend to experience objects as specific entities. In the third cycle, which encompasses children aged 10 months to about 1 year and 9 months, children begin developing their transportation systems (that is, crawling, walking, etc.), learning languages, and discovering space and time. Children within this third cycle begin to experience their self as an entity. The fourth cycle tends to span children aged 2 to approximately 4½ years old. Children within this fourth cycle begin to explore space and time, and begin to experience people as entities, as well as objects and themselves (Gesell Institute, 2011).

Table 3.1
Arnold Gesell's Maturational-Developmental Stages

Smooth Equilibrium	Breaking-up Disequilibrium	Sorting out Equilibrium	Inwardizing Disequilibrium	Expansion Equilibrium	Neurotic Disequilibrium
–	–	–	–	Birth	2 wks
1 mth	2–3 mths	4 mths	5 mths	6 mths	7–8 mths
9–10 mths	1 yr	1 yr 1 mth	1 yr 3 mths	1 yr 6 mths	1 yr 9 mths
2 yrs	2½ yrs	–	–	–	–

Description of stage					
Children are relatively calm, socially compliant, and can often be literal and concrete both in logic and in problem solving.	Children can be oppositional, can experience difficulty making decisions, are often at odds with themselves and their environment, and need structure.	Children demonstrate increased social awareness and physical development, and associate a specific result with a specific problem/task.	Children are fearful of the unexpected and comfortable with what they can control, can be territorial, approach problem solving by means of feelings, and demand stability.	Children are in constant motion, learning through movement, are often accident prone, and are more aware of the outside world than they are of their own world.	Children are concerned about and desire closure, often worrying about their relationships with others, and seeing problems paired with many solutions.

From his systematic exploration of children's growth and development, Gesell generated the Gesell Developmental Observation (GDO) in 1964 (Gesell Institute, 2011). The GDO is an assessment system that helps in understanding the characteristics of child behavior in relation to typical growth patterns. From 2008 to 2010, the Gesell Institute conducted a nationwide study to collect new technical data on the GDO assessment (Gesell Institute, 2012). Data from this study confirmed that present-day children continue to demonstrate and exhibit the same developmental stages and observations as originally determined by Gesell (Gesell Institute, 2012). Thus, even though educational expectations for children have changed drastically, development and learning across this short span of history has remained consistent (Gesell Institute, 2012).

BRAIN DEVELOPMENT/INTERPERSONAL NEUROBIOLOGY

Early in life and into adulthood, the brain works to integrate capacities, including thoughts, feelings, and behaviors, and organizes them to reflect an individual's environment (Siegel, 2012). Described by Thompson (2000, p. 1) as "the most complex structure in the known universe," the human brain grows at a critically rapid pace during the first two years. The brain communicates and transmits information through *neurons*, which are specialized nerve cells, and are the foundation of learning and memory (Siegel, 2012). Most neurons are generated prenatally, with the brain containing more than 100 billion neurons at birth (Siegel, 2012). The number of developed neurons at birth is much more than any individual will ever be likely to need (de Haan & Johnson, 2003). Through differentiation, neurons assume specific roles and functions whereby they form connections, or *synapses*, with other neurons that permit them to communicate and retain information. These neural systems are use-dependent, which means that these synaptic connections strengthen through repetition or wane with lack of use (Siegel, 2012). This gradual elimination of these little-used synaptic connections is referred to as *pruning* (Berger, 2011). The retained synapses are preserved in direct relation to stimuli and experiences in a child's world (Berger, 2011).

> By the age of 2, a child has achieved three-quarters of his or her adult weight (Berger, 2011).

Although a considerable amount of brain development is maturational by nature, healthy experiences and exposure are also essential (Berger, 2011). A child's early experiences profoundly affect the organizational structure of the brain in a use-dependent way – that is, if certain neural synapses are not stimulated, then that part of the brain will remain unorganized. This process can be recognized in a number of capacities early on: Thompson (2001) If an infant's hearing is somehow distorted or deprived for a prolonged period time during the early months of life, for example, perhaps because of a tumor on the hearing nerve, then those pathways will not form. Even if the distortion or deprivation is corrected, there may be an irreversible effect already in place, permanently distorting the infant's hearing ability. Greenough, Black and Wallace (1987) identified two experience-related characteristics of brain development: experience-expectant and experience-dependent. *Experience-expectant* refers to the common experiences to which infants are exposed early on that provide the stimulation necessary for typical brain development (Thompson, 2001). The brain is tailored to expect these experiences and to utilize them for growth, and they include such things as hearing, language, and vision development. *Experience-dependent* refers to those unique experiences that continue to foster brain development and growth throughout an individual's life, which continue to architecturally cultivate and tend to the existing structure of the brain (Berger, 2011). These experiences account for the acquisition of new knowledge and skills within individuals.

It is important to remember that, as the higher parts of the infant and toddler brain become increasingly more organized and functionally adept, children at this age lack the maturity of the prefrontal cortex (Thompson, 2000). Responsible for the most advanced cognitive functions in humans, including impulse control, emotional regulation, and social adaptability, the prefrontal cortex is the last part of the brain structure to mature (Siegel, 2012). This explains the developmentally appropriate impulse control struggles demonstrated by infants and toddlers. Entering into their second year, more executive abilities are developing within children,

Liz Ener

such as awareness of self as they become more conscious of their own feelings and intentions (Berger, 2011). When a 1-year-old observes himself or herself in a mirror, for example, he or she is increasingly able to recognize the reflection as his or her own. This beginning awareness is further supported by the child's increased use of personal pronouns, such as "I" and "me." By understanding these nuances of the developing brain, caregivers can work to promote optimal brain development to help children to achieve their full potential (Berger, 2011; Siegel, 2012).

PHYSICAL DEVELOPMENT

> At birth, a child's head is typically a quarter of his or her length (Berger, 2011).

Physical development includes observed physical changes and growth, as well as physiological aptitude, including the skills and coordination required to complete various motor tasks. At birth, a typical newborn has the capacity to breathe, eat, and regulate body temperature; however, these capacities are newly developed and much is dependent upon caregivers. Within these first few years, growth occurs in spurts, with periods of rapid change and development followed by periods of latency. Entering into the second year, growth slows in comparison to the first year; however, body proportions continue to change as the child's trunk and legs further develop (Berger, 2011; Perry, Piaget, & Inhelder, 1969).

The increase in infants' and toddlers' sensory dexterity further cultivates physical development (Berger, 2011). Although the degree to which they function largely depends upon the specific sense, all five senses are functional at birth. In fact, developed in utero, an infant's sense of hearing is particularly keen at birth (Berger, 2011; Santrock, 2014). Certain sounds evoke reflexive tendencies in infants, with loud noises startling them and making them cry, while soft, rhythmic sounds soothe them. Additionally, infants inherently turn their head toward the source of a sound and are particularly attuned to the human voice (Thompson, 2000).

> Newborns are able to focus on objects between 4 and 30 inches away (Berger, 2011; Santrock, 2014).

Whereas an infant's sense of hearing is acute at birth, an infant's sense of sight is the least mature of the five senses (Thompson, 2000). Remember that synapses are created in relation to environmental stimuli: Because the fetus is not exposed to visual stimuli in utero, the communication between an infant's eyes and cortex has not been formed, and begins developing only at birth (Berger, 2011; Siegel, 2012). Newborns prefer to fixate on faces and, as the visual cortex matures, infants are able to focus more intently. Over time, an infant's ability to visually scan becomes more organized and, at 3 months old, an infant is able to examine the eyes and mouths of those around them, which are the features that hold the most information related to communication and emotion (Berger, 2011; Santrock, 2014). *Binocular vision*, which is the capacity to focus on two things at once in a coordinated fashion, develops rapidly at about 14 weeks (Berger, 2011).

An infant's senses of taste, smell, and touch quickly adapt to the child's environment. Infants begin to recognize their caregivers' smells and touch, which results in their feeling relaxed when cradled by those familiar to them and uneasy in the arms of strangers. In fact, much of the sensory dexterity in young children appears to be oriented toward purposes of self-soothing and social connectedness to the world and those around them (Berger, 2011).

Motor Development

A number of significant changes occur within the first two years directly involving motor development. Infants develop a wide range of body movements and motor skills – that is, the learned abilities necessary to move and control the body (Berger, 2011; Santrock, 2014). A number of terms are utilized when describing general patterns of motor development, including "cephalo-caudal" and "proximal-distal" (Thompson, 2000). *Cephalo-caudal*, which means "head to tail," indicates that development typically progresses from the top of the body, or head, down to the legs. *Proximal-distal*, which means "from near to far," refers to developmental progression occurring outward, from the torso of the body to the extremities (Thompson, 2000).

32

The motor movements that an infant initially demonstrates are not skills, but rather *reflexes*, which can be defined as actions that are automatic in nature – that is, as direct, involuntary reactions to stimuli (Berger, 2011). Although newborns demonstrate a number of reflexes, three identified sets are particularly essential for survival (Berger, 2011). These include the reflexes required for breathing, regulating body temperature, and feeding. Some reflexes, which are not necessarily essential for survival past infancy, tend to disappear as a child ages; however, a number of reflexes remain and occur in adults, such as blinking, coughing, sneezing, and yawning (Brazelton & Sparrow, 2006).

Although physical and motor development typically occur in a patterned sequence for children, some variation in typical developmental periods can be attributed to differences in gender and culture (Berger, 2011). For example, girls are slightly shorter than boys in infancy. Additionally, cultural differences also affect motor development in young children depending upon exposure to certain environmental stimuli (Marotz & Allen, 2012).

Gross motor skills   Gross motor skills, which involve large body movements, allow children to move around on their own and to explore their environment (Berger, 2011). Specific to infants, gross motor skills tend to develop out of reflexes. For example, the swimming reflex comprises the involuntary movements that infants demonstrate when placed on their stomachs: They tend to move their arms and legs as though they are swimming (Berger, 2011; Brazelton & Sparrow, 2006). This reflex gives birth to *crawling*, with infants using their arms, legs, and developed strength to inch themselves forward by 5 months of age. By the time infants reach 8–10 months old, they are typically able to crawl on all fours (Marotz & Allen, 2012).

Walking is a developmental milestone typically occurring well within the first two years (Berger, 2011). Once a child is capable of walking without assistance, typically at around 12 months old, toddlerhood begins (Brazelton & Sparrow, 2006). By the age of 2, toddlers are able to climb and run, and have essentially reached full mobility, although they still lack coordination (Marotz & Allen, 2012). Once children reach this state, mobility expands speedily and tends to follow a predictable pattern. This pattern follows from the initial capacity of a child being able to lift his or her head and hold it erect and steady, through rolling over, sitting up without support, standing with assistance, and standing alone steadily, to walking, jumping, and kicking with relative precision (Berger, 2011).

Fine motor skills   Fine motor skills enable children to do such things as manipulate small objects, and the stem from an ability to control one's arms and hands (Ames & Ilg, 1976). The first fine motor skill to be developed is a child's ability to grasp an object. An infant's grasp is reflexive to some degree, because newborns have not yet mastered control over their hands and fingers (Brazelton & Sparrow, 2006). Grabbing hold of objects with precision requires coordination of the hands and eyes. By the age of 3 months, infants can typically touch objects, but not yet grasp them (Berger, 2011). By 4 months, infants can sometimes grasp objects; however, their hand–eye coordination continues to lack precision and their timing is often slow (Berger, 2011). It is not until 6 months of age that infants are able to master the ability to grasp and hold an object. Other fine motor skills that develop in the first two years include transferring an object from one hand to the other, holding an object in each hand, clapping hands, and scribbling (McDevitt & Ormrod, 2015).

> By 8 or 9 months of age, infants are able to reach out and try to catch an object moving towards them, and by 11 or 12 months, they are able to use both hands to grab hold of an object that is too large for one hand alone (Berger, 2011).

Throughout the second year, finger and hand coordination continue to mature (Berger, 2011). By the age of 2, children are working on mastering the pincer grasp, whereby they use their thumb and index finger to pick up objects (Ames & Ilg, 1976). Children at this age also begin to master the skills related to eating, such as first eating with their hands, then with their fingers, and finally beginning to manipulate utensils (Brazelton & Sparrow, 2006). Toddlers are able to turn pages in books and become increasingly more adept at handling small toys. In fact, in their second year, toddlers are able to engage with their environment in a much more selective manner as their movements become much less compulsive and much more intentional (Berger, 2011).

Toilet Training

The topic of toilet training typically arises within the first two or three years (Ames & Ilg, 1976). By 18 months, many children demonstrate the ability to control bladder and bowel function.

Children typically demonstrate an interest in toilet training by the age of 2; however, that age is not the be-all and end-all for toilet training (Thompson, 2000). Many parents and caregivers are uncertain regarding the time at which to start the toilet training process. Not all children are ready at a certain age. In fact, some children are ready before, or even after, the age of 2½. Gender-related differences are also noted in relation to toilet training, in that girls tend to toilet train at an earlier age on average as compared to boys (Ames & Ilg, 1976).

> The average age for toilet training for girls is 29 months; for boys, 31 months. By 36 months old, 98 percent of children are toilet trained (Boyse & Fitzgerald, 2010).

Some things can directly interfere with successful toilet training, including significant changes or an experienced trauma (Brazelton & Sparrow, 2006). When a child who had previously been completely potty trained becomes an older sibling for the first time, for example, caregivers might bear witness to regressed toilet training practices. During these times, children often become overwhelmed and stressed, and lose the ability to perform previous utilized skills (Brazelton & Sparrow, 2006). During these times, care and understanding must be rendered. Once children are able to reregulate, they will be likely to regain control over these previously mastered skills.

Toddlers yearn to gain control over their bodies and the world around them (Ames & Ilg, 1976). Toilet training, in particular, can therefore be a source of power struggles between caregivers and their children. Handling this process without care can result in young children attempting to regain control by withholding urine or bowel movements (Ames & Ilg, 1976). When parents are matter of fact about toilet training and suspend the typical emotionality surrounding the process, children are much more likely to experience a happy and fault-free toilet training process (Brazelton & Sparrow, 2006).

GENDER AND SEXUAL DEVELOPMENT

Similarly to most other aspects of development, such as learning how to walk, children additionally progress through typical milestones related to gender and sexual development. The increased interest in toilet training is likely to spur further interest in how children experience and feel about their bodies (Brazelton & Sparrow, 2006). Children from birth to age 2 typically demonstrate increased curiosity about their bodies, including their genitals. Toddlers and 2-year-olds additionally appear to lack inhibition related to nudity. In fact, many young children frequently remove their diapers or clothes. The curiosities of children continue to span their early development (Brazelton & Sparrow, 2006).

Self-stimulation is another component of developing toddlers and 2-year-olds. Both boys and girls tend to touch their genitals frequently; in fact, it is not out of the ordinary for toddlers and 2-year-olds to masturbate both in public and in private (AAP, 2005; Horner, 2004). A young child's curiosity continues to play a part as he or she begins to ask endless questions about the body and bodily functions (Horner, 2004).

Nearing age 3, children become more aware of gender differences and begin to develop a sense of gender identity. At this age, children additionally begin to associate certain behaviors with being male or female. These messages related to gender roles are received both inside and outside of the home (Brazelton & Sparrow, 2006).

COGNITIVE DEVELOPMENT

Jean Piaget, a developmental psychologist who was interested in how children learn, argued that children actively construct knowledge (Berger, 2011). His theory of cognitive development postulates that thinking and learning stem from interactions between individuals and their environment, and that it is human nature to organize knowledge and adapt to the surrounding world.

Through his work, Piaget determined that children cultivate knowledge following predictable age-directed patterns, which consequently affect their behaviors (Berger, 2011).

Piaget's initial stage of "intelligence," which beings at birth and extends to about 24 months, is sensorimotor (Berk, 2013). In this stage, young children begin cultivating knowledge by means of their senses and developing motor skills. Children additionally utilize their reflexes, motor skills, and abilities to explore and learn about their surrounding environment and world. Learning is an active process, although the ability for conceptual or reflective thought has not yet developed (Berger, 2011). It is within this stage that the concept of "object permanence" emerges. *Object permanence* is the awareness that objects continue to exist even when they can no longer be seen, heard, or touched. Nearing the end of this stage and entering in the next stage, children have begun to think through mental processes (Berk, 2013).

The next stage of Piaget's cognitive development theory is the "preoperational" stage, which spans the ages of 2 to 7 (Berger, 2011). Within this stage, children's cognitive capacities extend beyond the sensorimotor to include imagination and other forms of symbolic thought. This stage is marked by egocentrism, as children in this stage struggle to see the perspectives of others (Berk, 2013). This explains why toddlers and 2-year-olds focus solely on their own needs and desires, and struggle to understand the needs and feelings of others (Berger, 2011).

The environment to which a young child is exposed powerfully influences his or her developing cognitive abilities (Berger, 2011). Memory is contingent upon the maturation of the brain and specific experiences. This explains why a young infant's memory is fragile and lacks depth, whereas the memory of a 2-year-old is much richer (Berk, 2013).

Language

The ability to communicate through language differentiates humans from all other species. Theorists have historically argued about the way in which language learning actually occurs (Berger, 2011). Some, such as B. F. Skinner, argued that infants are taught language via exposure and reinforcement; others, like Noam Chomsky, argued that infants teach themselves. Proponents of an additional theory argue that language develops not out of reinforcement or innate ability, but rather for the reason of communication because humans are social beings and dependent upon one another (Berger, 2011).

Regardless of the theoretical perspective of language development to which one adheres, children across the globe appear to follow a similar pattern related to language development (Berger, 2011). Newborns engage in reflexive communication, including crying (Marotz & Allen, 2012). By 6–7 months old, infants begin engaging in *babbling*, which is the extended repetition of specific syllables. By 10–12 months, infants begin to produce sounds that are recognizable to those who know the infant well. The first spoken words that are recognizable as part of the infant's native language occur by 12 months. By 13–18 months, children accrue a vocabulary of about 50 words, then at or around 18 months, the child begins to learn three or more words a day. By 21 months, children speak their first two-word sentence, and by the age of 2, children speak in multiword sentences (Berger, 2011).

Moral Development

In his theory of moral development, Kohlberg contends that the progression of moral reasoning within individuals can be linked to certain developmental periods. Like Piaget, Kohlberg was interested in the way in which people reason, rather than the content or derivation of their reasoning (Berger, 2011). Kohlberg's theory of moral development revolves around six stages, with moral aptitude increasing with each mastered stage. Kohlberg additionally believed that children's moral reasoning and ethical behaviors would advance as they were confronted with maturational movements and experiences within the environment (Berger, 2011).

According to Kohlberg, newborns can be described as "amoral," in that they have not yet been exposed to nor do they have the cognitive capacity to respond in an ethical manner (Berger, 2011). However, very young children tend to fall in the "preconventional" level of moral reasoning, which is comparable to Piaget's preoperational stage of development. The preconventional level involves the first two stages of the moral development model and predominately revolves around young children's egocentricism. Children within these stages of development are concerned with external and immediate consequences, rather than with a more internalized convention of right and wrong.

WORLDVIEW/EGO DEVELOPMENT

An infant's worldview is directly related to the environmental stimuli to which he or she is exposed (Berger, 2011). As children mature, so does their worldview. Caregivers of children from birth to the age of 2 tend describe this period of time as chaotic, fast-paced, and tumultuous. An early 2-year-old is described as gentle and friendly, whereas an older 2-year-old can be described as tense and explosive (Ames & Ilg, 1976). The demonstrated behaviors between a child from birth to age 2 can feel much like a rollercoaster ride, with a steady stream of development milestones that must be met.

Known for his theory of psychosocial development, Erikson emphasized the importance of child–caregiver interaction (Berger, 2011). Children from birth to the age of 1 face the challenge of *trust vs. mistrust.* In this hallmark stage of ego development, infants learn to trust the caregivers around them to provide for them and to keep them safe, or they learn to lack confidence in the capacity of those caregivers to ensure optimal care (Santrock, 2014). Children this young are inherently dependent, because their survival relies on the need for their caregivers to take care of and provide for them. Children aged 1–3 years old tend to move into the stage of *autonomy vs. shame and doubt.* At this stage, children learn to be self-sufficient and capable, or they learn to doubt and lack confidence in their own abilities (Berger, 2011; Berk, 2013). A monumental developmental aspect occurring within this stage is toilet training, discussed earlier in the chapter. Children who experience difficulties during the course of toilet training are likely to be struggling to feel autonomous and capable, suffering shame at their inability to successfully toilet train (Berger, 2011).

According to Jane Loevinger's theory of ego development, newborns typically reside in the "prosocial" stage of ego development, in that early infants are unable to differentiate between themselves and the world (Loevinger, 1976). This stage quickly merges with the "symbiotic" stage, which is typically the stage at which infants and toddlers reside. The symbiotic stage is similar to Piaget's sensorimotor stage, and is marked by a lack of differentiation of self and a focus on immediate gratification. Children in this stage tend to experience an emotional and cognitive fusion between themselves and their caregivers. Those aged 2 and 2½ tend to progress into the second stage of ego development: the "impulsive" stage. This stage, which is comparable to Piaget's preoperational stage of cognitive development, is characterized by a preoccupation with bodily impulses and a continued focus on immediate needs (Berger, 2011). Children consider individuals who meet their needs at this stage to be "good" and those who do not meet their needs to be "bad." A child at this stage is so immersed in his or her own individualized world that he or she cares only about aspects directly affecting him or her specifically. Children typically remain in this stage well into their play years (Berger, 2011).

Racial/Ethnic Identity Development

The layperson often assumes that race and ethnicity is insignificant to young children (Van Ausdale & Feagin, 1996). Due to young children's egocentrism, a number of early child identity development theorists implied that children do not have the cognitive capacity to understand any degree of racial or ethnic terminology (Van Ausdale & Feagin, 2001). However, although traditional identity development theorists identify the period of adolescence as the peak of racial/ethnic identity development, several researchers have more recently suggested this process may arise earlier in a child's life (Cooper, Garcia Coll, Thorne, & Orellana, 2005; Cross & Fhagen-Smith, 2001; Hirschfeld, 1995; Kelly et al., 2007).

At birth, children begin to form a sense of self, based on their characteristics, dexterity, and preferences, as well as on their identification with specific social groups (Ruble et al., 2004). Quintana and McKown (2008) posited that children's understandings of overall ethnic differences are byproducts of their desire to understand the physical world, their ego development, and their inherent desire to identify with and understand their own social group. Therefore children's racial/ethnic identity development directly impacts on the way in which they experience their world (Graves & Graves, 2008).

Children can begin to identify and describe themselves using age, gender, and race labels as early as 2 years old, suggesting that they demonstrate an emerging understanding of racial/ethnic differences and concepts early in their lives (Cross & Cross, 2008; Van Ausdale & Feagin, 2001). Prior to the ages of 3 or 4, much of children's conceptual understanding of race/ethnicity is contingent upon physical qualities, such as skin color, facial features, or hair texture (Quintana, 1998). Research has indicated that very young infants are capable of processing faces that are of a different race from their own; however, between the ages of 3 to 6 months, infants' perceptions appear to narrow (Kelly et al., 2007). This narrowing – often referred to as "other race effect" – appears to result in infants becoming increasingly more sensitive to the facial features of their own ethnic group, thereby causing them to demonstrate an inability to recognize members from different ethnic groups (Kelly et al., 2007). Overall, concrete understanding of young children's racial/ethnic development remains somewhat obscure – but children's racial/ethnic identity development appears to parallel their development across other continuums, such as cognitive and emotional development.

EMOTIONAL DEVELOPMENT

Within the first few years, children's emotional aptitude and expression develop at a remarkably rapid pace (Berger, 2011; McDevitt & Ormrod, 2015). Very young children display more reflexive emotional responses, such as crying and being startled (Elkind, 1994). At 6 weeks old, infants manifest the social smile and, by 3 months, are able to engage in laughter (Santrock, 2014). At around 9 months old, infants are able to experience and express fear responses. It is at this time that parents and caregivers become acquainted with their children's wariness of strangers, or their "separation anxiety," which is marked by distress when familiar caregivers depart (Berger, 2011).

Emotions that are cultivated throughout infancy amass strength of expression within toddlers (Elkind, 1994). During this second year of life, emotional expression begins to take a more focused form and is targeted toward things that are actually scary or frustrating. Nearing the end of the second year, emotional expression progresses, and children are able to experience and express more advanced feelings, such as pride, shame, embarrassment, and even guilt (Berger, 2011; Elkind, 1994). Environmental and familial influences affect the degree of expression of certain feelings: If a particular family discourages the experience and demonstration of frustration or anger, for example, then a child will begin to understand that this particular emotional expression is rare (Berger, 2011).

Further, more advanced 2-year-olds begin to understand the difference between acceptable and unacceptable social behaviors (Elkind, 1994). This skill is directly related to an infant's degree of self-awareness, which begins to become differentiated within these later years. Children possess an emerging understanding of themselves and of themselves in relation to others (Berger, 2011). This emerging acquisition leads the way toward children's ability to experience emotions in direct response to others, as well as the ability to express these emotions toward those who evoked them (Elkind, 1994).

Temperament

Children are born with unique, distinguishable ways of being as they mature (Korner et al., 1985). Temperament is similar to personality, but it is inherently different, because personality is developed through learned processes, whereas temperament is thought to be genetic (Berger, 2011).

The typical categories attributed to temperament are "easy," "difficult," and "slow to warm up" (Kagan & Snidman, 2004).

- Infants described as *easy* are calm and relatively relaxed. This is the most optimal, or preferred, temperament in children and describes an estimated 40 percent of infants. These children follow predictable eating and sleeping schedules, and are often friendly and happy to engage with the world people around them.
- *Difficult* infants tend to be irritable and fussy. Children described in this way are marked by unpredictability when it comes to eating schedules and are easily upset. This type of temperament accounts for approximately 10 percent of infants.
- Infants described as *slow to warm up* are overwhelmed by new situations and are typically cautious of unfamiliar environments. Children with this temperament are occasionally fussy, but they are able to warm up to new experiences through repeated exposure. The temperament accounts for approximately 15 percent of infants.

A lesser known temperament description is "hard to classify" and accounts for approximately 35 percent of infants. As the name might suggest, infants with this described temperament may possess traits from among all three temperaments and are therefore difficult to categorize as one or the other (Kagan & Snidman, 2004).

SOCIAL DEVELOPMENT

At birth, infants begin to connect with and accrue information on those who surround them. Consistent with Erikson's stage of *trust vs. mistrust*, infants are working to develop a sense of trust in and safety with their caregivers (Berger, 2011). If trust and security is achieved within these first few years, then children will have mastered Erikson's initial psychosocial stage of development and will thereby be open to exploring their world.

Vygotsky (1978), a Russian psychologist, argued that a child's sense of self develops only after social interactions occur. Likening children to social actors, Vygotsky posited that children reflect on, interpret, and create patterns formulated by these routine social interactions. Children are not limited to learning only what is taught to them; rather, children can also glean meaning from experiences indirectly. Like Erikson's early stages, Vygotsky's work recognizes the influential role that adults have in the lives of young children: Early on, much of a child's social adaptability is learned from his or her experiences with, and imitation of, his or her caretakers.

Bronfenbrenner (1979), an American developmental psychologist, acknowledged the contextual importance that children's environments have on their development. More specifically, Bronfenbrenner recognized that children's development in impacted by, and contingent upon, the communities and historical eras to which they are exposed (Bronfenbrenner, 1979; Bronfenbrenner & Morris, 1998). Because of the contextual significance that environments have in development, children should be encouraged to experience situations that facilitate their social adeptness, such as learning to share with others.

Infants become conscious of social stimuli, such as facial expressions, by the age of 5 months (Berk, 2013). Coinciding with their ability to crawl, by 9–12 months, children's interest in the world around them and their desire to explore that world increases (Berger, 2011). Children this young will additionally begin to point to objects of interest: a skill that demonstrates a shared focus with another. Stranger anxiety can arise anywhere between the ages of 9 and 18 months, and is typically the result of feelings of worry and vulnerability in the face of unfamiliarity (Berk, 2013; Santrock, 2014).

Early on in toddlerhood, children begin to develop a sense of self, including a growing understanding that they are independent of others (Berk, 2013; Santrock, 2014). This understanding assists them in recognizing that other individuals have thoughts and feelings that are separate from their own thoughts and feelings (Berk, 2013). As they grow, toddlers begin to become more interested in connecting with their peers. They often engage in parallel play, or play in which they play alongside, but not with, their peers (Berger, 2011). In actuality, children do not typically self-initiate play with their peers until they are around 3 years old (Santrock, 2014).

Later toddlerhood typically includes expansive pretend play, in which children are working to strengthen their social skills (Berger, 2011). Pretend play allows children to handle their curiosity about the world around them by developing stories and ideas, as well as to practice problem-solving skills (Landreth, 2012). Children become more capable of demonstrating, experiencing, and understanding the feelings of others, for example an older toddler may be seen comforting a saddened peer (Landreth, 2012). However, older toddlers continue to experience difficulty with empathizing with others while also regulating themselves and therefore will continue to struggle to resolve conflicts with peers. Nearing the age of 3, children begin to become more adept at sharing with others and taking turns (Santrock, 2014).

RELATIONSHIP DEVELOPMENT

One of the most significant relationships in a child's life is the parent–child relationship. "Attachments" refer to the early connections established between children and their caregivers (Berger, 2011). These attachments take hold in infancy and persist throughout an individual's lifespan. More specifically, they are the building blocks for future relationships (Bowlby, 1969). The quality of these relationships profoundly affect a child's development, ability to express emotions, and ability to develop meaningful relationships (Berger, 2011).

Whereas Bowlby (1969) paved the way and identified healthy early attachments as paramount for optimal growth, Ainsworth (1973) furthered that research and identified four attachment styles: "secure," "anxious-ambivalent," "anxious-avoidant," and "disorganized".

- A *secure* attachment is marked by trust and confidence. This type of attachment allows an infant to feel happy, secure, and reassured in his or her relationships.
- An *anxious-ambivalent* attachment (also referred to in other texts as "resistant," or "insecure-resistant"/"insecure-ambivalent," attachment) is marked by anxiety and uncertainty (Berger, 2011; Santrock, 2014). This interaction in evidenced when an infant seeks contact from caregivers, but resists it at the same time.
- An *anxious-avoidant* attachment (also referred to as "insecure-avoidant" attachment) is marked by the infant avoiding contact with the caregiver, or seeking the contact only indirectly.
- A *disorganized* attachment style is marked by inconsistent behavior from the infant and is therefore difficult to classify (Berger, 2011).

Should an infant experience a significant degree of loss and/or trauma in early childhood, he or she may experience difficulty in connecting with others later in life (Bowlby, 1969). This trauma may lead to a history of attachment disruptions, which yield struggles related to feelings of insecurity when in relational contact with others. Significant attachment disruptions can oftentimes evoke significant stress within the parent–child relationship (Berger, 2011).

DEVELOPMENT IN THE AGE OF TECHNOLOGY

Fred Rogers, most notably known as "Mr. Rogers" from the television series *Mister Rogers' Neighborhood*, was an advocate for developmentally appropriate education and entertainment. He innovatively utilized available technology to create meaningful entertainment programs for children. Through his work, he was able to connect with families and each individual child viewing his programs, thereby demonstrating the constructive capacity of technology employed in positive ways.

Since the inception of *Mister Rogers' Neighborhood*, the world has undergone vast technological advancements. Children have become accustomed to technology and interactive media, and experience devices, such as televisions, computers, smartphones, and tablets, as staples in their homes and at school. Technological advancements have transformed the daily lives of children, including in terms of learning, entertainment, and social connectedness, and have increased communication between parents and teachers due to the ease of networking. Because of this surge in access to, and use of, electronic media, children may spend a large portion of their time sitting in front of a variety of screens (Brazelton & Sparrow, 2006).

The presence and use of technologically based devices in the home and at school is a tumultuous topic – especially in relation to very young children. Many parents and teachers are opposed to children's prevalent use of electronic media, believing that it can stunt social and emotional health; others are proponents for, and endorse the use of, such media, asserting its potential for enlarging children's learning processes (Brazelton & Sparrow, 2006; Elkind, 2001). Because of the conflicting evidentiary support both for and against children's use of technology, and the continued division amongst research findings, parents and teachers are often left confused and unsure of how to best navigate the digital age (Christakis, Zimmerman, DiGiuseppe, & McCarty, 2004; DeLoache et al., 2010; Elkind, 2001; Hsin, Li, & Tsai, 2014).

The American Academy of Pediatrics (AAP, 2011) discourages any type of screen time for children aged, or under the age of, 2 and recommends a maximum of only two hours of screen time per day for children older than 2. In fact, a number of negative outcomes have been found to be correlated with children's overuse of technology, including irregular sleep patterns, behavioral issues, problems with focusing/attending, and disruption in language development (AAP, 2011; Brooks-Gunn & Donahue, 2008; Christakis et al., 2004; DeLoache et al., 2010; Lee, Bartolic, & Vandewater, 2009; Vandewater et al., 2007). Digital programs specifically targeted for infants and toddlers, such as *Baby Einstein*, are often advertised as important educational material even though research does not necessarily support the effectiveness or appropriateness of these programs (DeLoache et al., 2010). Such marketing tools can pressure parents, who feel compelled to take every necessary measure to set their children up for success, yet fail to understand that these materials are educationally relevant and appropriate only when children are capable of understanding their content (AAP, 2011). Because children from birth to age 2 do not yet have the cognitive capacities required to understand the content and context of such materials, these media may not be the most developmentally appropriate modalities for children. The AAP argues that young children learn best from unstructured play, because they are freed to be better able to think creatively, to problem solve, and to develop small and gross motor skills.

Although the value inherent to children's use of digital media is debatable depending on their stage of development, most literature suggests the use of such media with very young children to be inappropriate. When considering children's use of technology, parents and teachers are encouraged to consider the appropriateness of the medium, while also making informed decisions regarding the most optimal environments to induce healthy development in young children (AAP, 2011; Brooks-Gunn & Donahue, 2008; Brazelton & Sparrow, 2006; Elkind, 2001).

BEST PRACTICES IN COUNSELING/THERAPY

When Counseling/Therapy Is Indicated

Recognizing typical and atypical behaviors in children under the age of 3 can be a challenging process. Often, these behaviors do not fully materialize until children are well beyond the age of 3. The responsibility for recognizing any cause for concern among young children typically resides with parents, caregivers, and teachers. Because parents play such a vital role in the lives of young children, determining the cause of such concerns is equally as important as defining the concerns. Often, atypical and/or problematic behaviors are symptoms of an internal struggle. Care must be taken to determine the causes of such behaviors, which may be a function of delayed development or the result of a rupture within the parent–child relational system, both of which would cause children to demonstrate concerning atypical or maladaptive behaviors.

Specifically with regard to developmental expectations, some children demonstrate behaviors that fall outside what would be considered typical development. More specifically still, these atypical behaviors or milestones may manifest in a way that is drastically different from the pace at which their peers are developing, such as in a young child who, at 18 months, has not yet begun to crawl. This would be of concern because children typically learn to crawl by 7–10 months. Children who have not yet learned to crawl by 18 months begin to fall behind in other aspects of development, because their abilities to physically and visually explore their world are stunted, which in turn can further affect their learning and exploration.

Ways in which parents and caregivers might determine areas of concern include noting the time at and sequence with which certain skills emerge, and then the demonstrated quality and skill level of such skills. Parents can consult developmental experts or early child interventionists to determine whether atypical behaviors should be causes for such concern, and can then decide a plan of action that best supports the child's forward development.

Caretakers must additionally take care when considering whether children's atypical behaviors are a function of a rupture in the parent–child relationship. Research has shown that a parent's history of attachment directly influences his or her relationship with his or her children; therefore, should parents have experienced fractures in their own parental relationships, they should consider how their own process might be impacting on their child. Parents who misread the cues of their children, perhaps failing to respond to their child's cry or misunderstanding why their child is crying, can negatively affect the way in which the young child learns to regulate his or her own affect. Typical behaviors that young children might demonstrate should they be experiencing an unhealthy attachment with the parent or caregiver include frequent illnesses, temper tantrums, and aversion to touch, amongst other things.

Developmentally Appropriate Approaches

Because typical therapeutic approaches with children begin around age 3 due to the cognitive and emotional capacities required for individual therapeutic work, parents concerned with their young child's psychological adjustment are encouraged to seek out therapeutic interventions specifically intended primarily for parental support. A number of avenues can provide such services, including personal counseling and parent–child relational therapy, amongst others.

Moreover, parents might also be interested in pursuing specific parental education intended to provide them with a better understanding of developmentally appropriate expectations for children. This specific intervention may ease parents' and caregivers' concerns as they learn what they should be expecting and/or experiencing. Parental education might involve attending a formal educational training workshop or course, often facilitated by community agencies or within school districts, or it might involve borrowing or buying reading material specifically addressing child development (some of these which can be found in the references list at the end of this chapter).

Personal Counseling

A parent who is experiencing difficulty with connecting or feeling attuned to his or her child might benefit from attending and engaging in his or her own therapeutic work. If parents experienced interpersonal struggles with their own attachment figures, the chances are that these struggles will arise as the parent rears his or her own children. Personal therapeutic work could help the parent to process his or her experiences, leading to a higher and more adjusted expression of the self.

As Landreth (2012) affirmed, a parent in distress is of no help to his or her child. Should parents be experiencing any kind of personal emotional dysregulation, such as a mother experiencing postpartum depression, personal counseling will be encouraged in an effort to support and anchor the parent to work toward his or her own healthy functioning. Parental health directly affects parental capacity to be with and connected to their children. Any disruption to these processes can yield disastrous results and it is essential that these struggles be mediated as early as possible so as not to interfere further in a child's development.

Parent–Child Relational Therapies

Parent–child relational therapies are broadly defined, and encompass a number of therapeutic practices and approaches, including: filial therapy, child–parent psychotherapy (CPP), didactic developmental psychotherapy (DDP), and the development, individual-differences, and relationship-based (DIR) model. Although these approaches vary considerably in terms of their philosophies, and how they can be used to facilitate change and healing, most of them have an overarching primary goal of strengthening the parent–child relational system.

Filial therapy   The overarching goal of "filial therapy" is to promote the parent as the agent of change within a child. Parents and caregivers are viewed as holding the most significant and impactful role in the lives of children. With this philosophy, filial therapists work to train parents, providing them with skills such as reflective listening, to help them to gain understanding and acceptance for their child, thereby strengthening the parent–child connection.

Traditionally two approaches have been most well regarded in the world of filial therapy: the Guerney filial therapy model, and child–parent relationship therapy (CPRT) (Landreth & Bratton, 2006). Although the Guerney model and CPRT have comparable philosophies, they vary procedurally. The Guerney model is traditionally less structured, whereas CPRT includes a manualized protocol typically facilitated through group sessions, lasting two hours, once a week, for ten weeks. Although filial therapy and CPRT are designed for children over the age of 2, therapists can modify the approach to meet the developmental needs of children between birth and 2 years old.

Child–parent psychotherapy (CPP)   A relationally based treatment, CPP is intended for use with children from birth through to the age of 6 who have experienced trauma, resulting in emotional and/or behavioral struggles (Lieberman & Van Horn, 2008). Similarly to other models for working with young children, the goal of CPP is to promote healing within and strengthen the parent–child relationship. Child–parent psychotherapists work to support the parent–child relationship by addressing misperceptions of both caregivers and children, as well as targeting maladaptive patterns of behaviors. The intervention additionally allows therapists to tailor treatment to a family's cultural context.

Didactic developmental psychotherapy (DDP)   Originally developed by Daniel Hughes, DDP is an approach intended to be used when working with children whose emotional struggles are a direct result of early parent–child separation (Becker-Weidman & Hughes, 2008). The primary goal of DDP is to promote children's healing by establishing a safe and trusting parent–child relationship; because DDP is never coercive, children enter therapy by choice. Didactic developmental psychotherapy traditionally involves three components:

1   initially meeting with parents to create support and to transmit information regarding healthy attachment and parenting approaches;
2   conducting therapy with the child of focus to establish attunement and to restructure cognitions, in which sessions cognitive-behavioral approaches are often used and at which parents are either present or observing through a two-way mirror; and
3   conducting periodic meetings with parents/caregivers without the child present to process the prior session and to plan further treatment.

Development, individual-differences, and relationship-based (DIR) model   The DIR model, designed by Dr. Stanley Greenspan, is a method of analysis specifically targeted toward helping clinicians and educators to develop an informed intervention or an approach to treatment (Greenspan & Wieder, 2006). The DIR model assists by:

- identifying a child's current developmental functioning;
- exploring the child's individual differences as pertaining to such things as sensory processing; and
- examining the functioning of the child's current relationships with caregivers, including their patterns of interaction (Greenspan & Wieder, 2006).

Following the DIR assessments, clinicians and educators are better equipped to design an intervention program that meets the specific needs of each child and family member (Greenspan & Wieder, 2006).

In closing, it is imperative that caregivers remember that relationships matter and are not immune to disruptions. Focusing on these disruptions can be countertherapeutic and caregivers might benefit instead from recognizing these ruptures as a normal relational byproduct. Systematic change can occur only within the confines of a trusting relationship; therefore, given that attention is paid to establishing just such a trusting relationship, repair is both possible and essential to the future well-being of both parents and children.

CONCLUSION

Much of infants', toddlers', and 2-year-olds' domain-specific individual neurological, physical, cognitive, emotional, and social developmental accomplishments support advancements in, and the sophistication of, their overall development. Infants are endearing and temperamental as they work to establish trust and security within their primary attachments. Toddlers often experience bouts of defiance and temper tantrums as they make efforts to achieve mastery over their environment. Two-year-olds are experiencing an exciting period, full of new discoveries, as they begin to develop confidence and increased self-awareness. These first few years of a child's life signify a period of rapid growth, with children moving from being infants fully dependent on those around them toward development of autonomy and independence. The expansive growth that pervades these extraordinary beginning years paves the way for, and promotes, future development.

REFERENCES

Ainsworth, M. D. S. (1973). The development of infant–mother attachment. In B. M. Caldwell & H. N. Ricciuti (Eds.), *Review of child development research, vol. 3* (pp. 1–94). Chicago, IL: University of Chicago.

American Academy of Pediatrics (AAP). (2005). *Sexual behaviors in children*. Elk Grove, IL: AAP. Retrieved from http://www.aap.org/pubserv/PSVpreview/pages/behaviorchart.html

American Academy of Pediatrics (AAP). (2011). Policy statement: Media use by children younger than 2 years. *Pediatrics, 128*(5), 1–7.

Ames, L. B., & Ilg, F. L. (1976). *Your two-year-old: Terrible or tender*. New York, NY: Dell.

Becker-Weidman, A., & Hughes, D. (2008). Dyadic developmental psychotherapy: An evidenced-based treatment for children with complex trauma and disorders of attachment. *Child and Family Social Work, 13*(3), 329–337.

Berger, K. S. (2011). *The developing person through childhood and adolescence* (8th ed.). New York, NY: Worth.

Berk, L. E. (2013). *Development through the lifespan* (6th ed.). New York, NY: Pearson.

Bowlby, J. (1969). *Attachment and loss, vol. 1: Attachment*. New York, NY: Basic.

Boyse, K., & Fitzgerald, K. (2010). Toilet training. Retrieved from http://www.med.umich.edu/yourchild/topics/toilet.htm

Brazelton, T. B., & Sparrow, J. D. (2006). *Touchpoints: Birth to three – Your child's emotional and behavioral development* (2nd ed.). Cambridge, MA: De Capo.

Bronfenbrenner, U. (1979). *The ecology of human development*. Cambridge, MA: Harvard University Press.

Bronfenbrenner, U., and Morris, P. (1998). The ecology of developmental processes. In W. Damon and R. M. Lerner (Eds.), *The handbook of child psychology: Theoretical models of human development, vol. 1* (pp. 993–1028). New York, NY: John Wiley.

Brooks-Gunn, J., & Donahue, E. H. (2008). Introducing the issue. *Future of Children, 18*(1), 3–10.

Christakis, D. A., Zimmerman, F. J., DiGiuseppe, D. L., & McCarty, C. A. (2004). Early television exposure and subsequent attentional problems in children. *Pediatrics, 113*(4), 708–13.

Cooper, C. R., Garcia Coll, C. T., Thorne, B., & Orellana, M. F. (2005). Beyond demographic categories: How immigration, ethnicity, and "race" matter for children's identities and pathways through school. In C. R. Cooper, C. T. Garcia Coll, W. T. Bartko, H. Davis, & C. Chatman (Eds.), *Developmental pathways through middle childhood: Rethinking contexts and diversity as resources* (pp. 181–206). Mahwah, NJ: Erlbaum.

Cross, W. E., & Cross, T. B. (2008). Theory, research, and models. In S. Quintana & C. McKown (Eds.), *Handbook of race, racism, and the developing child* (pp. 154–181). Hoboken, NJ: John Wiley & Sons.

Cross, W. E., & Fhagen-Smith, P. (2001). Patterns of African American identity development: A life span perspective. In C. L. Wijeyesinghe & B. W. Jackson, III (Eds.), *New perspectives on racial identity development: A theoretical and practical anthology* (pp. 243–270). New York, NY: New York University.

de Haan, M., & Johnson, M. H. (2003). Mechanisms and theories of brain development. In M. de Haan & M. H. Johnson (Eds.), *The cognitive neuroscience of development: Studies in developmental psychology* (pp. 1–18). New York, NY: Psychology.

DeLoache, J. S., Chiong, C., Sherman, K., Islam, N., Vanderborght, M., Troseth, G. L., Strouse, G. A., & O'Doherty, K. (2010). Do babies learn from baby media? *Psychological Science, 21*(11), 1570–1574.

Elkind, D. (1994). *A sympathetic understanding of the child* (3rd ed.). Needham Heights, MA: Allyn & Bacon.

Elkind, D. (2001). *The hurried child: Growing up too fast too soon* (3rd ed.). Cambridge, MA: Perseus.

Gesell Institute of Child Development. (2011). *Gesell Developmental Observation–Revised examiner's manual.* New Haven, CT: Gesell Institute.

Gesell Institute of Child Development. (2012). *Gesell Developmental Observation–Revised and Gesell early screener technical report.* New Haven, CT: Gesell Institute.

Graves, D. A., & Graves, S. B. (2008). Multicultural issues in the lives of developing children in the 21st century. In J. K. Asamen, M. L. Ellis, & G. L. Berry (Eds.), *The Sage handbook of child development, multiculturalism, and media* (pp. 83–99). Los Angeles, CA: Sage.

Greenough, W. T., Black, J. E., & Wallace, C. S. (1987). Experience and brain development. *Child Development, 58*(3), 539–559.

Greenspan, S. I., & Wieder, S. (2006). *Infant and early childhood: Mental health – A comprehensive developmental approach to assessment and intervention.* Washington, DC: American Psychological Association (APA).

Hirschfeld, L. (1995). The inheritability of identity: Children's understanding of the cultural biology of race. *Child Development, 66*(5), 1418–1437.

Hornor, G. (2004). Sexual behavior in children: Normal or not? *Journal of Pediatric Health Care, 18*(2), 57–64.

Hsin, C., Li, M., & Tsai, C. (2014). The influence of young children's use of technology on their learning: A review. *Educational Technology & Society, 17*(4), 85–99.

Kagan, J., & Snidman, N. C. (2004). *The long shadow of temperament.* Cambridge, MA: Belknap.

Kelly, D. J., Quinn, P. C., Slater, A. M., Kang, L., Liezhong, G., & Pascalis, O. (2007). The other-race effect develops during infancy: Evidence of perceptual narrowing. *Psychological Science, 18*(22), 1084–1089.

Korner, A. F., Zeanah, C. H., Linden, J., Berkowitz, R. I., Kraemer, H. C., & Argras, W. S. (1985). The relation between neonatal and later activity and temperament. *Child Development, 56*(1), 38–42.

Landreth, G. L. (2012). *Play therapy: Art of the relationship* (3rd ed.). New York, NY: Routledge.

Landreth, G. L., & Bratton, S. C. (2006). *Child–parent relationship therapy (CPRT): A 10-session filial therapy model.* New York, NY: Routledge.

Lee, S. J., Bartolic, S., & Vandewater, E. A. (2009). Predicting children's media use in the USA: Differences in cross-sectional and longitudinal analysis. *British Journal of Developmental Psychology, 27*(1), 123–143.

Levine, P. A., & Kline, M. (2006). *Trauma through a child's eyes: Awaking the ordinary miracle of healing.* Berkley, CA: North Atlantic.

Lieberman, A. F., & Van Horn, P. (2008). *Psychotherapy with infants and young children: Repairing the effects of stress and trauma on early attachment.* New York, NY: Guilford.

Loevinger, J. (1976). *Ego development: Concepts and theories.* San Francisco, CA: Jossey-Bass.

Marotz, L. R., & Allen, K. E. (2012). *Developmental profiles: Pre-birth through twelve* (7th ed.). Belmont, CA: Wadsworth.

McDevitt, T. M., & Ormrod, J. E. (2015). *Child development and education* (6th ed.). Upper Saddle River, NJ: Pearson.

Perry, B., Piaget, J., & Inhelder, B. (1969). *The psychology of the child.* New York, NY: Basic Books.

Quintana, S. M. (1998). Development of children's understanding of ethnicity and race. *Applied & Preventative Psychology: Current Scientific Perspectives, 7*, 25–45.

Quintana, S. M., & McKown, C. (2008). Introduction: Race, racism, and the developing child. In S. Quintana & C. McKown (Eds.), *Handbook of race, racism, and the developing child* (pp. 1–15). Hoboken, NJ: John Wiley & Sons.

Ruble, D. N., Alvarez, J., Bachman, M., Cameron, J., Fuligni, A., Coll, C. G., & Rhee, E. (2004). The development of a sense of "we": The development and implications of children's collective identity. In M. Bennett and F. Sani (Eds.), *The development of the social self* (pp. 29–76). New York, NY: Psychology Press.

Santrock, J. (2014). *Child development* (14th ed.). New York, NY: McGraw-Hill.

Siegel, D. J. (2012). *The developing mind: How relationships and the brain interact to shape who we are* (2nd ed.). New York, NY: Guilford.

Siegel, D. J., & Bryson, T. P. (2011). *The whole-brain child: 12 revolutionary strategies to nurture your child's developing mind.* New York, NY: Bantam Books.

Sprenger, M. (2008). *The developing brain: Birth to age eight.* Thousand Oaks, CA: Corwin.

Thelen, E., & Adolph, K. E. (1992). Arnold L. Gesell: The paradox of nature and nurture. *Developmental Psychology, 28*(3), 368–380.

Thompson, R. A. (2001). Development in the first years of life. *Future Child, 11*(1), 20–33.

Thompson, R. F. (2000). *The brain: A neuroscience primer* (3rd ed.). New York, NY: Worth.

Van Ausdale, D., & Feagin, J. R. (1996). Using racial and ethnic concept: The critical case of very young children. *American Sociological Review, 61*(5), 779–793.

Van Ausdale, D., & Feagin, J. R. (2001). *The first R: How children learn race and racism.* Lanham, MD: Rowman & Littlefield.

Vandewater, E. A., Rideout, V. J., Wartella, E. A., Huang, X., Lee, J. H., & Shim, M. (2007). Digital childhood: Electronic media and technology use among infants, toddlers, and preschoolers. *Pediatrics, 119*(5), 1006–1015.

Vygotsky, L. S. (1978) *Mind in society: The development of higher psychological processes.* Cambridge, MA: Harvard University.

4

THE EXTRAORDINARY 3-YEAR-OLD

Kasie R. Lee

Source: Used with permission from Shutterstock

THE 3-YEAR-OLD

When a child reaches 3 years old, parents experience a welcome reprieve from the "terrible 2s." At 3, children experience what the prominent scholar of child development, Dr. Arnold Gesell, termed a state of "equilibrium" (Gesell Institute, 2011). The child's behavior, along with his or her internal state of being, have typically reached a balanced stage of smooth, integrated development. Three-year-olds are happy within themselves and in their relationships with others (quite a markedly different experience from that of those aged 2½). Unlike 2-year-olds, 3-year-olds are quite pleasant to be around and parents typically experience very few concerns about them. Three-year-olds often have cooperative, easy-going attitudes. They love to please others by following rules, sharing, and attempting to help with household chores and other tasks. However, their desire to do things the "right" way leads them to frequently ask for help or reassurance. They are typically compliant, having developed a new fondness for the word "yes," which seemed nonexistent in their vocabulary at the age of 2½. Three-year-olds enjoy being with others – particularly primary caregivers – and often ask parents and siblings to read to them and play with them. They have an increased security in their relationships, which now expands beyond their immediate family members, and they love making new friends (Gesell Institute, 2011).

> Unlike 2-year-olds, 3-year-olds are quite pleasant to be around and parents typically experience very few concerns about them.

This internal sense of security and stability is also reflected in the child's physical development. At 3, children experience improvement in both fine and gross motor skills, allowing for more success in play activities and other daily tasks that were frustrating for them at 2. Three-year-olds walk and run with confident ease. They also experience increased excitement about learning new words, and their vocabulary and communication with others improves substantially. Three-year-olds generally have a positive outlook toward the world, and enter most experiences with a sense of wonder and curiosity (Gesell Institute, 2011).

THE 3½-YEAR-OLD

At 3½ years old, children experience a dramatic period of instability. During this time, children appear to lose the stability that they achieved at 3, and their bodies begin to prepare for an intense period of growth set to begin at 4. This transition brings about disequilibrium in many areas for the child. Children often experience instability in their social, emotional, physical, and cognitive development. Three-and-a-half-year-olds typically experience great difficulties in their relationships with others. They feel much less secure within themselves compared to how they felt at 3, and this can typically translate into more crying, whining, and difficulty separating from their parents. Three-and-a-half-year-olds become much more demanding, attempting to direct the behaviors of adults, as well as friends, and to ensure that everyone's attention is upon them. Three-and-a-half-year-olds are often determined to control their environment at all costs; at the same time, they are highly inconsistent and experience dramatic emotional extremes, vacillating from being loud, boisterous, and demanding to being shy and withdrawn. They are often very determined and strong-willed, frequently refusing to follow rules. Even trivial requests can prompt a rebellious tantrum from a 3½-year-old and he or she can be very difficult to please. For example, if presented with yogurt as a snack, a 3½-year-old may cry loudly in disappointment – and continue to cry and refuse all other options presented. Meal times in general tend to be difficult for them. At other times, 3½-year-olds can be very friendly, loving, creative, and delightful, and they like to be included. This is also a time marked by an incredible sense of fantasy, imagination, and playfulness. This unpredictable quality makes relationships with 3½-year-olds much more strained than they were at the age of 3 (Gesell Institute, 2011).

> Three-and-a-half-year-olds feel much less secure within themselves compared to 3-year-olds, leading to more crying, whining, and difficulty separating from their parents.

This instability in the child's internal and social self is mirrored in his or her physical abilities. It is normal at this age for children to become clumsier, frequently stumbling and falling. Certain play activities, such as drawing or block building, become more difficult, because muscle control is weaker and the 3½-year-old experiences hand tremors. Despite the increased verbal abilities achieved at 3, 3½-year-olds often stutter as their communication and use of language becomes unstable, along with their senses of sight and sound. At 3½, children may report difficulties seeing and hearing. As a result of this increase in instability, children at 3½ often feel insecure and anxious, and rely much more heavily on self-soothing behaviors, such as nail-biting, nose-picking, thumb-sucking, chewing on their clothes, and rubbing their genitals. Children may also develop facial or other tics, or may excessively blink their eyes. These behaviors can often be particularly worrisome for parents, causing many to seek advice and guidance (Gesell Institute, 2011).

BRAIN DEVELOPMENT

At 3 years old, children experience tremendous changes in their brain development. Indeed, the brain of a 3-year-old is two-and-a-half times more active than the adult brain, making this a prime time for learning. Three is an age at which physical development begins to slow down, and emotional and cognitive growth progress dramatically (Sprenger, 2008). To avoid the use of technical neuroscience language, we will

> The brain of a 3-year-old is two-and-a-half times more active than the adult brain!

only summarize the specifics regarding the physical changes happening in the brain at this age. Sprenger (2008) offers a more technical, yet accessible, discussion regarding brain development in young children (Sprenger, 2008).

Increased blood flood and connections throughout multiple parts of the brain cause dramatic changes in the 3-year-old's brain. An "explosion" in language development occurs as higher level thinking skills are acquired. At 3, children develop the ability to store episodic memories, as well as long-term semantic memories. Physical development occurs as visual–motor coordination improves, along with emotional regulation and self-control (Sprenger, 2008). These changes occurring in the 3-year-old's brain directly influence the physical, cognitive, emotional, and social growth that will be described in further detail in the rest of this chapter.

Three is a particularly important age at which to stimulate brain growth in children. During this time, the brain experiences a period of "pruning," during which connections that are used remain active and those that are not used die. Providing materials that invoke opportunities for play, such as sand and water tables, and art supplies. such as paint, crayons, and markers, promotes stimulation, growth, and integration for multiple parts of the 3-year-old's brain (Sprenger, 2008). Typical brain-based developmental milestones of the 3-year-old include: clear speech, sentences of five or six words, running, climbing, hopping, balancing on one foot, stacking up to six blocks, knowing some colors, understanding numbers and counting, remembering stories, engaging in pretend play, and moving back and forth from fantasy to reality (Sprenger,

> Three-year-olds sleep 10–12 hours a night and may need rest times during the day, instead of naps (Petty, 2010).

2008). While 3-year-olds should be provided with multiple activities designed to promote brain development to foster appropriate milestones, they should also be given an adequate amount of unstructured time to allow integration to occur. Overly stimulating the 3-year-old – and indeed children of all ages – with too many structured activities for the sake of promoting development can have deleterious effects (Stamm & Spencer, 2007).

PHYSICAL DEVELOPMENT

At 3 years old, children begin to develop taller, thinner, and more adult-like bodies. They have a full set of teeth and they typically sleep through the night for 10–12 hours. They have achieved greater independence, being able to feed themselves, dress themselves, put on their shoes, wash their hands, and brush their teeth (with some help from adults) (Gesell Institute, 2011).

Motor Skill Development

Three-year-olds experience improved coordination and a greater sense of control over their muscles, and they can walk, run, jump, kick, climb, and swing with ease. They can easily walk

> Three-year-olds are typically very active, like to keep up with older children, and will play until they are exhausted.

forward and backward. They have good balance, can walk up and down stairs, walk on their tiptoes, and stand and hop on one foot. They can also ride a tricycle, catch a large ball, throw a ball overarm, and kick a ball forward (Petty, 2010). They are typically very active, like to keep up with older children, and will play until they are exhausted. They can become tired quickly, which tiredness is often accompanied by a cranky mood (Gesell Institute, 2011).

The fine motor skills of 3-year-olds are becoming more developed. Three-year-olds can now hold crayons and markers with their fingers, instead of their fists, and can complete puzzles with large pieces with ease. However, sustained fine motor coordination requires effort and causes 3-year-olds to become easily fatigued. Three-year-olds are also able to pour their own drinks with little support from adults, but they continue to experience frequent spills.

Three-year-olds experience increased motor coordination, strength, and balance. They have a greater mastery over their bodies, are full of energy, and are in constant motion. Three-year-olds should be encouraged to use their arms, legs, and fingers and hands to explore the world. However, accidents are frequent because they fail to watch where they are going and crash into things. They are also often overly bold in their actions, lacking a sense of reality about their abilities, and therefore require close supervision (AAP, 2009).

Potty Training

Typically, by 3 years of age, children have successfully mastered toilet training. Boys are more likely to master potty training later than girls, but most are typically accident-free by 3½ (Brazelton & Sparrow, 2006). In preparation for a preschool setting, it is important for 3-year-olds to become comfortable using toilets away from home with little assistance from adults (AAP, 2009).

Many 3-year-olds may sleep through the night without accidents, while others may continue to have occasional nighttime accidents. Accidents should be approached with acceptance because 3-year-olds may be very hard on themselves. Accidents are also common for 3-year-olds who are engaged in play with their friends and who withhold urine in an attempt to avoid missing out on the fun. Again, these accidents should be not be responded to with punishment, because they are a typical part of child development that the 3-year-old will eventually grow out of (AAP, 2009).

Three-year-olds who have successfully mastered potty training may regress if they experience dramatic changes in their environment, such as the birth of a sibling or their parents' divorce. Others may experience regressions as a result of medical issues. As with accidents, 3-year-olds should be approached with empathy and understanding, and should not be pressured to regain control. Should dramatic regressions not gradually subside, parents are advised to consult with a pediatrician or other child development expert (AAP, 2009; Brazelton & Sparrow, 2006).

GENDER AND SEXUAL DEVELOPMENT

Not unlike other areas of development, sexual development is not only based on the physical changes occurring in a child's body, but also influenced by what a child is exposed to in his or her familial environment. Sexual development is particularly dependent upon what a child witnesses and is taught in regards to cultural and religious values regarding sexuality and personal boundaries (NCTSN, 2009). While the typical patterns of sexual development will be described here, these behaviors are likely to vary depending on each child's individual experiences.

By 3 years old, children have typically developed a sense of gender awareness, distinguishing the differences in boys and girls, and identifying themselves appropriately. They find pleasure in touching their genitals or rubbing against other objects, and this behavior often increases when they are tired or upset. Masturbating is sometimes done in private or in public, because 3-year-olds have little sense of modesty. They also enjoy being naked and they frequently take off their clothes. Three-year-olds are curious about the differences between the bodies of children and adults, and they may attempt to watch their parents change clothes or go to the bathroom. They also may attempt to touch their mother's, or other women's, breasts. They frequently ask questions about their private parts and where babies come from. They are also curious about bodily functions, like to talk about bowel movements and urination, and are fond of words such as "poop" and "pee" (NCTSN, 2009).

Although it can be alarming to many parents, it is common for 3-year-olds to be curious and to explore the bodies of their peers by engaging in games such as "doctors." Sexual play is considered normal when it occurs between children who play together regularly, who know each other well, and who are of the same general age and physical size. Normal sexual play occurs infrequently, and it is spontaneous, unplanned, and voluntary, with neither child feeling upset or uncomfortable. Sexual play that does not fit these criteria can be harmful to children and often indicates underlying concerns, and should therefore be addressed with the help of childcare professionals (NCTSN, 2009).

> Sexual play is considered normal when it occurs between children who play together regularly, who know each other well, and who are of the same general age and physical size. Normal sexual play occurs infrequently, and it is spontaneous, unplanned, and voluntary, with neither child feeling upset or uncomfortable.

COGNITIVE DEVELOPMENT

Three-year-olds are very curious and love to talk, and they spend most of their days asking questions about everything including "who," "what," "where," and "why" questions. However, complex answers from parents can be confusing and 3-year-olds will prefer simple, concrete answers. They now have a greater sense of mastery over their world. They can follow simple directions with no more than three steps, such as: "It's time to put your toys away and put your shoes and coat on." They begin to understand that their actions can cause things to happen, but they continue to struggle with problem-solving skills, lacking the ability to see more than one solution. They begin to have a clearer sense of time, and they know their daily rituals. Some other common milestones achieved by the age of 3 are naming common colors, recalling parts of a story, beginning to understand numbers and counting, and understanding the concepts of "same" and "different" (AAP, 2009).

Communication increases tremendously at the age of 3. At this age, most speech is sufficiently understandable for children to communicate clearly with adults in their families and with strangers. At 3 years old, children begin to talk in complete sentences of between three and six words. Their vocabulary increases tremendously, allowing them to express their needs more easily. They have now mastered basic grammar rules and can properly use "I," "me," "we," and "you." While they can now communicate more clearly with adults, however, they may have difficulty taking turns in conversations. Three-year-olds love to listen attentively to stories, and their memories are now well developed, allowing them to remember their favorite parts of stories and movies. They enjoy repetition – especially rhymes, sounds, and new words (AAP, 2009).

At 3 years old, children often play make-believe using dolls, animals, and other children and adults. Toys and play materials that allow for manipulation foster further development and creativity. For 3-year-olds to reach their fullest potential, they should be exposed to stimulating environments that allow for multiple opportunities for exploration. Further, they should be encouraged to try difficult tasks previously beyond their level of mastery, and their accomplishments should be acknowledged and their efforts applauded (Georgia Department of Early Care and Learning, n.d.).

WORLDVIEW/EGO DEVELOPMENT

Ego Development

According to Erikson's (1963) stages of psychosocial development, 3-year-olds are in the process of transitioning from the *autonomy vs. shame* stage to the *initiative vs. guilt* stage. During this time, 3-year-olds are developing a sense of autonomy, self-efficacy, and mastery. This causes them to be very curious and constantly trying new things. However, 3-year-olds continue to approach the world in a very self-centered way, and others may now see their behaviors as intrusive and demanding. Three-year-olds love to talk, and enjoy sharing their thoughts and feelings with others. The 3-year-old has a greater sense of individuality and truly believes that he or she is the center of the universe. Yet 3-year-olds are sensitive to the opinions that others have of them, because they now understand the difference between right and wrong, and want to do what is right. As 3-year-olds are exploring their worlds and trying new tasks, parents should be encouraged to applaud their efforts, even when mistakes and messes occur. Frequent disapproval from parents can cause 3-year-olds to inhibit their curiosity and to feel an inflated sense of guilt, and have a negative impact on their developing self-concept.

Racial/Ethnic Identity Development

By the age of 3, children are becoming more aware of how people look. They are aware of differences between boys and girls, and they notice differences in skin color, and hair color and texture, as well as other physical traits. They may prefer to be around people who look similar to them and may show fear in approaching people that look different. They may prefer to play with dolls that look like them. They may begin to model prejudices to which they are exposed by family members or the media, but they do not yet understand the true meanings of racism and stereotypes. Between the ages of 3 and 4, children begin to ask for explanations for differences, and seek to understand where their skin, hair, and eye colors came from – and whether they will remain constant. They may be curious about how people with different skin colors can be in the same family. At 3, children are unable to understand a scientific reason behind racial differences and they are typically unable to identify their own racial/ethnic groups (PBS, 2015).

EMOTIONAL DEVELOPMENT

Three-year-olds experience a wide variety of emotions. Feelings such as love, joy, fear, and anger are felt very intensely, and 3-year-olds make no attempt to hide their feelings. They are often very silly and enjoy making others laugh. They are able to identify many of their own feelings, as well as the feelings of others, by interpreting facial expressions and tone of voice. They understand that others have thoughts and feelings, and are able to show care and concern by offering hugs to those who are crying or informing a parent when a sibling is upset. Three-year-olds have a greater ability to identify and articulate their wants and needs when they are upset, and they have fewer tantrums than they did as 2-year-olds. However, they may continue to struggle with self-control and emotional regulation, and may fall apart during stressful situations or when there are sudden changes to their normal routines (AAP, 2009).

Three-year-olds frequently move back and forth between fantasy and reality, sometimes having difficulty distinguishing the difference. They may have imaginary friends and assign feelings to inanimate objects such as a flower or the moon. Three-year-olds can create very vivid fantasy worlds and may be convinced that they are the characters in their stories. It is common for 3-year-olds to don costumes and proclaim "I am Spider-Man," and or "I am a princess." They may even desire to wear these costumes for weeks on end. Although it may seem funny, their fantasies should be respected and not belittled, even unintentionally. Parents should be encouraged to play along, within reason (Miller, 2001). Further, parents should be careful with jokes or idle threats such as "I'm leaving you here" when a 3-year-old refuses to leave a store: Because of their difficulties distinguishing fiction and fact, the child may believe that the parent is serious and feel terrified, inciting a tantrum (AAP, 2009).

> Play materials that allow for maximum imagination, such as boxes, dress-up clothes, and household utensils, meet the pretend play needs of 3-year-olds.

Because 3-year-olds are becoming more independent, they are better able to make choices for themselves. Their independence can be encouraged by offering choices such as what to drink with dinner or what to shirt to wear. For example, appropriate choices for a 3-year-old might be "Would you like milk or juice with dinner?" or "Do you want to wear the yellow shirt or the purple shirt?" Options should be minimized to avoid overwhelming the 3-year-old, but even benign choices can offer very young children the opportunity to learn to make decisions and to feel competent in their abilities (AAP, 2009).

> Three-and-a-half-year-olds have a larger vocabulary with which to express refusal (Gesell Institute, 2011).

SOCIAL DEVELOPMENT

At 3, children begin to identify themselves as unique individuals, with thoughts and feelings separate from those of others. They understand the idea of "mine" and "his" or "hers." This transition allows them to become more concerned about their relationships with others. Three-year-olds are often able to identify their friends, although they do not completely understand the concept of friendship. Three-year-olds enjoy being with peers, and they are beginning to develop an increased ability to play with other children rather than simply alongside them. However, they experience difficulties sharing and engaging in cooperative play. They understand the concept of taking turns and have an awareness of others' feelings, but they have difficulty putting others' wants and needs above their own. Because sharing is sometimes difficult, 3-year-olds may often prefer to play alone (Petty, 2010). Playtime for 3-year-olds often results in yelling and crying, and sometimes pushing, hitting, or other physical aggression. When social conflicts arise, the 3-year-old lacks the ability to problem solve and often looks to adults for help. Three-year-olds are, however, capable of prosocial behavior and conflict resolution when encouraged and supported by adults. They are more likely to accept compromises during conflicts with peers when those compromises are facilitated by adults. Cooperative play increases as children become more familiar with their peers or when playing

Three years old is the peak age for imaginary companions.

with siblings. Three-year-olds are also observant during playtimes, closely watching other children, particularly in new situations, and they often imitate the behaviors of other children. Three is an ideal age for a child to begin preschool or to participate in a playgroup, because these provide prime opportunities for further developing social skills (AAP, 2009).

RELATIONSHIP DEVELOPMENT

Three is the age at which friendships begin to develop. Three-year-olds have a strong desire for friendship and love playing with other children. However, their concept of friendship is often temporary and constrained to those with whom they happen to be playing at the current moment. They have difficulty sharing and taking turns. It is not uncommon to hear a 3-year-old angrily shout "You're not my friend anymore!" (Miller, 2001).

In relationships with their parents, 3-year-olds display a desire to please and cooperate. At 3, a child may prefer to be with one parent more than the other, and most often it is the parent of the opposite sex. Further, they often imitate the actions of their parents and other adults. Three-year-olds spend lots of time observing others' behaviors and are often very aware of what adults expect from them. They are also aware of what adults say about them, and they can be particularly aware when parents complain about their behaviors to others. A greater sense of independence allows 3-year-olds to separate more easily from their parents, but they need caregivers nearby to serve as a secure base as they explore, play, and meet new children (AAP, 2009).

DEVELOPMENT IN THE AGE OF TECHNOLOGY

The American Academy of Pediatrics (AAP, 2011) recommends that screen time for children under the age of 2 should be discouraged. "Screen time" includes all televisions, smartphones, and tablets, including programs and apps specifically designed for young children. Some research suggests that screen time can be harmful to children's language development (Lapierre, Piotrowski, & Linebarger, 2012). For children over the age of 2, parents should be encouraged to use screen time with their children as a way in which to interact and play together. Children's development of language is often directly related to the amount of time that parents spend talking with them, and the same growth is not experienced by hearing people talk on television (Wong, Hall, Justice, & Hernandez, 2015). If parents are unable to interact with children during screen time owing to other responsibilities, such as household chores, parents should be encouraged to provide their children with opportunities for unstructured free play. Free play is more beneficial for child development than exposure to social media. There is no evidence to support the benefits of exposing babies and toddlers to media, and some evidence to suggest that it may be harmful (AAP, 2011). Those parents who choose to expose their 3-year-olds to media should be familiar with the programs to which their children are exposed; all adult content should be avoided; and, ideally, parents should be participating in these activities with their children. Additionally, exposure should be limited and highly regulated by parents, and children's bedrooms should be screen-free environments (AAP, 2011; Wong et al., 2015).

BEST PRACTICES IN COUNSELING/THERAPY

When parents share their concerns about a child with a therapist, it is the responsibility of the mental health professional to discern which behaviors are typical developmental issues and which behaviors may represent more serious concerns. Understanding the normal patterns of child development is crucial for appropriate clinical decision making and the selection of effective interventions.

The age of 3 often represents a very calm and pleasant stage of child development; thus therapists are likely to encounter a parent with concerns regarding a typically developing 3-year-old only rarely. It is more likely that those 3-year-olds referred for therapy will have encountered environmental circumstances or biological influences that have disrupted their development, caused problematic symptoms, and impeded their healthy functioning. Furthermore, because 3½ can be a much more challenging phase of child development, it may be more common for therapists to hear alarm expressed by parents of 3½-year-olds who are experiencing developmentally appropriate milestones. While these struggles can be considered normal, they are no less disconcerting and stressful for parents to navigate. As this chapter has described, because the age of 3½ is often a tumultuous time in a child's life, parents may be more likely to reach out for help and support from therapists.

Case Conceptualization and Treatment Planning

To help families most effectively, it is vital that therapists have a comprehensive understanding of normal development of 3-year-olds and 3½-year-olds. Only in understanding typical child development can therapists understand the extent to which development has gone awry. When parents report concerns regarding their children, therapists must conduct a careful and thorough assessment of each individual family's needs before deciding upon the most appropriate treatment approach. During the treatment planning process, therapists must decide upon the most appropriate approach based on their theoretical conceptualization of the underlying cause of the concerns and needs of the child.

A primary treatment consideration is the decision to work with the child individually, the parent(s) individually, the parent(s) and child together, or a combination of these modalities. The relationship between primary caregivers and a 3-year-old is the ideal focus for therapy. Parents who are attuned with their young children and who can respond in relationally enhancing ways serve as therapeutic agents for children, safeguarding them from emotional and behavioral obstacles. A second treatment consideration is the specific treatment modality: Any therapeutic approach directly involving children aged 3 or 4 should be based on play. Three-year-olds are limited in their abilities to think abstractly and to communicate verbally; thus play offers young children opportunities to express themselves concretely using toys. Three-year-olds use play in concrete ways, typically playing out mastery skills or using play to explore relationships. Psychoeducation and talk therapies that require verbal communication should be reserved for modalities involving only parents.

In the following sections, we share two case examples of therapeutic approaches directly involving 3-year-olds.

Filial Therapy/Child–Parent Relationship Therapy (CPRT)

Because parents serve as primary attachment figures for their children, working with children and parents together can be extremely beneficial. Research indicates that involving parents in the therapy of their children, when appropriate, is much more impactful than working with the child individually (Bratton, Ray, Rhine, & Jones, 2005). By working with parents and children in sessions together, therapists can help parents to improve their communications skills with their children and to develop more empathic relationships, and can further facilitate healthy attachment and a stronger sense of security. When the child's presenting concerns are developmentally normal, therapists may use parent–child therapy to help to normalize that child's behaviors, and to encourage parents to develop more developmentally appropriate expectations and responses to that child.

Case study 1   A mother, "Samantha," sought counseling services for help with her 3-year-old daughter. Samantha reported that her daughter was disrespectful and constantly interrupting adult conversations. She was also quite defiant, frequently saying "no," demanding that things be done her way, and was easily frustrated and angry when things went otherwise. Samantha expressed frustrations with her daughter's clumsiness and reported that she frequently made messes around the house. Samantha was a young, single mother, working full-time, and when we first met she had recently decided to return to college. Samantha felt that working full-time while going to college had put a strain on her relationship with her daughter, because they were spending less time together and, on most days, her daughter was cared for by her grandmother (Samantha's mother). Samantha expressed a desire to develop a closer relationship with her daughter and to learn a more developmentally appropriate approach to discipline.

Samantha and I discussed the benefits of participating in filial therapy (see Chapter 2). I met with Samantha and her daughter for approximately four months. Our sessions included teaching Samantha developmentally appropriate behavior for 3-year-olds, normalizing her stressful experience as a single mother, providing emotional support for her, and teaching her the skills with which to facilitate nondirective play sessions with her daughter. Samantha and her daughter participated in weekly play sessions at the clinic, while I observed behind a two-way mirror. After the play sessions, Samantha and I met individually to discuss her experience, and to further develop her parenting skills. Samantha often felt overwhelmed with the responsibility of providing for her daughter, working full-time, and advancing her education. Participating in filial therapy helped Samantha to develop more developmentally appropriate expectations for her daughter. While her daughter's behavior continued to be stressful, Samantha developed an increased level of empathy and understanding toward that behavior as being developmentally normal. This attitude of acceptance helped her to respond in healthier ways and to trust that the behaviors would pass with time. The play sessions helped Samantha to feel more connected to her daughter, and her daughter, in turn, felt a safer connection to her mother. The playtimes provided much-needed quality time for the two to spend together that was difficult to obtain at home.

Filial therapy is thus demonstrably an ideal intervention for 3-year-olds because they love to play, particularly with their primary caregivers. It provides both parent and child a safe way in which to tackle challenging issues and to develop stronger, healthier connections.

Child-Centered Play Therapy (CCPT)

The previous case study represented a parent who, although stressed, was able to be present-minded and emotionally available for her child in therapy sessions. Often, when parents are struggling with their own mental health issues or have experienced the same environmental stressors as those to which their children are being exposed, filial therapy may be less successful — or, at worst, harmful. In circumstances such as these, therapists will find it more beneficial to begin treatment working with young children and parents separately.

Typically, individual therapy is be contraindicated for children under the age of 3 because of development considerations. When considering individual therapy with a 3- or 4-year-old, it is vital that therapists consider the development of the child. Around the age of 3, children begin to develop more trusting relationships with adults outside their immediate family members. Three-year-olds are typically able to easily separate from their parents, allowing them to comfortably accompany therapists to an individual counseling environment such as a playroom. Additionally, because 3-year-olds are typically fully toilet trained, being in a 30–45-minute counseling session is less of a concern than it is with younger children. Individual therapy may not, however, be appropriate for children who have not yet achieved these developmental milestones.

Further, as already noted, any individual therapeutic approach involving young children should be based in play, and this is particularly true for 3-year-olds. Three-year-olds are typically eager to play. They approach life with wonder and curiosity. They have a strong sense of imagination and playfulness, priming them to engage with toys in the playroom. Additionally, they love to engage in fantasy, and they are eager to make new friends, both of which allow them to use toys to quickly develop trusting relationships with therapists. When considering individual play-based therapies for a 3-year-old, however, therapists' options are limited. Owing to developmental considerations, approaches requiring talk therapy and psychoeducation are not ideal for 3-year-olds. Child-centered play therapy (CCPT) represents the most appropriate approach for very young children because it allows the child to participate in a process of self-guided healing and to communicate with a therapist in the child's natural language of play. Attempts by a therapist to guide or direct sessions with a 3-year-old often prove fruitless, because this typically requires the child to engage in activities beyond his or her developmental capabilities.

Case study 2   The mother of "Ethan," a 3-year-old, sought counseling services because of his aggressive and defiant behavior. Ethan was hospitalized in an inpatient psychiatric facility after being expelled from multiple preschools on grounds of violent behavior toward other children. Ethan's parents had recently divorced after several episodes of domestic violence that Ethan witnessed. A restraining order was issued and Ethan's father's parental rights were terminated. Ethan expressed anger toward his mother and sadness about the loss of his father. Ethan's mother was exhausted and overwhelmed with his behavior and the grief regarding the loss of her marriage. Further, the trauma that she had experienced in the abusive relationship with her ex-husband prevented her from being the emotionally supportive parent that Ethan desperately needed.

I conducted weekly individual CCPT with Ethan over the course of two years. As his therapy progressed, Ethan disclosed several detailed experiences of sexual abuse that he had sustained at the hands of his father. Initially, Ethan's mother was unable to face the extent of Ethan's pain and play therapy provided an environment in which Ethan could safely process his traumatic experiences. While I met individually with Ethan, I conducted periodic parent consultation sessions with Ethan's mother; she also participated in her own individual counseling with another therapist. As she began to heal, she developed a greater capacity to be emotionally supportive for Ethan, and I therefore suggested that she participate in a child–parent relationship therapy (CPRT) group specifically aimed at divorced parents. After participating in the group, Ethan's mother expressed a desire to continue her filial training, and I conducted individual weekly filial sessions with her, in addition to Ethan's weekly play therapy sessions, for several months. Following the filial sessions between Ethan and his mother, I met with her individually to provide parenting support, to help her to further develop empathy and acceptance toward Ethan, and to guide her toward more developmentally appropriate communication strategies.

Over the course of two years, Ethan's aggression, anger, and sadness ceased, he successfully entered kindergarten, and he and his mother developed a safe, nurturing, and supportive relationship.

Parent Involvement Interventions

The Incredible Years (IY)   The Incredible Years (IY) program is intended specifically for children who are at risk of developing behavioral problems. The IY parent program exposes parents to specific strategies for young children, starting at 2 years old. Through the use of child-directed play sessions, parents learn how to respond in developmentally appropriate ways when interacting with their children (Webster-Stratton, 2012). Because IY uses play and relationship components, it is well matched to the needs of 3-year-olds.

Child–parent psychotherapy (CPP)   Child–parent psychotherapy (CPP) is designed as an intervention for young children, from birth to the age of 6, who have experienced at least one traumatic event (that is, abuse, loss, disaster, etc.) (Lieberman & Van Horn, 2008). The intervention focuses on helping parents to develop relationships with their children to help build safety, attachment, and adaptive responses to trauma. For young children, CPP uses parent–child play sessions to help parents to learn beneficial methods of communication that will guide the child through the trauma event and response. Specifically, for 3-year-olds who have experienced trauma, CPP provides a developmentally appropriate intervention.

Positive discipline   Positive discipline teaches Adlerian-based parenting skills with which to build effective communication between parent and child (Nelsen, Erwin, & Duffy, 2007a, 2007b). The positive discipline approach to young children helps parents to understand their child's developmental needs, goals of behavior, and how to best encourage him or her. Positive discipline is designed as a parent education program for typically developing children, teaching skills by means of books, group training sessions, and videos.

CONCLUSION

Three-year-olds can present unique challenges for the therapist. For some children in this age group, typical developmental milestones such as frequent tantrums, defiance, and general moodiness can be challenging for parents. Working with these children requires therapists to provide emotional support for parents, while educating them on developmentally appropriate expectations for their children. At other times, children in this age group who have experienced trauma or other factors negatively impacting on their development require therapists to provide more intensive individual approaches for both child and parent. As with children of all ages, therapists must carefully consider the unique needs of each family and select interventions appropriately. This chapter described the typical developmental milestones of 3-year-olds and 3½-year-olds and suggested interventions, as well as provided case examples to illustrate the selection of effective treatment interventions.

REFERENCES

American Academy of Pediatrics (AAP). (2009). *Caring for your baby and young child: Birth to age 5* (5th ed.). New York, NY: Bantam Books.

American Academy of Pediatrics (AAP). (2011). Media use by children younger than 2 years. Retrieved from http://pediatrics.aappublications.org/content/early/2011/10/12/peds.2011-1753.full.pdf

Bratton, S., Ray, D., Rhine, T., & Jones, L. (2005). The efficacy of play therapy with children: A meta-analytic review of treatment outcomes. *Professional Psychology: Research and Practice, 36*(4), 376–390.

Brazelton, T. B., & Sparrow, J. D. (2006). *Touchpoints: Birth to three – Your child's emotional and behavioral development* (2nd ed.). Cambridge, MA: De Capo Press.

Erikson, E. (1963). *Childhood and society* (2nd ed.). New York, NY: Norton Press.

Georgia Department of Early Care and Learning. (n.d.). Georgia Early Learning Standards: Birth through age 3. Retrieved from http://decal.ga.gov/documents/attachments/GELSComplete608.pdf

Gesell Institute of Child Development. (2011). *Gesell Developmental Observation–Revised examiner's manual*. New Haven, CT: Gesell Institute.

Lapierre, M. A., Piotrowski, J. T., & Linebarger, D. L. (2012). Background television in the homes of US children. *Pediatrics, 130*(5), 839–846.

Lieberman, A. F., & Van Horn, P. (2008). *Psychotherapy with infants and young children: Repairing the effects of stress and trauma on early attachment*. New York, NY: Guilford.

Miller, K. (2001). *Age and stages: Developmental descriptions and activities – Birth through eight years*. West Palm Beach, FL: TelShare.

National Child Traumatic Stress Network (NCTSN). (2009). Sexual development and behavior in children: Information for parents and caregivers. Retrieved from http://nctsn.org/nctsn_assets/pdfs/caring/sexualdevelopmentandbehavior.pdf

Nelsen, J., Erwin, C., & Duffy, R. (2007a). *Positive discipline: The first three years – Infant to toddler*. New York, NY: Three Rivers.

Nelsen, J., Erwin, C., & Duffy, R. (2007b). *Positive discipline for preschoolers*. New York, NY: Three Rivers.

Petty, K. (2010). *Developmental milestones of young children*. St. Paul, MN: Redleaf Press.

Public Broadcasting Service (PBS). (2015). How racial identity and attitudes develop in young children. Retrieved from http://www.sesamestreet.org/parents/topics/getalong/getalong05

Sprenger, M. B. (2008). *The developing brain: Birth to age eight*. Thousand Oaks, CA: Corwin Press.

Stamm, J., & Spencer, P. (2007). *Bright from the start*. New York, NY: Gotham Books.

Webster-Stratton, C. (2012). The incredible years: Parents, teachers, and children training series. In S. Pfeiffer and L. Reddy (Eds.), *Innovative mental health interventions for children: Programs that work* (pp. 31–45). New York, NY: Routledge.

Wong, D. W., Hall, K.R., Justice, C. A., & Hernandez, L. W. (2015). *Counseling individuals through the lifespan*. Los Angeles, CA: Sage.

5

THE EXTRAORDINARY 4-YEAR-OLD

Jenifer W. Balch

Source: Used with permission from Shutterstock

It is a Saturday afternoon and Kaylee is entertaining herself by playing with various toys in her playroom. She discovers her older sister's dance uniform, sees the shiny sequins on the uniform, and immediately puts it on. Kaylee then finds costume jewelry and a glitter wand left over from the previous Halloween. She puts on the jewelry and fastens a bow in her hair to complete her look. In full costume, Kaylee twirls into the living room, where her parents are watching television, and performs a dance routine for them. With a big smile on her face, she tells them she is a fairy princess with magical powers. Kaylee's parents smile and tell her how cute she looks when she is dressed up and pretending to do magic. Kaylee becomes frustrated, throws down her wand, and insists that she *is* a fairy princess with *actual* magical powers.

Kaylee's love for fantasy and make-believe play is typical of a 4-year-old child. Four-year-olds are often described as adventurous, active, talkative, and curious. They are ready for just about anything that comes their way, taking on new adventures with high energy and excitement. They constantly take in new information and are ready to explore the world.

According to Arnold Gesell's model of development, maturity occurs in a cyclical pattern of *equilibrium* and *disequilibrium* (Gesell Institute, 2011). The first six months of a 4-year-old's life is characterized as vigorous and expansive, with strikingly outgoing behavior, to the extent of possible dangerous behavior at times. Children of this age have active imaginations and high amounts of energy. They are talkative and loud, which can be seen in both playful excitement and angry tantrums. As 4-year-olds mature to 4½, they typically grow less outgoing and tend to worry. They are often working to understand the world and separate what is real from what is not real.

> Four-year-olds are full of energy and excitement during the first six months, and then become less outgoing and tend to worry during the last six months.

BRAIN DEVELOPMENT

> Four-year-olds have extremely active brain growth owing to their reaching a peak in cerebral energy metabolism.

The brain grows substantially throughout a child's fourth year of life, aiding in increased language, improved number sense, and curiosity about a multitude of things around them. Brain-imaging studies have revealed that cerebral energy metabolism reaches a peak around the age of 4, indicating extremely active brain growth during this time (Berk, 2009). Due to the high amount of input received by the brain, it uses approximately 30 percent of the body's energy (Sprenger, 2008).

During the first three years of life, children are right-hemisphere dominant, focusing on the big picture, emotional information, and living in the present moment (Siegel & Bryson, 2011). At 4 years old, children start accessing the left hemisphere of the brain, allowing them to start to use logic, to understand cause and effect, and to put their feelings into words. You can see evidence of this when a child begins to ask "why?" over and over again: His or her brain is developing at a new level that spurs curiosity and the search for a more logical understanding of the world.

By 4 years old, many cortical regions have overproduced synapses, resulting in a high energy need. This overabundance of synapses also contributes to the plasticity of the brain – that is, the ability of the brain to reorganize neural pathways based on new experiences. Neurons that are rarely stimulated lose their connective fibers: a process called "pruning." At 4 years old, pruning of the prefrontal cortex occurs to decrease the number of synapses. As formation of synapses, myelination, and synaptic pruning continue, preschoolers improve in a wide variety of skills, including physical coordination, perception, attention, memory, language, logical thinking, and imagination. Myelination is the formation of myelin around the neuron, enabling nerve cells to transmit information faster and allowing for more complex brain processes. At age 4, myelination continues in the limbic area, contributing to emotional development and the ability for children to have more intimate relationships. The cerebellum is also continuing myelination, and the frontal and parietal lobes are growing, helping the child to make improvements in gross and fine motor skills and visual–motor coordination.

By the age of 4, the hippocampus is developed and forming semantic memories that deal with factual information and concepts unrelated to personal experiences. During this fourth year of life, neurons produce acetylcholine, assisting in long-term memory formation. Dendrites continue to grow in the Broca's area, contributing to improvements in using language – particularly the importance of speech intonation in conveying meaning and emotions (Kagan & Herschkowitz, 2005). The frontal lobes continue connecting, allowing the child to make associations between small details and the overall picture. The frontal lobe and cerebral cortex are devoted to planning and organizing behavior, and these develop rapidly during this time. The corpus callosum also grows quickly throughout early childhood and is involved in many aspects of thinking, such as perception, attention, memory, language, and problem solving.

PHYSICAL DEVELOPMENT

Four-year-olds are extremely active, tiring less easily and recovering more quickly than adults. Parents and other adult caregivers often have trouble keeping up with the energy of a 4-year-old child. It is common for children to ask adults to play with them and to continue playing as long as the adult is willing, without showing any signs of getting tired. This high energy level is a result of a rapid metabolism and a heart rate that pumps proportionately more oxygen into the blood than is present in adults (Elkind, 1994). Energy is high; physical growth, however, actually slows down during the preschool years. Preschool children grow an average of 3–4 inches per year in height. At 4 years old, it is common to observe children running into other people and objects, stepping on things, and spilling whatever is in their hands or nearby. This clumsiness is a result of children focusing their attention on visual objects in the far distance, as opposed to objects close in proximity.

> As a result of large and frequent physical action, 4-year-olds need lots of room in which to move.

Motor Abilities

Children master the motor skills of early childhood during everyday play. They eagerly engage in playful activities when they have a place in which to run, climb, jump, and throw, or have access to puzzles and art supplies that promote manipulation, drawing, and writing. At 4 years old, children gradually become more coordinated and graceful, demonstrating improvements in their gross motor skills. Their balance improves and they are able to start developing athletic abilities. As children become steadier on their feet, they are able to experiment with new skills using their arms and torsos, such as throwing and catching a ball. Four-year-olds have improved arm and leg coordination, and demonstrate a new confidence and willingness to try new things. At this age, children can learn to climb, jump, kick, and throw with accuracy.

Fine motor skills are also improving at a rapid pace during a child's fourth year. At this age, children have more control over their hands and fingers, allowing them to have more responsibility in taking care of their own bodies. They become more self-sufficient, developing the capability to feed and clothe themselves without as much help from adults. Improved fine motor skills also allow children to engage in art and creative play, such as stringing beads, building with blocks, and using scissors. Although 4-year-olds demonstrate improved fine motor skills, they are not yet fully developed. For example, 4-year-olds still usually hold their pencil with their fist, and use their arm, hand, and fingers as a single unit. Young 4-year-olds tend to hold the pencil toward the eraser and write with lighter strokes, whereas older 4-year-olds tend to write more firmly (Wood, 2007). At this age, children are typically using lines to represent the boundaries of an object when they draw: Many children draw people in a tadpole-like way, for example, drawing a circular shape with lines attached.

> Four-year-olds use their whole forearms when drawing and typically have a wobbly pencil stroke (Gesell Institute, 2011).

The development of motor skills varies among males and females. Boys have greater muscle mass and are slightly more developed than girls in skills that emphasize force and power. They usually jump and run slightly farther, and throw much farther, than girls. Girls have a greater overall physical maturity, and are more advanced in fine motor skills and certain gross motor skills that require a combination of balance and foot movement, such as hopping and skipping.

GENDER AND SEXUAL DEVELOPMENT

At 4 years old, children are becoming more aware of their own bodies and start noticing gender differences. Because of the curious nature of children this age, it is common for them to ask questions about body parts, sex, and where babies come from. Children often learn attitudes about sexuality and gender roles by observing their parents or primary caregivers. For example, it would be common for a girl to dress up in an apron and "cook dinner" for the family if she were to observe her mother engaging in these behaviors. Typically developing 4-year-olds have a vague understanding of how babies are born, but lack knowledge regarding adult sexual behavior (Volbert, 2000).

Masturbation is common among girls as they explore their bodies and find self-stimulation exciting. Parents can allow these explorations to occur in private without worry, because this is developmentally normal. Masturbation is also common among boys at this age as they discover their penis. Boys often react to a full bladder with an erection and then play with their newly discovered penis, finding that it causes an exciting sensation. It is not uncommon for boys to hold on to their penis while sucking their thumb, finding it both comforting and stimulating. Although masturbation can be an uncomfortable subject for many adults, it is important to recognize the developmentally normal and appropriate nature of children exploring their bodies. When talking with their children about masturbation, parents need to help their children to understand that masturbation is something that is done in a private place and avoid conveying disapproval.

If masturbation occurs for prolonged periods of time, the child may be demonstrating a heightened need for self-soothing: a situation that may warrant further exploration with a mental health professional. The child may need help developing more appropriate coping skills and alternative ways in which to self-soothe. Masturbation can also be a result of being overly sexually stimulated or traumatized, in which case consultation with a mental health professional is needed to determine the appropriate plan of action.

As children discover their own bodies, they often become curious about the bodies of others. A common way in which children explore each other's bodies is to play "doctors." This is a familiar concept for children, because they have experienced doctors examining them. Many 4-year-old children will ask a friend to play doctor and examine that friend's body. After a few safe explorations, the child's curiosity will be met and this behavior will go away. When parents find out about this behavior, they are often embarrassed and worried. It is important to recognize that this behavior is normal, and parents should avoid overreacting in ways that will elicit fear or shame in their children. Parents should also be aware that the behavior may increase if it attracts too much attention, since the child may find that attention increasingly exciting. Instead, parents should talk with each child individually about this behavior in a way that is not condemnatory, but which sets appropriate boundaries.

An important difference to note is if a child reports playing doctor or any other activity when he or she did not want to do so, or reports feelings of coercion to do or witness something that felt uncomfortable. A child needs an adult's help in this type of situation to ensure his or her physical and emotional safety. It is important to help children to understand that such coercion is not appropriate. Moreover, because of the sensitivity of this subject and the emotions involved, it is important that the adult remain aware of his or her responses because overreacting may cause the child to feel uncomfortable talking about this subject in the future.

COGNITIVE DEVELOPMENT

Language skills are rapidly increasing during this age as children develop more complex ideas and the ability to put those thoughts into words. This increased language ability supports children's increasing control over behavior, because they can now use language to gain self-control when feeling intense emotions, such as anger and excitement. The ability to formulate and verbalize more complex ideas gives children an increased ability to express themselves and to feel powerful. Responses are no longer black and white. While 4-year-olds still look to parents or other adults for help, they can also find a solution on their own and take pride in doing so.

The fourth year of life is a time of rapid intellectual growth. Children of this age need stimulating learning environments that allow for flexibility and creativity. They have short attention spans and therefore should not be expected to stay focused on one task for too long. Four-year-olds often get excited about and learn best through methods that allow them to be physically active, such as drama, dance, and outdoor play. They should also be given the opportunity to use objects that they can manipulate, such as clay, paint, and building blocks. Children learn best by doing, because learning goes from the hand to the head, not the other way around (Wood, 2007). At 4 years

Children learn best when engaging in physically active experiences, such as drama, dance, and outdoor play.

old, children can typically count between five and seven items, compare sets of items, and accurately name four or more colors. At 4½, children can recite their names, addresses, and phone numbers, may be able to write their own names, and can draw people with basic large body parts (Sprenger, 2008).

According to Piaget, young children are not yet cable of thinking logically. Their thinking is rigid, focused on the present, and simply limited to one aspect of a situation at a time. A 4-year-old child would be in the "preoperational" stage of Piaget's cognitive development model, starting to utilize language and engage in symbolic play. Although Piaget acknowledged the importance of language, he believed that sensorimotor activity led to internal images of experiences, which were then labeled with words (Piaget & Inhelder, 2000). He believed that children practiced and strengthened newly acquired representational schemes by pretending through make-believe play. An essential part of preoperational thinking is egocentrism, whereby children focus on their own points of view, assuming that others think and feel the same way as they think and feel. At this age, children struggle to understand that others can have a perception that is different from their own.

Increased verbalization and reasoning abilities make fantasies more detailed and elaborate (Brazelton & Sparrow, 2001). By 4 years old, children can pretend with less realistic toys and have a more flexible imagination. Their worlds are full of fantasy, serving to protect their dreams, wishes, and ability to relate to the future. This type of magical thinking allows the child to go back and forth between recognizing how the world is and how he or she wants it to be.

Consider Tommy, a 4-year-old boy, who is practicing his pitching and accidentally throws a baseball through a window. When Tommy's parents ask about the broken window, he denies breaking it and blames it on his imaginary friend, Adam. In this way, magical thinking has given Tommy the power and ability to believe that he is the good boy who did not break a window. As children engage in magical thinking, it is not uncommon for them to tell a lie. Few defense mechanisms have developed by this age, so a child uses what is available to him or her, such as denial or avoidance, causing him or her to escape from reality. Four-year-old children often lie when a strong wish is at risk or when they do not know how to face the reality of a situation.

> It is normal for 4-year-olds to lie to escape reality or as a form of play, because they have creative imaginations and have developed few coping strategies to deal with reality by this age.

When a child really wants something, lying becomes a way of protecting the wish and avoiding confrontation. Children feel the need to lie as a result of intense wishes, important fantasies, and limited ways of facing reality (Brazelton & Sparrow, 2001). Many 4-year-olds have stolen candy from a candy store, for example, because they have not quite developed the morality to know that it is not acceptable behavior. In a situation such as this, parents should explain that the candy is not for stealing and find a way in which to teach the child to take responsibility for his or her wrongdoing without overly shaming him or her. Fortunately, the lies told by 4-year-olds are usually transparent.

Sociodramatic play continues to increase at this age, because children have a better understanding of relationships with others and story lines. Children engage in animistic thinking, assigning human qualities to inanimate objects, such as thoughts, wishes, feelings, and intentions. They often focus on one aspect of a situation and neglect other important features. Children are not typically capable of irreversibility at this age, unable to go mentally through a series of steps in a problem and then reverse the direction to return to the starting point. They struggle with hierarchical classification – that is, organizing objects into classes and subclasses based on similarities and differences.

WORLDVIEW/EGO DEVELOPMENT

Loevinger (1976) created the developmental sequence of ego development to describe how the ego matures through sequential stages as a result of the interaction between self and the environment (Loevinger, 1976). Most 4-year-olds are in the "impulsive" or "self-protective" stages.

- Although the *impulsive* stage is most common in toddlers, some children – and even adults – may become fixed in this stage. The impulsive ego is focused primarily on the body's feelings, basic impulses, and immediate needs. The individual's impulses help him or her to perceive his or her identity as separate from those of the people around him. Children in the impulsive stage have simple and dichotomous thoughts, and are demanding and dependent, not taking into consideration the needs of others.

- The *self-protective* stage follows the impulsive stage, and is most common in early and middle childhood. Children with a self-protective ego are more cognitively advanced, and capable of understanding cause and effect, rules, and consequences. The primary concern at this stage is for the child to do whatever it takes to get what he or she wants. Hence 4-year-olds may respond to rewarding behavioral measures by displaying the desired behavior. In this stage, children protect themselves by externalizing and blaming others for anything that goes wrong.

Racial/Ethnic Identity Development

Byrd (2012) identified three components to racial/ethnic identity: awareness, identification, and attitudes. She defined *awareness* as the ability to differentiate between races according to commonly accepted norms, *self-identification* as the ability to correctly label one's own race/ethnicity, and *attitudes* as beliefs about characteristics of various racial groups. Of these components, the first to develop is awareness. At 4 years old, children are becoming more aware of others and the world around them. They are starting to notice physical differences and are likely to be able to categorize groups of people based on skin color (Byrd, 2012; Swanson, Cunningham, Youngblood, & Spencer, 2009). Swanson and colleagues (2009) explained that cultural identity follows a progression similar to a child's cognitive development: As children develop more advanced cognitive skills, they can better differentiate themselves from others and can better understand more abstract concepts associated with various classifications of people (Swanson et al., 2009).

EMOTIONAL DEVELOPMENT

Although 4-year-olds have the language with which to more adequately express themselves, they are still trying to learn about and understand themselves. It is common for children at this age to become overwhelmed with feelings, and to struggle with self-regulation and managing their emotions. It is during this fourth year that children can make advances toward this ability to regulate themselves. As internal control over behavior becomes more advanced, children can use internal dialogue to make choices about their behavior. Although children can learn to keep themselves under control, the temperament of each child is different. Some children are easily overwhelmed or hypersensitive, while others are more strong-willed. Each child has a unique way of responding to a stressor and must use tools for self-management. Parents can help by maintaining awareness that children are more vulnerable to losing control when in a particular state of mind or a particular physiological state (Brazelton & Sparrow, 2001). When a child is struggling for an unknown reason, Siegel and Bryson (2011) suggested that parents check to see if their child is hungry, angry, lonely, or tired.

It is not uncommon for 4-year-olds to throw temper tantrums. This is often a child's effort to make the world his or her own, learning to live in reality and trying to understand it intellectually. Sometimes, temper tantrums are a result of a child keeping his or her feelings inside until he or she simply cannot hold them in any longer: A child may display good behavior all day at school, for example, and then come home and unload where he or she feels safe enough to do so.

Four-and-a-half-year-olds have an increased number and intensity of fears, which may result in nightmares, negative communication with others, or periods of solitary thoughtfulness.

Older 4-year-olds are sometimes fearful or worry and may have nightmares. At this age, children become more aware of being small, dependent on their parents or other caregivers. They start to understand that they are part of a bigger world and they are increasingly aware of their own limitations. As children become more cognizant and understanding of the world, they also become more aware of their own feelings. Additionally, they develop increased concern for right and wrong, good and bad. Escalating feelings can overwhelm children at this age, and often emerge in the form of fears and nightmares. Parents are typically unaware that this is a normal reaction to new feelings. This age brings new capabilities for mental representation and children tend to project their fears onto objects in the environment (Elkind, 1994). Nightmares are serious for children, and they often struggle at night when in the dark and separated from caregivers. Children need to feel understood in the context of their perceptions. Adult assurance that there is nothing to fear ("There are no monsters under the bed") is therefore less effective than assurance that the adult is available and will keep the child safe.

SOCIAL DEVELOPMENT

Imagine two boys playing in the backyard. Both boys want to play with the ball that they have spotted and their mother tells them to share or take turns. Immediately, the boys begin arguing, each saying that it is his turn and that the ball belongs to him. At 4 years old, children often regard toys as extensions of themselves and asking them to share is similar to asking them to give away a part of themselves (Elkind, 1994). They have little sense of ownership, and possession means that all things are for them.

Typically, 4-year-old children want to please others and often seek praise. Friends are important and they want to be liked. At this age, children would rather play with others than alone and are likely to base friendships on shared activities. Although children will play with both boys and girls, it is more common to see children playing with their same gender. Children are easily influenced by their friends' behaviors and want to conform, often excluding children that they perceive as "different."

At this age, children have active imaginations, and love to play make-believe and dress up. Most children enjoy singing and dancing, and can be seen doing these things just about anywhere. They can become easily immersed in fantasy play as a way in which to problem solve and test out magical solutions. Children often feel torn between dependency on others and wanting to explore and master the world around them. Fantasy is a way to work through this struggle.

It is not uncommon to see children call others names or to tattle. At 4 years old, children start engaging in self-assertive and aggressive behaviors, with the goal of increased independence. Children start to feel that they have more control over their worlds. Boys are more aggressive than girls, and are more frequently the initiators and victims of aggressive behaviors. They also tend to be less compliant to adult authority, but there appears to be no gender difference in the frequency of compliance with peers.

At 4 years old, boys and girls play together, and often model adult behavior. Children will often imitate others, walking and talking like them. For example, a boy may spend time outside using his toys to "mow the yard" if he has watched his father do so many times. It is generally accepted that many behaviors that distinguish boys from girls are learned and do not reflect innate, genetic, or physiological differences (Elkind, 1994). In general, girls conform less to gender role stereotypes compared to boys.

Four-year-olds are curious, active, and creative. They love to explore and fantasize, often creating their own games and activities. Like Piaget, Erikson (1963) believed that children developed in a predetermined order, going through a series of stages. He was interested in the socialization patterns of children and the affects that these have on an individual's sense of self. In Erikson's psychosocial theory, he emphasized that the ego does not just mediate between id impulses and superego demands, but at each stage acquires attitudes and skills that make the individual an active, contributing member of society.

A 4-year-old is in the stage of *initiative vs. guilt*, whereby children begin to assert their power and control by directing their play and social interactions. In the appropriate environment, children have the opportunity to develop a sense of initiative, feeling secure in their abilities to lead others and to make decisions. Consequently, if this does not happen, either as a result of criticism or the imposition of control by others, children can develop a sense of guilt. Children need to be able to assert their power and take the initiative by facing diverse challenges and accomplishing tasks. During this stage, it is important that caregivers encourage this exploration and also offer appropriate guidance to help children to make appropriate decisions. When parents support their child's newfound sense of purpose, the child can then feel a sense of responsibility.

Jenifer W. Balch

RELATIONSHIP DEVELOPMENT

Children often learn by observing others. They are curious, inquisitive, and want to understand and master the world around them. They are often excited about new tasks, yet unaware of boundaries. Often, a 4-year-old initiates goals, engaging in elaborate fantasies to find his or her own solutions, or at least to think about the possibilities. The child is becoming more independent in his or her decision-making and power is a major issue: A 4-year-old wants to be the boss.

At 4 years old, children start moving away from relationships with their parents and start forming relationships with peers. They are friendly and talkative with others, and love being with friends. Children at this age often view friends as those whom they like and with whom they spend time, enjoying similar play activities. Consider Joey, who comes home from school one day and describes a game of tag that he played with his new "best friend," David – only, the following week, to decide that they are no longer best friends, because David no longer wants to play tag: This behavior is typical, because children typically associate friendship with activities in which they are involved together. Although children have a simple definition of friendship at this age, they demonstrate noticeably different behaviors with those whom they perceive as friends, giving them more attention, reinforcement, and emotional expression (Berk, 2009). Friendships offer social support for children, making it easier for them to adjust to new environments, such as school.

Four-year-olds cooperate more with family members when not feeling challenged or rushed (Gesell Institute, 2011).

Although 4-year-olds start drifting away from their parents, parents still play an important role. After all, the family environment is where the child first learned about social interaction. Children often have mixed feelings toward their parents as they start to figure out that they can love someone and also not like something that person does. It is typical for children of this age to experiment with triangular relationships, playing parents against one another: When Aiden wants to stay up late, past his bedtime, and his dad has told him "no," he will go and ask his mom, hoping for a different answer.

Children can sometimes feel jealous of their parents spending time with each other or another sibling, wanting their undivided attention. Sibling rivalry is a typical and well-known concept, and fairly common in most families. When new children are born into a family, it is typical for older children to feel pushed aside or left out. When a child has younger siblings, he or she is forced to give up the position of "the baby," and may be viewed as more capable and given more responsibilities. Children often compete with each other with the goal of gaining attention from their parents. Although conflict and rivalry exist in sibling relationships, they can also be characterized by play, prosocial behavior, caretaking, and teaching (Benson & Haith, 2009).

Vygotsky's (1986) sociocultural theory stressed the social context of cognitive development. Increased use of language allows children to participate in social dialogues with more knowledgeable individuals who encourage them to master culturally important tasks. Children start to communicate with themselves in the same ways as they do with others, enhancing the complexity of their thinking and ability for self-control. Vygotsky believed that children speak to themselves for self-guidance, helping them to think about their mental activities and behavior: a foundation for all higher cognitive processes. This self-directed speech is termed "private speech." Vygotsky believed that play was the leading source of development in early childhood, allowing the child to move into the world of ideas, free from the boundaries of reality. This freedom is essential for cognitive development at this age, because children are no longer able to make reality align with their desires and need to use their imaginations.

DEVELOPMENT IN THE AGE OF TECHNOLOGY

Technology and media have become highly integrated into our society for people of all ages, The American Academy of Pediatrics (AAP, 2013) reported that children use entertainment media, including televisions, computers, smartphones, and other electronic devices, an average of seven hours a day. This is a much higher figure than recommended, and can lead to obesity, developmental delay, anxiety, depression, aggression, lack of socialization, attention problems, and poor grades (Rowan, 2014). While technology use has its risk factors, it is important to note the benefits that technology can provide to children, such as learning opportunities and connecting with others. Technology, in general, is not good or bad, but it is important for parents to find the right balance for their children.

In its most recent report on media, the AAP (2013) recommended no more than two hours a day of technology screen time for children. It also suggested that parents monitor the media accessed by their children, and keep televisions and devices with Internet access out of children's bedrooms. Additionally, the AAP recommended that parents create firm rules about media devices within the home, establishing set times at which media devices will not be used.

> The American Academy of Pediatrics recommended children engage in no more than two hours of technology screen time per day (AAP, 2013).

BEST PRACTICES IN COUNSELING/THERAPY

When Counseling/Therapy Is Indicated

Common emotions and behaviors have been described about a typical 4-year-old child, but it can be difficult to assess whether a child needs professional help. The most immediate indicator of a child's need for counseling is suspicion or knowledge that he or she has experienced any type of trauma or abuse (physical, sexual, or emotional). Because abuse can have lasting effects on an individual, early intervention is imperative to help to heal the hurt associated with the experience. In addition to abuse, adults should take notice of any drastic behavioral changes for a child: Is he or she suddenly complaining of aches and pains? Does he or she seem more argumentative than usual, or beyond developmental expectations? Is he or she aggressive toward others at school, at a developmentally unexpected level? Any of these behaviors, especially if prolonged, may be indicators of developing concerns with which counseling could help.

In additional to behavioral changes, adults should also take notice of a child's changing emotions. Although it is normal for children of this age to experience various emotions as they come to know and try to understand the world, counseling may be necessary if a child experiences overly intense emotions or prolonged sadness, anxiety, or fear. Nightmares are a typical experience for a 4-year-old child, for example, but if a child has so many nightmares that he or she is afraid to be alone or go to sleep at night, then professional help may be warranted.

Most importantly, parents and other caregivers should understand normal behaviors, emotions, and patterns of their specific children, and seek help if they observe a marked change in these emotions or behaviors for an unknown reason.

Developmentally Appropriate Approaches

Play therapy is the most effective form of counseling for 4-year-olds because it allows the child to use his or her natural mode of communication (play) to work through stressors, and to explore feelings about himself or herself and his or her experiences. Play therapy provides an age-appropriate environment that allows a child to create his or her reality through play. At 4 years old, children cannot yet comprehend abstract concepts, such as feelings, and are unable to accurately express thoughts and feelings verbally. It would be unrealistic and too much pressure for the child if we were to expect him or her to match an adult's cognitive and verbal abilities in expressing his or her thoughts and feelings. Therefore cognitive-behavioral approaches to counseling are not appropriate for children at this age. Play therapy, however, meets children at their level and allows for communication in ways that are most comfortable for children.

Children can learn about themselves and the world through play in a way that nurtures a 4-year-old's need for imagination and fantasy. Four-year-olds are active beings, and play therapy allows them to expend their energy and explore in a way that makes sense for them. Additionally, play is concrete, whereas words are abstract. Because 4-year-olds do not yet understand abstract reasoning, play allows them to use concrete objects to represent individual experiences within their environments. It gives them manageable ways in which to discover their inner worlds, allowing increased feelings of security and control. Concrete play gives a child the opportunity to explore and learn to cope by transforming unmanageable situations into manageable ones, bridging the gap between concrete experience and abstract thought.

Child-centered play therapy (CCPT)   Child-centered play therapy (CCPT) is the most developmentally appropriate approach for a 4-year-old child. A child of this age thinks concretely, is present-focused, learns by doing, and struggles to see another person's point of view. A counselor using CCPT would provide a relationship and environment that allows the child to move forward internally as he or she is ready, embracing the developmental needs of the child. This approach is sensitive to the changes that are taking place in a 4-year-old as he or she explores the world to gain a sense of purpose. Additionally, CCPT provides a nondirective environment to match the 4-year-old's quest for initiative and autonomy, while allowing for communication through symbolic, fantasy-driven play.

Adlerian play therapy (AdPT)   Adlerian play therapy (AdPT) has both directive and nondirective elements, and allows for flexibility, depending on the phase and lifestyle of the child (Kottman, 2011). Active parent involvement is needed in order to effectively employ this approach. Traditionally, AdPT requires children to have more developed cognitive skills than a 4-year-old has, such as abstract reasoning skills, but AdPT can be adapted for preschool-age children with the involvement of caregivers (Dillman Taylor & Bratton, 2014).

1 In the first phase of AdPT, the play therapist works to build a collaborative, therapeutic relationship, which has many benefits for a child of any age.
2 In the second phase of AdPT, information can be gathered from parent consultations to better understand the lifestyle of the child.
3 During the third phase, the play therapist works with parents to gain insight about the child's behaviors, as well as with the child in the playroom to increase his or her self-understanding.
4 The last phase of AdPT can involve both the parents and child to help the child to integrate his or her new perceptions of self, others, and the world.

Working with Parents, Caregivers, and Teachers

Parents, teachers, and other caretakers can benefit from exploring the normal development of 4-year-olds to better understand the children in their lives. Not only can education and understanding provide insight into a child's emotions and behaviors, but it may also allow for some patience and forgiveness when things do not go as the adult expected. While 4-year-olds can be fun and full of fantasy, there are also times of impulsivity and intense emotions. Caregivers can help children to better understand their experiences by naming the feeling and validating the child's experience. For example, when a child wakes up scared from a nightmare, a parent might say "You feel scared because you had a bad dream," thereby providing comfort to their child by assuring him or her that the parent is there to protect and keep the child safe.

During this time of rapid development, it is important that 4-year-olds have time to play. While play can be fun for children, it also serves other purposes, such as learning about and exploring themselves, as well as the world around them. Parents and caregivers should embrace this discovery period for children by ensuring that they have opportunities to engage in nondirected play.

Filial therapy   Filial therapy is an age-appropriate intervention that is highly recommended for a 4-year-old child. At this age, parents and caregivers typically have a high amount of emotional significance for their children, and therefore are ideal agents of change. In filial therapy, parents learn how to facilitate a growth-promoting atmosphere in which the child can reach his or her full potential. In child–parent relationship therapy (CPRT), a form of filial therapy, a trained play therapist teaches parents the basic principles and methods of child-centered play therapy (Landreth & Bratton, 2006).

This form of counseling is especially helpful for young children. Even though children are limited in their social, emotional, and cognitive abilities, parents are able to learn the skills and concepts with which to help their child to feel understood. As the parent–child relationship improves, it has the potential to positively impact on the daily interactions of those in the relationship. It can empower parents and give them the tools with which to create long-lasting changes in the daily environment of the child.

Parent–child interaction therapy (PCIT)   Parent–child interaction therapy (PCIT) is an evidence-based treatment approach that was originally developed for children with disruptive behavioral problems (Brinkmeyer & Eyberg, 2003). With roots in attachment and social learning theories, PCIT teaches parents new ways of interacting with their children. It involves live coaching of parents, with two phases.

1 In the first phase, parents learn how to give positive attention using praise, reflection, imitation, description, and enthusiasm.
2 In the second phase, parents learn to provide effective and consistent instructions, using praise for compliance and time out for noncompliant behavior.

This approach can be helpful for parents of 4-year-olds as a result of its emphasis on improving the parent–child relationship through *positive* interactions and play. At this age, children are frequently unable to fully comprehend their emotions and verbalize their needs; PCIT helps parents to increase positive interactions with their children in ways that help them to feel more securely attached, which can lead to increased self-esteem and self-regulation. However, the application of the parent-directed phase of PCIT may be limiting to the needs of a 4-year-old who craves free play, symbolic expression, and initiation of activity.

Parent education   More often than not, parents can benefit from general education about child development in order to better understand their child and to form realistic expectations about behavior. *The Whole-Brain Child* (Siegel & Bryson, 2011) and *No-Drama Discipline* (Siegel & Bryson, 2014) are helpful resources to help parents to understand brain development, and its influence on emotions and behavior (Siegel & Bryson, 2011, 2014). With accurate information about child development, parents can make informed decisions about parenting strategies and discipline that are purposeful and developmentally appropriate for their child.

Specific parent programs also exist to help parents to build effective skills to use with their children.

• Carolyn Webster-Stratton (2013) developed a set of programs titled The Incredible Years. Her preschool basic parenting program is for children aged 3–6, aiming toward improved parent–child interactions, a reduction of behavioral and emotional problems, and the promotion of positive attributes and emotional regulation.
• Jane Nelsen (2006) has also developed a set of programs entitled "positive discipline," which is based on the teachings of Alfred Adler and Rudolph Dreikurs. It is a positive approach that uses concepts such as encouragement and respect to help to foster a sense of belonging. There are books, DVDs, and training courses that parents can attend to learn this model of parenting.
• Nelsen, Erwin and Duffy (2007) wrote *Positive Discipline for Preschoolers*, which is particularly applicable for parents of 4-year-olds. In this book, the authors teach parents about mutual respect, understanding the purpose of a child's behavior, effective communication strategies, and understanding the child through the lens of his or her development.

CONCLUSION

The fourth year of life can appear magical and exciting for a child. He or she is full of energy and full of life, becoming increasingly aware and exploring himself or herself, as well as the world around him or her. This is a time of rapid growth and development in in the brain, affecting many areas of life, including emotions, social behaviors, and relationships with others and the world. While 4-year-olds can appear overly energetic at times and have endless questions about the world, it is a special time in life as they increase their awareness and their ability to learn and understand many dynamics around them.

REFERENCES

American Academy of Pediatrics (AAP). (2013). Children, adolescents, and the media. *Pediatrics*, *132*(5), 958–961.

Benson, J. B., & Haith, M. M. (Eds.). (2009). *Social and emotional development in infancy and early childhood*. San Diego, CA: Academic Press.

Berk, L. E. (2009). *Development throughout the lifespan* (5th ed.). Boston, MA: Allyn & Bacon.

Brazelton, T. B., & Sparrow, J. D. (2001). *Touchpoints three to six: Your child's emotional and behavioral development*. Cambridge, MA: Perseus.

Brinkmeyer, M. Y., & Eyberg, S. M. (2003). Parent–child interaction therapy for oppositional children. In A. E. Kazdin & J. R. Weisz (Eds.), *Evidence-based psychotherapies for children and adolescents* (pp. 204–223). New York, NY: Guilford Press.

Byrd, C. M. (2012). The measurement of racial/ethnic identity in children: A critical review. *Journal of Black Psychology*, *38*(1), 3–31.

Dillman Taylor, D., & Bratton, S. C. (2014). Developmentally appropriate practice: Adlerian play therapy with preschool children. *The Journal of Individual Psychology*, *70*(3), 205–219.

Elkind, D. (1994). *Understanding your child: Birth to sixteen*. Needham Heights, MA: Allyn & Bacon.

Erikson, E. (1963). *Childhood and society*. New York, NY: Norton.

Gesell Institute of Child Development. (2011). *Gesell Developmental Observation–Revised examiner's manual*. New Haven, CT: Gesell Institute.

Kagan, J., & Herschkowitz, E. C. (2005). *A young mind in a growing brain*. Mahwah, NJ: Lawrence Erlbaum.

Kottman, T. (2011). *Play therapy basics and beyond*. Alexandria, VA: American Counseling Association.

Landreth, G. L., & Bratton, S. C. (2006). *Child–parent relationship therapy (CPRT): A 10-session filial therapy model*. New York, NY: Routledge.

Loevinger, J. (1976). *Ego development*. San Francisco, CA: Jossey-Bass.

Nelsen, J. (2006). *Positive discipline*. New York, NY: Ballantine Books.

Nelsen, J., Erwin, C., & Duffy, R. A. (2007). *Positive discipline for preschoolers: For the early years – Raising children who are responsible, respectful, and resourceful* (3rd ed.). New York, NY: Three Rivers Press.

Piaget, J., & Inhelder, B. (2000). *The psychology of the child*. New York: NY: Perseus.

Rowan, C. (2014). Risk vs. benefit: Technology use by young children. Retrieved from http://www.zoneinworkshops.com/risk-vs-benefit-technology-use-by-young-children.html

Siegel, D. J., & Bryson, T. P. (2011). *The whole-brain child: 12 revolutionary strategies to nurture your child's developing mind, survive everyday parenting struggles, and help your family thrive*. New York, NY: Bantam Books.

Siegel, D. J., & Bryson, T. P. (2014). *No-drama discipline: The whole brain way to calm the chaos and nurture your child's developing mind*. New York, NY: Bantam Books.

Sprenger, M. (2008). *The developing brain: Birth to age eight*. Thousand Oaks, CA: Corwin Press.

Swanson, D. P., Cunningham, M., Youngblood, J., & Spencer, M. B. (2009). Racial identity development during childhood. In H. A. Neville, B. M Tynes, & S. O. Utsey (Eds.), *Handbook of African American psychology* (pp. 269–281). Thousand Oaks, CA: Sage.

Volbert, R. (2000). Sexual knowledge of preschool children. *Journal of Psychology & Human Sexuality*, *12*(1–2), 5–26.

Vygotsky, L. S. (1986). *Thought and language* (A. Kozulin, ed.). Cambridge, MA: MIT Press.

Webster-Stratton, C. (2013). The Incredible Years parent, teacher and child programs fact sheet. Retrieved from http://incredibleyears.com/about/incredible-years-series/

Wood, C. (2007). *Yardsticks: Children in the classroom ages 4–14* (3rd ed.). Turners Falls, MA: Northeast Foundation for Children.

Part III

MIDDLE CHILDHOOD

6

THE EXTRAORDINARY 5-YEAR-OLD

Dalena L. Dillman Taylor

The playful innocence of a 5-year-old child that captivates his or her parents can seemingly devolve overnight as the child turns 5½. At 5½ years old, this shift in behavior and emotion is frustrating, and often confusing, for parents and teachers alike. Around this age, children enter school for the first time. Although this transition is becoming less drastic as more children enter preschool prior to kindergarten, for many children this time marks the transition to becoming a "big kid" and embracing the new adventures that will arise in an environment outside of their primary family.

Consider Lucy, a typical 5-year-old, who likes to spend much of her time trying to be like "mommy," mimicking her every move and wanting to do the things that her mother does. Lucy likes her home life, and the routines associated with home or school, and doing simple things such as playing with her dog, helping her mom, and reading her favorite books or having them read to her. She has become a sponge for knowledge and is excited to learn how things work in the world. Lately, Lucy enjoys staying home and being told stories about her family by her mother. Lucy is very good about asking for permission to stay up a little past her bedtime for just one more story.

At 5½ years old, Lucy is no longer that sweet little girl of only six months earlier. She still asks for one more story – but instead of accepting a denial of her request, she battles her family using whatever tools she has: crying and screaming. Instead of accepting the rules as they are, Lucy will argue with her parents and has lately taken to chewing on her crayons or pencils to deal with her frustration. Although her teachers have nothing but good things to say, Lucy is a very different girl at home.

BRAIN DEVELOPMENT

Children's brains grow at exceptional rates (Sprenger, 2008) and, by the end of his or her fifth year, a 5-year-old's brain will reach about nine-tenths of its potential adult size (Santrock, 2001). A child's brain is continuing the myelination of the corpus collosum of the frontal lobe and of the limbic system, which means that a protective layer is developing to increase the speed of messages being delivered from these areas. As a result of this continual growth, greater connections are made in the hippocampus, amygdala, and both hemispheres of the brain; thus a child's short-term memory and abilities to read and to understand language are improved.

> By the end of the fifth year, a child's brain reaches approximately 90 percent of its fully grown size.

At this age, children begin to connect both the emotional and factual concepts of memories, and are expected to be able to plan and organize in at least simple ways. Another aspect that helps to facilitate the formation of memories is the increase in the dendritic complexity: At age 5, the child not only has the ability to connect the factual and emotional aspects of memories and events, but he or she may also be experiencing more diversity in his or her memories, which leads to a greater connection and capability to remember events.

Integration of different parts of the brain (right to left, brain stem to frontal lobe) help the child to make sense of events, emotions, and thoughts that occur throughout the day (Siegel & Payne Bryson, 2011). Also around this time, dendritic growth becomes evident in Broca's area, located in the left hemisphere, which is associated with language development. Simultaneously, a child's blood flow throughout the left hemisphere continues to increase, which further leads to a greater ability to expand his or her vocabulary and to comprehend more through communication with others. In combination, the brain also gains "coherence," in which synchronization of neural activity occurs (Sprenger, 2008).

With all of these factors combining, the brain begins to work to make greater connections. Five-year-olds tend to retell stories to integrate events into their worldviews. For example, most children can be seen playing "school" after the first few days of kindergarten. This repetition of events helps children to make sense of their new experiences. Because of this development, parents can play a crucial role in enhancing these connections in the brain and the child's ability to remember events by listening and responding actively when their child struggles with conflicting feelings or messages, experiences a new situation, and/or discloses a problem.

PHYSICAL DEVELOPMENT

Five-year-olds also begin changing physically: Their bodies begin to slim down and lengthen. At this age, boys and girls are still relatively of similar size and stature (Santrock, 2001). At age 5, children are more poised and controlled in their movements, but by 5½ these same children become more awkward and clumsy (Miller, 2001). Five-year-olds are typically described as busy beings, learning to do many new things both academically (such as to color within the lines, to write letters, to draw) and physically (such as tip-toeing, riding a bicycle, jumping, kicking, and skipping) (see Davies, 2010; Gesell Institute, 2011; Miller, 2001). Free play is therefore crucial for children's physical development at this period of time. Children who learn through play at this age "flourish, providing them ultimately with a greater flexibility in thinking and coping skills" (Miller, 2001, p. 170).

Motor Development

A 5-year-old's motor coordination is continually improving, especially his or her fine motor skills. In comparison to their 4-year-old selves, 5-year-olds can grasp a pencil, fold paper in half, trace their hands, and cut interior shapes from a larger paper. Yet 5½-year-olds may struggle to do many of these same tasks: Five-and-a-half-year-olds have less balance, are less organized, and tend to be more restless than their younger counterparts.

Six months makes a difference: Motor skills that came easily to 5-year-olds prove to be difficult for 5½-year-olds.

Sitting for extended periods of time is another challenge for 5½-year-olds. The Gesell Institute of Child Development (2011) reports that, at this age, children might struggle more academically, especially in reading and writing, because of their loss of visual orientation and the frequency with which they reverse letters and numbers. Children also become more aware of these inconsistencies in their behaviors, yet lack the awareness of how to make changes – and this difficulty can create feelings of inferiority and inadequacy if a child is pushed beyond his or her limits of ability, potentially leading him or her to "give up," or quit. It is therefore critical for the caregivers (that is, parents, teachers, counselors) involved in these children's lives to be aware of this discrepancy, to encourage the child to continue to try, and to maintain realistic expectations of this age. A school environment that allows children to move more freely (that is, a center) can be also be helpful in keeping children engaged in learning.

GENDER AND SEXUAL DEVELOPMENT

Five-year-olds experience an increase in sexual interest, although their desires decrease (Wurtele & Kenny, 2001). Like other areas of growth and maturation, sexual development is a process that appears to be continual throughout an individual's lifetime, during which he or she connects sexual meaning based on the experiences with and attitudes of those people with whom he or she is in close contact (that is, his or her primary support system) (see Francoeur, Koch, & Weis, 1998). However, unlike adults, 5-year-olds' sexual development involves curiosity about their own bodies, as well as those of others who are either similar to or different from themselves. Their interest appears to be less in sex play as it was at age 4, and more geared toward talking about the topics of death, sex, and reproduction.

> Five-year-olds tend to be modest, want more privacy, and want to cognitively understand the difference between sexes.

At the age of 5, children can now explain gender identity based on genital differences, thereby noticing the physical characteristics of girls and boys (Volbert, 2000). If 5-year-olds are around older children, they are more likely to try out sexual behaviors and to ask more developmentally mature questions about sex. Yet very few have knowledge of, or can describe, sexual behavior of adults. Parents should respond with developmentally appropriate answers, because if they fail to do so, the child will either not understand the answer and/or may be overwhelmed by the answer given. Some researchers have found common sexual behaviors of 5-year-olds to include, among other things:

- masturbating purposefully, sometimes in the presence of others;
- attempting to see others naked;
- mimicking dating behaviors (such as kissing and holding hands);
- discussing private parts;
- using "naughty" words, even without knowing their meaning; and
- exploring private parts with others (for example while playing "doctors") (see Kellogg, 2009, 2010; NCTSN, 2009; Wurtele & Kenny, 2001).

Because sexual development has been a taboo topic in our society, it is important for caregivers to understand the difference between normal sexual development and behaviors and abnormal ones, so that they can respond appropriately to support the healthy development of the child.

COGNITIVE DEVELOPMENT

As mentioned in previous chapters, children aged 2–6 fall into the "preoperational" stage in cognitive development (Santrock, 2001). Given this shift in cognition, children are now capable of mentally representing objects with symbols, mostly occurring as language develops (Piaget, 1932/1997). As their memories sharpen, their ability to think in terms of categories and to generalize also increases (Davies, 2010). This process makes it easier for 5-year-olds to store and access knowledge (Davies, 2010). With this increase in ability, children at this age also begin to apply causality to situations and events so that they can make sense of these occurrences. However, 5-year-olds are also bound by magical thinking, in which reality infuses with fantasy, making it easier to confuse causal events. Five-year-olds are prone to drawing false conclusions because they might elide two actions occurring closely together and attribute one as the cause of the other. Life events can therefore be challenging for a child at this age: If a child disobeys her mother by not picking up her toys and that caregiver then hardly speaks to her throughout the afternoon, the child may link the two events and believe that her mother no longer loves her because of her disobedience (Davies, 2010). This type of egocentric logic occurs even if her mother is observably busy with other tasks or explains to the child that she is not angry.

Because of the increase in their abilities to understand and utilize language resulting from further brain development, children can now express their inner states and feelings – although

Because 5-year-olds can understand cause and effect, they become more effective problem solvers (Miller, 2001).

this expression is limited by an inadequate ability to attach words to their cognitions. Five-year-olds may find it difficult to prolong actions or even to reverse them because of a lack of mental capacity. Given that their thoughts are led mainly by their perceptions, they view the world, and think, in terms of mental images specific to imitations of their perceived environments. Children develop a strong attachment to these symbols and mental images, and their egocentric nature makes it is difficult for them to comprehend how another person may view similar events. For example, one child may associate a red octagon with stopping and not be able to understand how that symbol could represent anything else. This said, it becomes more apparent that play is the preferred modality to communication, given the importance of symbols at this age.

WORLDVIEW/EGO DEVELOPMENT

Five-year-olds are transitioning from being egocentric, focused more on self, and ruled by physical and emotional impulsivity, paying little attention to others' needs, to focusing on controlling their impulses and understanding how their actions impact on others (Loevinger, 1966). Children at this age develop a conscience and guilt emerges as a distinct emotion. Consequently, 5-year-olds begin to apply standards of morality to monitor their behaviors in hopes of minimizing punishment, albeit inconsistently (Davies, 2010).

Five-year-olds become attuned to others' feelings and often take action if they see a friend hurting (Petty, 2010).

Children at this age often struggle between wanting to avoid punishment and wanting the approval of their peers (Kohlberg, 1981). Often, they will go as far as to blame others for their wrongdoings to avoid the negative consequences of their actions, even though this behavior directly contradicts their desire to maintain friendships with peers. They are susceptible to behavioral techniques that offer rewards for good behavior – and *extreme* caution must be taken here. Although children can follow behavioral modifications, these approaches do not emphasize expression of emotion, which is crucial for child development at this age given that their thinking is still grounded in symbolism. Therefore children at this age may be able to understand the consequences of rewards and punishments, but will not be able to fully express their own thoughts and feelings, which could impact on their emotional development.

With 5 being such an impressionable age, parents can provide positive influences and direction (such as consistent monitoring, setting of limits, encouraging positive behaviors, increasing expectations as the child's ability for self-control increases, and increasing peer orientation) to align the child's moral compass to one that more closely fits with the parents' and society's expectations.

Racial/Ethnic Identity Development

A child's ethnic and cultural identity is found to be one element in their emerging sense of self (Davies, 2010). Five-year-olds can differentiate between obvious physical differences (such as gender, or skin color) (see Sue & Sue, 2003), and they tend to group individuals based on these characteristics, because of the point at which they are developmentally – that is, they have an increased capacity for categorization and generalization, as discussed earlier in the chapter. Parents can play a crucial role in healthy development by discussing differences in an educational way, and discussing the family's culture as only one way in which to act and view the world.

Children at this age begin to internalize others' perspectives, but, because of the egocentric nature of 5-year-olds, they still struggle to see the abstract aspects of culture without it being represented visually. It is important for parents to help 5-year-olds to understand their own culture so that they can continue the development of their identity. Similarly, if parents teach and embrace other cultures with care and compassion, children at this age are likely to learn to respect and value all cultures and races equally. This responsibility is challenging, especially since children at this age are interpreting the world through their lens as their capacity for language increases. Cultural identity development is therefore difficult to categorize by ages and stages for children as a whole, because it may be different for each child.

EMOTIONAL DEVELOPMENT

Children begin their fifth year emotionally calm and serene. But, by mid-year, children's emotionality shifts to brash, disobedient, overly demanding, and explosive outbursts. Children's emotional development is in a period of growth. Their abilities to relate to others continues to improve, along with their abilities to communicate, imagine, and think (Greenspan, 1993). Children become more capable of experiencing, understanding, managing, and reflecting on emotions to meet social standards (Santrock, 2001). As their egocentric nature shifts, 5-year-olds also begin to understand that different people feel differently, even in relation to a similar event.

Most children develop emotional regulation in the first year of life; therefore, with parental help and an increase in cognitive skills, children can find balance during this period of emotional instability. Five-year-olds begin to become less dependent on one caregiver as they start to share feelings and emotions with both parents. Children at this stage learn that each parent accepts expression of emotion differently and children work to bring balance in these relationships. Children then develop greater emotional flexibility, less dependence on one caregiver, and greater security when needs are met.

> Five-and-a-half-year-olds often feel torn between choices and will try to choose multiple options in play, possibly leading to frustration (Gesell Institute, 2011).

SOCIAL DEVELOPMENT

Children at this age are at a crossroad for their psychosocial identity (Erikson, 1963). Five-year-olds either add to their autonomy, beginning to undertake, plan, and attack a task, or they develop guilt, which can lead to an overly controlled or overly constricted attitude, creating unhealthy expectations in their social relationships with others. Gender role socialization may influence how children approach this stage: Boys appear to find more pleasure in the attack and conquest of tasks, whereas girls tend to play chase and catch.

In addition, 5-year-olds begin to develop prosocial behavior (that is, sharing, comforting, helping, controlling aggression, and cooperating), and this interaction with others becomes more elaborate and frequent over the year (Davies, 2010). As in emotional development, the shift in their egocentric nature enables 5-year-olds to begin to accept another's perspective and leads to an increase in empathy.

> An increase in interaction through school further enables 5-year-olds to develop cooperation, sharing, and problem-solving skills.

Social skill development is interlinked with relational development for 5-year-olds. The majority of children at this stage develop social skills and competence within relationships with their peers. This development occurs as verbal ability increases through interactions with peers. Interactions such as negotiating play scenarios, competing and excluding within a triangular relationship, and arguing grounded in egocentrism and possessiveness provide 5-year-olds with opportunities to play well without adult supervision (Davies, 2010).

Although 5-year-olds are developing prosocial behaviors, they still exhibit internal conflicts. One common problem at this age tends to be that 5-year-olds often take things that are not theirs and lie about it to authority figures (Miller, 2001). However, parents who are consistent and who enforce socially appropriate behavior can help to eliminate this problem, and can create opportunities for children to understand fairness. Children respond well to rules; thus parents can make this process smoother for 5-year-olds.

RELATIONSHIP DEVELOPMENT

Five-year-olds try out a triangular relationship first with parents (Greenspan, 1993). This type of relationship enables children to work through more complicated relationships. If children develop secure attachments with one or both parents, they are more likely to develop secure relationships with peers. They practice balancing the relationship needs of both parents before generalizing outward to peers.

Balancing others' needs can be challenging at times as 5-year-olds transition out of an egocentric phase. Early in the year, children find it difficult to differentiate their thoughts and feelings from those of others because those of others are not observable. Children tend to associate

Five-year-olds still recognize another's subjective state only by observable behaviors or physical observation.

more wrongdoings with acts that are observable, because they lack the cognitive ability to take into account the intention behind the act. Children transition during this year toward an understanding that each person has a unique, subjective perspective on life. However, the thoughts, opinions, and feelings of each individual are viewed by children at this stage as one unit and not mixed. Although children at this stage are beginning to understand others' different perspectives, another's subjective state is still recognized only in terms of observable behaviors or physical observation, and is understood only in one direction, rather than from multiple perspectives.

Once this balancing of needs is practiced with parents, 5-year-olds generalize this process to their peers, given that peer relationships are becoming increasingly important. These new relationships enable 5-year-olds to increase their social skills and to transition to cooperative play (Davies, 2010). Friendships therefore develop based on common interests in play. This transition also signifies early development of social hunger. Children begin to gain and name their best friends, and exclude those children who do not have similar play interests (Sprenger, 2008). This exclusion may be partly a result of children at this age preferring smaller groups.

In addition, children's fantasy lives expand as a result of better balanced relationships. The child now feels more secure to play out dramas or fictional happenings without being fearful of losing the security of one relationship. Similarly, children play out this pattern with peers – real or imagined. Although children at this age begin to increase in their capacity for logic, their imaginative side is more prominent than their rational side. In other words, children are still capable of getting lost in fantasy, although they can now usually differentiate between fact and fantasy.

DEVELOPMENT IN THE AGE OF TECHNOLOGY

The American Academy of Pediatrics (AAP, 2013) recommends that children aged 5 should be limited to no more than two hours a day of technology use. This figure excludes handheld devices (such as smartphones or tablets) because, according to the AAP, children aged 5 should not use handheld devices at all. In moderation, technological advances benefit a 5-year-old's development of curiosity about the world and prosocial behavior (Clifford, Gunter, & McAleer, 1995). However, many children at this age are exceeding this recommendation by up to as much as four or five times (Active Healthy Kids Canada, 2015). With excessive use of technology, 5-year-olds are more susceptible to several long-term negative consequences.

Typical 5-year-olds undergo potentially the last major growth of their brain, leaving them vulnerable during this period. A link between children's brain development and the overuse of technology has been established, indicating an increased risk of developing several major problems (such as executive functioning and attention deficit, cognitive delays, impaired learning, increased impulsivity and decreased ability to self-regulate, child depression, anxiety, attachment disorder, attention deficit, autism, bipolar disorder, psychosis, and problematic child behavior) (see Mentzoni et al., 2011; Robinson & Martin, 2008; Small & Vorgan, 2008). Further, excessive use of technologies has been linked to developmental delays, with nearly a third of children entering kindergarten with a developmental delay. Specifically, decreases in concentration and memory have been found to result from the pruning of the neuronal tracks that link to the frontal cortex (Christakis et al., 2004; Small & Vorgan, 2008). With each of these factors impacting on a child's brain and cognitive development, 5½-year-olds are projected to have a more difficult transition in school given the academic difficulties already at play.

In addition to brain and cognitive difficulties, children at this age may also experience social skill deficits. Computer games are typically designed for a single player, thus creating opportunities for children to play alone, detach from others, increase time spent away from parents, siblings, and peers, and decrease time spent on homework. Children who spend an excessive amount of time using technologies (including television, tablets and PCs, and smartphones) are often passive learners and have unrealistic views of the world (for example of "fairy tale" endings). Correlations between child aggression and violent media content have also been a hotly debated topic, resulting in mixed reviews. Some researchers have linked child aggression and violent media content (Anderson, Gentile, & Buckley, 2007; Davies, 2010), whereas

Szalavitz and Perry (2010) asserted that potential moderators are at play (such as time spent watching violent shows and innate tendencies toward violence) (Szalavitz & Perry, 2010). It is therefore crucial that parents monitor the use and content of the technologies that their children pursue, so as to mitigate any long-term negative consequences on the child's health and development. The AAP (2013) suggests that young children learn best by interacting with people, rather than with technology.

BEST PRACTICES IN COUNSELING/THERAPY

The age of 5 marks a year of transition for many children. This shift from preschool to elementary school can be trying for parents and children alike. Children typically enter school with enthusiasm, excitement, and an eagerness to learn. Halfway through this year, children experience difficulty academically, physically, and emotionally. However, most children still express happiness regularly, feel confident in their ability to try new things, love to learn, and genuinely express curiosity about their self and others. Parents and caregivers should consider counseling services when children appear unusually sad, are overtly disobedient (especially as a younger 5-year-old), experience a disconnect between parent and child, exhibit overly anxious behaviors, express a dislike for school, and/or display sexual behaviors beyond the realms of usual curiosity.

It is important for counselors to understand a child in the context of his or her development so as to select the most appropriate intervention. The development of a child can be impacted by his or her history and context, and by instability in his or her family structure. However, the process of development cannot be sped up because it is a natural process that is impacted on by the environment in which a child lives and grows. Gathering developmental information is one part of a larger puzzle when working with children and not all counseling approaches are appropriate for children at the age of 5. (For an extensive list of the most-used play therapy modalities, see Lambert et al., 2007.)

Developmentally Appropriate Approaches

Given that most children "under the age of 10 do not have abstract reasoning and language skills to verbally process their thoughts, feelings, reactions, and attitudes" (Kottman, 2001, p. 2), it is recommended that counselors who work with children of this age use expressive media such as toys, art, and play. Play is the language of children and toys are their words; therefore children at the age of 5 will benefit greatly from therapy in which play is the modality (Landreth, 2012). This section will consequently focus on only those approaches deemed appropriate for 5-year-olds within theoretical frames, literature, and current research.

Child-centered play therapy (CCPT) In child-centered play therapy (CCPT), the child and counselor develop a dynamic interpersonal relationship that facilitates safety and freedom in the playroom, whereby the child comes to feel free to explore and express himself or herself through the developmentally appropriate modality of play (Landreth, 2012). Child-centered play therapy stands apart from other play therapy approaches in that the focus remains on the child's innate tendency toward growth and the deep belief of the therapist in the child's ability to self-direct (Landreth & Bratton, 2006; Ray, 2008). In response to the rigid thinking and desire to follow rules that are common among 5-year-olds, CCPT provides a safe place in which children can test those beliefs without fear of punishment. This freedom for growth and exploration allow for the child to grow in a way that fits with his or her need to develop autonomy at this age. Further, 5-year-olds develop a strong attachment to symbols; thus this self-directed approach to counseling enables children at this age to express themselves symbolically.

Additionally, a child who is brought to play therapy at the age of 5 will be able to work through significant changes, traumatic events, or developmental challenges in his or her life in the context of a relationship that accepts that child exactly as he or she is. This acceptance and understanding within the therapeutic relationship gives the child the freedom to work toward his or her own enhancement and at his or her own pace, usually leading to change. Consider a child aged 5½, at which age children can be explosive: If the caregiver asks him or her to behave in any other way, a power struggle is likely to ensue. However, if the child's explosive behavior is accepted or allowed for a temporary time, without an audience and with no request that it stop, power struggles are likely to decrease and the child is more inclined to try a behavior that is more self-enhancing. Therefore this freedom found in CCPT is developmentally appropriate and has been shown to be effective (Lin & Bratton, 2015).

Adlerian play therapy (AdPT)   In Adlerian play therapy (AdPT), counselors apply the concepts derived from individual psychology (Adlerian therapy) to conceptualize both their child clients and parents through the use of play, art, and toys, using the child's natural expression of language to communicate most effectively with children through play (Kottman, 2003; Kottman & Ashby, 2015). Adlerian play therapists "believe that the therapeutic powers of play will facilitate the process of working with children by creating a bond between the therapist and the client based on shared fun" (Kottman, 2001, p. 2). To facilitate exploration of the child's beliefs about himself or herself, the world, and others, the play therapist communicates with the child mostly through metaphor. Because 5-year-olds have developed a strong attachment to symbols, working with metaphor is congruent with their developmental level. In addition to the benefits of using symbols and metaphor in play, this communication style allows the play therapist to understand the child's method for obtaining significance and belonging within his or her family, and allows the play therapist to understand the link between the child's current behaviors and his or her perception about how to act, based upon whether his or her beliefs about himself or herself, the world, and others were proven to be true.

A child's lifestyle is not fully formed until the age of 8; AdPT therefore provides an environment in which a 5-year-old can grow and develop by means of using encouragement as a primary tool of change (Kottman & Ashby, 2015). Further, Adlerian play therapists maintain a proactive and positive view of children and their ability to change (Kottman, 2003). Given that 5-year-olds are typically optimistic and excited for new challenges, the use of encouragement and a belief in their abilities are beneficial to their development of autonomy. Play at the age of 5 appears to be imaginative and focused on the problem as perceived by the child. If the therapist respects and does not derail that play, then the child's perception of the problem is revealed. It is therefore cautioned here that play therapists work in a more nondirective approach initially, given that the child lacks perspective taking, viewing objects and actions concretely, and is only beginning to develop emotional expression (Dillman Taylor & Bratton, 2014). If they implement cognitive and/or behavioral interventions before they have gathered a full developmental history and developed a solid, therapeutic relationship, counselors who use these techniques are likely to limit the child's expression of self, which mostly occurs in nonverbal metaphor. However, once the therapist can fully conceptualize the child's worldview and believes that a solid, trusting therapeutic alliance has been developed, the therapist can incorporate more cognitive-based interventions, such as role-playing, mutual storytelling, and others. These interventions are always used sparingly at this age, matched to the specific child's needs, and sandwiched between reflections and meta-communications.

Although AdPT is one of the most widely used play therapy modalities (Lambert et al., 2007), little empirical research has been conducted at time of writing. Research that has been conducted is promising: The first randomized control trial (RCT) demonstrated that children (aged 5–10) who participated in AdPT had a statistically significant increase in on-task behavior and a decrease in total problems, as compared to the active control group (Meany-Walen, Bratton, & Kottman, 2014). Of this sample, 14 children were aged 5 at the time of the intervention.

Parent Education/Therapy Models

Child–parent relationship therapy (CPRT)   Child–parent relationship therapy (CPRT) is a ten-week filial model, defined as a unique approach by professionals trained in play therapy to teach parents child-centered principles and the skills with which to be therapeutic agents with their own children (Landreth & Bratton, 2006). It would be an appropriate intervention if the child were to present with parent–child relationship issues. However, it is important to assess the parent's emotional readiness for this group: If the parent is emotionally unstable, then CPRT will not be an appropriate method of intervention. The therapist may choose to work with the child first in individual play therapy and to use parent consultations to lay the foundation for future CPRT trainings. In this instance, both the child and parent are getting their needs met within the safety of a therapeutic relationship with the counselor.

Similarly to CCPT, child–parent relationship therapists work with the parents to develop empathy and patience with children, allowing the parent to explore and experience the child's world. Given that 5-year-olds value following rules and avoiding punishment even at the cost of lying, parents who employ this approach provide children with an accepting environment that encourages children to be themselves and not to feel inhibited, allowing them to fully experience and learn from their environment, the consequences of their actions, and their interactions with others. The ten-session CPRT model has demonstrated a large effect size in repairing or nurturing the parent–child relationship (Landreth & Bratton, 2006). It has therefore been shown to be effective for children at age 5 and can be deemed developmentally appropriate. Child–parent relationship therapy is an affordable parenting program and all parent materials come free with the facilitator materials.

Positive discipline   Similar to the parallel between CCPT and filial therapy, positive discipline, a parenting education model, is heavily influenced by an Adlerian framework (Nelsen, 1996). The developer of this model summarized its premise as:

> [T]ogether, [parent and child] we will decide on the rules for our mutual benefit. We will also decide together on solutions that will be helpful to all concerned when we have problems. When I must use my judgment without your input, I will use firmness with kindness, dignity, and respect.
>
> – Nelsen (1996, p. 8)

This collaboration enables children to begin practicing and developing social interest at a level that is appropriate for the age of the child – a key aspect of developing into a contributing member of society.

Positive discipline is especially suited to 5-year-olds because of its developmental match to their needs. The approach enables parents to better understand their child, their child's goal of misbehavior, and how to approach their child in a way that he or she will understand based on his or her age. For a 5-year-old, this model enables parents to give the child an opportunity to make choices and to learn responsibility. Given that 5-year-olds tend to avoid punishment, parents are taught to provide developmentally appropriate consequences with firmness and kindness – two key aspects of this model – to mutually decide on a solution to a problem between the parent and child. Parents keep the focus on collaboration and decision making, thus providing opportunities for the child to learn to live with the consequences of his or her choices without instinctually avoiding punishment.

As for 5½-year-olds, who are eager to disobey, this method provides parents with opportunities to respond with choices and consequences to teach their child more appropriate ways of behaving without the power struggle or the "4 'R's," as outlined by Nelsen (1996): resentment, revenge, rebellion, and retreat. (If working through this model with teachers, see Nelsen & Lott, 2013.) This approach also encourages positive development by means of demonstrated trust and respect for the child. At this age, 5-year-olds are building their confidence and self-esteem, and parents who implement this parenting model encourage this development by using encouraging statements and mutually working with their child to solve a particular issue.

In addition, Nelsen (1996) designed positive discipline to help parents to recognize and reorient those of their own behaviors that may impact on their ability to parent effectively. Siegel and Hartzell (2013) emphasized the importance of parents learning to recognize when their own "stuff" gets in the way of parenting. They affirmed that parents could more effectively respond and build positive attachments when they processed those of their histories and events that may have significant impact on their ability to be present with their child. Cross-discipline research supports the focus of this parenting education model. Positive discipline is also an affordable parenting intervention.

Parent–child interaction therapy (PCIT)   Parent–child interaction therapy (PCIT) is an evidence-based program for young children (from birth to age 5) who are experiencing conduct disorders or externalizing behavioral disorders (NREPP, n.d.). This approach would therefore be most appropriate if the child's presenting concern (disobedient behavior) were to be beyond the normal explosive behaviors of a 5-year-old. Like the other parenting programs outlined, the focus of PCIT is on improving the quality of the parent–child relationship, and enhancing the positive interactions between parent and child. In PCIT, parents are taught nondirective play skills with which to build or strengthen a supportive relationship with the child. Parents typically implement these skills during the first phase of this program: child-directed interaction (CDI). During the second phase, parent-directed interaction (PDI), parents develop the skills with which to encourage prosocial behaviors and discourage negative behaviors. Parents take the lead in this phase, directing their child's behavior by communicating clearly age-appropriate, consistent instructions and consequences to increase their child's compliance. This parent education program is generally conducted in 15 weekly, one-hour sessions by a licensed mental health professional. Unlike other programs, the materials for PCIT are costly and less affordable even for professionals. Although this program is considered evidence-based for this age group, the cost associated with this parent education intervention therefore makes it less feasible than other options previously presented.

Working with Parents, Caretakers, and Teachers

Five can be a challenging age for parents, caretakers, and teachers. The once energetic, sweet 5-year-old can be explosive, clumsy, and hard to manage at 5½. It is important for parents to develop patience not only for their child, but also for themselves. Landreth and Bratton (2006, p. 174) teach parents that "you cannot give away that which you do not possess" (2006).

Not only is the child emotionally different half a year later, but he or she also begins to pull away from his or her parents, becoming less dependent on them and more interested in building peer relationships. This shift can be challenging for parents and caretakers alike. It is crucial that the therapist provide parents with support, empathy, and a space for debriefing the loss of their caring 5-year-old. This short section therefore highlights the presence that a therapist must have with the parent to be successful and offers helpful hints to guide parent–teacher consultations. Although some of these ideas have been discussed in parenting education models previously, this section emphasizes basic skills for parents and teachers to strengthen their relationship and to minimize behavioral difficulties that result, in large part, from developmental milestones.

Parents and teachers can develop patience by means of a greater understanding of child development. If knowledge is gained, typically the parent and/or teacher will exhibit greater empathy because some of the problems at hand (such as explosions, tantrums, and disobedience) are normal for this age. Therefore therapists can educate parents on the milestones that 5-year-olds will experience.

Parents can also be on the lookout for these milestones and can recognize early if the child is experiencing any concerning behaviors. Therapists can teach parents how to respond in a positive, encouraging manner. This skill will be particularly helpful as a child becomes clumsier and experiences difficulty in bringing himself or herself under control, both of which were milestones that he or she achieved at an earlier stage. Parents and teachers might consider using encouragement when their child is struggling, for example "You're really working hard to figure that out."

Parents can also use reflective responding to enable their children to begin to understand their emotions and to learn to express them in socially appropriate ways. When the child is getting increasingly upset because he or she cannot figure out how to work a toy, for example, the parent might simply respond, "You feel mad right now." This reflection helps the child to recognize his or her own feelings in the moment. Sometimes, this frustration can lead to inappropriate behavior such as throwing things or screaming at the parent. When this happens, it is important for parents to remain calm and to provide logical consequences. Children at this age are beginning to understand short-term consequences; therefore parents can implement this skill to help their child to develop consciousness of, and responsibility for, his or her actions.

Parents are highly encouraged to spend quality one-on-one time with their child. This time can help children to feel important and cared for – especially if they have younger siblings. During this time, parents can create opportunities for children to learn about their own culture and others in an accepting and inclusive environment, or parents might empower the child to come up with activities that they might do together.

CONCLUSION

Five-year-olds are in a period of transition. Many aspects change for them over the course of this year. Therapists, parents, caregivers, and teachers will support children's healthy growth and development during this period if they have a firm grasp of the developmental changes that occur between the ages of 5 and 6. Although the explosiveness of a 5½-year-old may appear abnormal, these new behaviors are temporary and to be expected at this age. Therapists, in particular, must be aware of the child's developmental functioning if they are to find the most appropriate intervention for the child's presenting concern and age. With children's transition from parental dependence toward an increased interest in peers, it is important to include parents in the therapy process to help to support their feelings during these transitions and to provide approaches that they can use at home to best meet their child's needs.

REFERENCES

Active Healthy Kids Canada. (2015). Particip-ACTION report card on the physical activity of children and youth. Retrieved from http://www.participaction.com/report-card-2015/report-card/

American Academy of Pediatrics (AAP). (2013). Children, adolescents, and the media. *Pediatrics*, *132*(5), 958–961.

Anderson, C. A., Gentile, D. A., & Buckley, K. E. (2007). *Violent video game effects on children and adolescents: Theory, research, & public policy*. Oxford: Oxford University Press.

Christakis, D. A., Gilkerson, J., Richards, J. A., Zimmerman, F. J., Garrison, M. M., Xu, D., Gray, S., & Yapanel, U. (2009). Audible television and decreased adult words, infant vocalizations, and conversational turns. *Archives of Pediatrics & Adolescent Medicine*, *163*(6), 554–558.

Clifford, B. R., Gunter, B., & McAleer, J. L. (1995). *Television and children*. Hillsdale, NJ: Erlbaum.

Davies, D. (2010). *Child development: A practitioner's guide* (3rd ed.). New York, NY: Guilford.

Dillman Taylor, D., & Bratton, S. C. (2014). Developmentally appropriate practice: Adlerian play therapy with preschool children. *Journal of Individual Psychology*, *70*(3), 205–219.

Erikson, E. (1963). *Childhood and society*. New York, NY: Norton.

Francoeur, R. T. Koch, P. B., & Weis, D. L. (1998). *Sexuality in America: Understanding our sexual values and behaviors*. New York, NY: Continuum.

Gesell Institute of Child Development. (2011). *Gesell Developmental Observation–Revised examiner's manual*. New Haven, CT: Gesell Institute.

Greenspan, S. (1993). *Playground politics: Understanding the emotional life of your school-aged child*. Reading, MA: Harvard University Press.

Kellogg, N. D. (2009). Clinical report: The evaluation of sexual behaviors in children. *Pediatrics*, *124*(3), 992–999.

Kellogg, N. D. (2010). Sexual behaviors in children: Evaluation and management. *American Family Physician*, *82*(10), 1233–1238.

Kohlberg, L. (1981). *The philosophy of moral development: Moral stages and the idea of justice*. San Francisco, CA: Harper & Row.

Kottman, T. (2001). Adlerian play therapy. *International Journal of Play Therapy*, *10*(2), 1–12.

Kottman, T. (2003). *Partners in play: An Adlerian approach to play therapy* (2nd ed.). Alexandria, VA: American Counseling Association.

Kottman, T., & Ashby, J. (2015). Adlerian play therapy. In A. Stewart & D. Crenshaw (Eds.), *Play therapy: A comprehensive guide to theory and practice* (pp. 32–47). New York, NY: Guilford.

Lambert, S. F., LeBlanc, M., Mullen, J. A., Ray, D., Baggerly, J., White, J., & Kaplan, D. (2007). Learning more about those who play in session: The national play therapy in counseling practices project (phase 1). *Journal of Counseling & Development*, *85*, 42–46.

Landreth, G. L. (2012). *Play therapy: The art of the relationship* (3rd ed.). New York, NY: Routledge.

Landreth, G. L., & Bratton, S. (2006). *Child–parent relationship therapy (CPRT): A 10-session filial therapy model.* New York, NY: Routledge.

Lin, Y.-W., & Bratton, S. C. (2015). A meta-analytic review of child-centered play therapy approaches. *Journal of Counseling & Development, 93,* 45–58.

Loevinger, J. (1966). The meaning and measurement of ego development. *American Psychologist, 21*(3), 195–206.

Meany-Walen, K. K., Bratton, S., & Kottman, T. (2014). Effects of Adlerian play therapy on reducing students' disruptive behaviors. *Journal of Counseling and Development, 92*(1), 47–56.

Mentzoni, R. A., Brunborg, G. S., Molde, H., Myrseth, H., Mar Skouveroe, K. J., Hetland, J., & Pallesen, S. (2011). Problematic video game use: Estimated prevalence and associations with mental and physical health. *Cyberpsychology, Behavior, and Social Networking, 14*(10), 591–596.

Miller, K. (2001). *Ages and stages: Developmental descriptions and activities birth through eight years.* West Palm Beach, FL: Telshare.

National Child Traumatic Stress Network (NCTSN). (2009). Sexual development and behavior in children: Information for parents and caregivers. Retrieved from http://www.nctsn.org/resources/audiences/parents-caregivers

National Registry of Evidenced-based Programs and Practices (NREPP). (n.d.). Parent–child interaction therapy. Retrieved from http://www.nrepp.samhsa.gov/ViewIntervention.aspx?id=23

Nelsen, J. (1996). *Positive discipline.* New York, NY: Ballantine Books.

Nelsen, J., & Lott, L. (2013) *Positive discipline for the classroom.* New York, NY: Three Rivers Press.

Petty, K. (2010). *Developmental milestones of young children.* St. Paul, MN: Redleaf Press.

Piaget, J. (1932/1997). *The moral judgment of the child.* New York, NY: Free Press.

Ray, D. (2008). Impact of play therapy on parent–child relationship stress at a mental health training setting. *British Journal of Guidance & Counselling, 36*(2), 165–187.

Robinson, J. P., & Martin, S. (2008). What do happy people do? *Journal of Social Indicators Research, 89*(3), 565–571.

Santrock, J. W. (2001). *Child development* (9th ed.). New York: McGraw-Hill.

Siegel, D. J., & Hartzell, M. (2013). *Parenting from the inside out: How a deeper self-understanding can help you raise children who thrive.* Los Angeles, CA: Tarcher.

Siegel, D., & Payne Bryson, T. (2011). *The whole-brain child: 12 revolutionary strategies to nurture your child's developing mind.* New York, NY: Bantam Books.

Small, G., & Vorgan, G. (2008). *iBrain: Surviving the technological alteration of the modern mind.* New York, NY: Harper Collins Publishers.

Sprenger, M. (2008). *The developing brain: Birth to age eight.* Thousand Oaks, CA: Corwin Press.

Sue, D., & Sue, D. (2003). *Counseling the culturally diverse: Theory and practice* (4th ed.). New York, NY: Wiley.

Szalavitz, M., & Perry, B. D. (2010). *Born for love: Why empathy is essential and endangered.* New York, NY: William Morrow.

Volbert, R. (2000). Sexual knowledge of preschool children. *Journal of Psychology & Human Sexuality, 12*(1–2), 5–26.

Wurtele, S. K., & Kenny, M. C. (2011). Normative sexuality development in childhood: Implications for developmental guidance and prevention of childhood sexual abuse. *Counseling and Human Development, 43*(9), 1–24.

7

THE EXTRAORDINARY 6-YEAR-OLD

Kimberly M. Jayne

Source: Used with permission from Shutterstock

THE 6-YEAR-OLD

Six-year-olds are complicated creatures who are growing and changing rapidly. The disequilibrium of the 5½-year-old peaks at age 6 (Gesell Institute, 2011). At times, the 6-year-old may seem oppositional and stubborn, and may even appear to be at odds with himself or herself and his or her environment. A 6-year-old may have frequent mood swings and may frequently change his or her mind (Wood, 2007). He or she may adamantly demand a red popsicle, only to cry when you deliver it, declaring: "I wanted vanilla ice cream. I hate red popsicles!"

While they are becoming more independent and adventurous, 6-year-olds also demand routine and ritual to provide a sense of security. Bedtime and mealtimes may become more difficult, and 6-year-olds may often seem messy and disobedient (Gesell Institute, 2011; Wood, 2007). Six-year-olds cry frequently and may also complain or whine more frequently than their 5-year-old selves. When 6-year-olds throw tantrums, they may hit or kick and can be difficult to comfort. They are very sensitive to criticism and correction, and earnestly seek approval from parents, teachers, and friends (Petty, 2010).

Six-year-olds are imaginative, curious, and enthusiastic, and are often buzzing about talking and making noise. They love jokes and guessing games, and are animated in their speech. They take great pleasure in practicing and showing off their skills and abilities, and their enthusiasm for learning and life is contagious. Six-year-olds are moving toward abstract thinking and reasoning, and have an expansive vocabulary to support their constant chatter. Six-year-olds are often either travelling a mile a minute or completely stopped in their tracks, fluctuating between noisy, frenetic activity and fatigue (with moodiness).

THE 6½-YEAR-OLD

The 6½-year-old is much calmer and more easygoing than his or her younger counterparts. As they enter a state of equilibrium, 6½-year-olds blossom into likeable, affectionate, and humorous companions (Gesell Institute, 2011). Six-and-a-half-year-olds love to demonstrate their knowledge for others: from counting to 100, to reading books at bedtime. They get along well with parents, teachers, and friends, and enjoy new places, new information, and new ideas. Six-and-a-half-year-olds are a delight to those around them, and less at odds with themselves and their environment, with less frequent and intense fluctuations in mood and behavior.

BRAIN DEVELOPMENT AND INTERPERSONAL NEUROBIOLOGY

A child's brain is constantly being wired and rewired, with each experience helping to determine its structure (Siegel & Bryson, 2011). Relational experiences and social interactions are the primary context for early brain development (Kestly, 2014). Unnecessary synaptic connections are pruned throughout childhood, with the biggest reduction happening between the ages of 5 and 11. At 6 years old, the brain is still growing and will not reach its adult size for another year or two. The healthy, developing 6-year-old's brain is becoming more integrated as communication between the left and right hemisphere increases.

Six-year-olds' dopamine levels in the prefrontal cortex are now similar to those of an adult brain, and promote the 6-year-old's increasing ability to focus, concentrate, and set goals (Sprenger, 2008). Six-year-olds often show gains in executive functioning that are critical for mastering new skills and performing well in school. Links between the temporal and parietal lobes support the 6-year-old's burgeoning vocabulary and reading abilities. Play contributes to the development of one of the most important brain functions: self-control (Aamodt & Wang, 2011; Kestly, 2014). The prefrontal cortex helps to shape the 6-year-old's goal-directed behavior by activating or inhibiting other regions in the brain. The ability to self-regulate behavior is important for both academic and interpersonal success. Succeeding at challenging tasks that require self-control, such as puzzles, multistep art projects, board games, and imaginary play, builds more success for the 6-year-old, while repeated failure may teach the child to stop trying. Six-year-olds are especially susceptible to the powers of success and failure, and need encouragement and support from parents and teachers as they learn to self-regulate, and as they develop cognitive processes such planning, concentration, working memory, self-control, and motivation.

Six-year-olds often enjoy and thrive in the structured and engaging environment of school, but need opportunities for self-directed free play to support healthy brain development.

Neglect, trauma, or disrupted attachment in early childhood can affect brain development and how the body responds to stress throughout childhood (Davies, 2011). A child who experiences trauma before the age of 6 may continue to show deleterious effects, including higher cortisol levels in the brain, hyperarousal, challenges to concentration, and difficulty in self-regulating behavior and emotions (Kestly, 2014).

PHYSICAL DEVELOPMENT

Just as their emotional worlds are expanding, 6-year-olds are also experiencing rapid physical growth and may get sick frequently, complain about aches and pains, and be more clumsy and accident-prone overall (Gesell Institute, 2011; Wood, 2007). They are highly active and always in a hurry, but also get tired easily. Six-year-olds often chew on their pencils and fingernails, because they are starting to lose their baby teeth and their permanent teeth begin to come in. Six-year-olds are often great eaters and sleepers, but at times they may be defiant at mealtimes and bedtimes. They may be more fearful at bedtime and may need the comforting presence of their parent, a night light, or a familiar stuffed animal to ease their anxiety. Most 6-year-olds no longer take an afternoon nap, but bedtime routines are essential. Six-year-olds usually wake up easily, but may resist getting dressed, brushing their teeth, or taking a bath, and seem very uninterested in their own personal hygiene. They often have lots of opinions about what to wear and dislike having their hair combed or fixed (Petty, 2010). As they become more independent, most 6-year-olds are able to tie their own shoelaces.

> Six-year-olds experience rapid physical growth correlated with rapid physical activity, but they tire easily (Gesell Institute, 2011).

Bathroom accidents are rare by the age of 6, but accidents or bedwetting under times of stress are normal. Six-year-olds are often highly embarrassed and ashamed when they have accidents, and will be very sensitive to criticism or punishment. They may need reminding or help with scheduling bathroom breaks, especially when they are busy playing or engaged in a new activity. An average 6-year-old boy or girl is 45 inches tall and weighs 46 pounds (Davies, 2011).

Motor Development

A 6-year-old is learning to distinguish his or her right hand from his or her left, but may have difficulty translating this skill to other people (Wood, 2007). When writing and reading, a 6-year-old may still reverse letters and numbers, but most are able to print the alphabet, write their first and last names, and write numbers from one (1) to ten (10) (Gesell Institute, 2011; Berk, 2007). Their writing is often large and they may use their entire arm to make each stroke when they are writing. Six-year-olds engage in more fine motor activities, including painting, cutting with scissors, playing with clay, and drawing, and value these forms of expression (Petty, 2010).

In terms of gross motor development, 6-year-olds are seldom successful at hitting a thrown ball and will be much more successful at T-ball than baseball. Six-year-olds are almost never completely still, even when they are sitting, and are often clumsy and awkward. Six-year-olds are able to skip, jump rope, ride a bicycle without training wheels, and bounce and catch a ball (Sprenger, 2008). Whereas the 6-year-old will often work more quickly than carefully and will be concerned more with quantity than quality, the 6½-year-old begins to slow down. At 6½, most reversals of letters and numbers are resolved, and children have better hand–eye coordination overall (Gesell Institute, 2011).

GENDER AND SEXUAL DEVELOPMENT

By the age of 6, children increasingly adopt socially constructed gender-specific behavior and avoid behavior associated with the opposite gender (Davies, 2011). Six-year-olds will often discriminate between "boy" colors and "girl" colors, or identify specific toys as for use by girls or boys. Gender constancy is established at the age of 6, and, during this phase of development, children may be more rigid in their understanding and allegiance to gender. While they often play in groups separated by gender, they also continue to identify with their classmates based on age and grade across genders. Some children may express a strong interest in opposite-sex behavior at this age. Identification with the opposite sex may strengthen or become less pervasive as the child continues to develop. Parents and teachers should communicate acceptance and support for the 6-year-old's developing gender identity, and exploration of both masculine and feminine characteristics. Sexual or affectional orientation typically emerges more clearly just before or during puberty.

Kimberly M. Jayne

When considering a 6-year-old's sexual development, it is important to remember that children do not assign the same meaning to erotic behavior or sexual events as do adults (AAP, 2005; Weis, 1998). Six-year-olds may play with their genitals and discover that it provides a feeling of pleasure. Once this is discovered, the child is likely to repeat this behavior simply because it feels good, without any sense of the act as sexual. Children may also use masturbation as a way to self-soothe, and they often masturbate more frequently when they are anxious or under stress. Although childhood masturbation may be a surprising or uncomfortable for parents, it is important to respond with sensitivity and acceptance toward the 6-year-old. Because children do not understand the social implications of public masturbation, they should not be punished or shamed for doing it. Parents can set limits about when and where children masturbate, and should redirect or distract children as needed. Parents should also be aware of what sexual content children are exposed to at this age, providing supervision over media that is accessed and used on television, social media, video games, music, and online. Although 6-year-olds may see displays of kissing and hand-holding, exposure to other forms of sexual intimacy and behavior are not developmentally appropriate.

Six-year-olds may also engage in some sexual play, which usually involves mostly looking and some touching, and may begin to develop some feelings of affection toward other children (Greenspan, 1998). It is within normal developmental limits to find a 6-year-old and his or her

> Six-year-olds may still play with an imaginary friend or use a security object such as a "blankie" or stuffed animal at bedtime.

friend undressing with each other in order to examine each other's bodies. They may also attempt to see other people naked, or undress and talk about private parts, or use "sexual," or "naughty," words even when they do not comprehend their meaning. Six-year-olds may also talk about having a "girlfriend" or "boyfriend," or may develop a crush on a teacher. They may ask many questions about where babies come from or why parents sleep together in the same room. It is important for parents to be accepting of the child's curiosities, while teaching the child about privacy and setting appropriate limits to avoid sexual overstimulation.

For typically developing 6-year-old males, the penis, scrotum, and testicles will grow in proportion to the rest of the body (Madaras & Madaras, 2007). Growth in the genital area is typically slow and the testicles are usually less than 3 milliliters in size. Uncircumcized males at this age may or may not be able to retract their foreskin. Foreskin retraction is a slow process that varies individually, but most uncircumcised boys will be able to retract their foreskin to reveal the urinary opening and about halfway to the corona; full retraction is completed during puberty and should never be forced. Although 6-year-old females grow taller, begin to lose fat, and gain more muscle overall, there are no demonstrable physical signs of development to their genitalia or breast tissue at this age.

COGNITIVE DEVELOPMENT

According to Piaget, children actively construct reality out of their experiences with the environment, and the way in which they make meaning out of their experience evolves as they develop more complex ways of thinking (Piaget & Inhelder, 1969). Six-year-olds are transitioning from the "preoperational" period of cognitive development toward the "concrete operational" period:

> Six-year-olds will pretend and model the romantic behaviors of characters on television or adults whom they observe.

from concrete to abstract thought. In the preoperational stage, children are actively acquiring language, and are able to use symbols to represent their experiences and realities. It is during this period that children express their life experiences primarily through symbolic play. Younger 6-year-olds may still have the sort of magical thinking that leads them to believe that a beloved stuffed animal is the source of comfort or security necessary to keep monsters away at bedtime, or that something that they did, such as color on the wall, caused their parents to get divorced. As 6-year-olds move into concrete operations, they acquire the ability to manipulate symbols mentally and visually. Instead of having to sort colored blocks into separate piles, the child is now able to sort them mentally without moving a finger.

It is at the stage of concrete operations that children truly begin to conceptually understand numbers and letters, and are able to decode words, rather than simply to memorize them or sight-read (Elkind, 2006). Six-year-olds also develop the ability to learn and operate according to rules, including rules of etiquette, such as saying "Thank you" when someone helps them to tie their shoelaces. Using manners is more than memorizing what to say: it reflects the 6-year-old's ability to progress through a reasoning process to determine when specific rules apply. Six-year-olds are often captivated by knock-knock jokes because they are able to follow the prescribed rules of this form of humor, but they fill in the gaps with gibberish or spoil the punchline because they are yet to grasp the subtle nuances and sophistication of verbal comedy. Children in concrete operations are also able to learn the rules of reading (reading from left to right), spelling ("i before e except after c") and arithmetic (2 + 4 = 6 and 4 + 2 = 6). As concrete thinkers, children are able to create games and make up rules of their own. Six-year-olds can learn the social rules of childhood such as "Last one there is a rotten egg!" or "You get what you get and you don't throw a fit." They can also differentiate between fantasy and reality, and rapidly enter in and out of pretend play.

Six-year-olds begin a major transition in intellectual growth. They love to ask questions and are often heard endlessly asking their parents "why?" without constraint. They learn best through discovery, and are eager for new experiences and adventures (Gesell Institute, 2011; Petty, 2010; Sprenger, 2008). Six-year-olds crave structure and routine in the classroom, and often get distressed by the slightest change in their schedules or when transitioning from one activity to the next. Most 6-year-olds have an attention span of 20–30 minutes and prefer structured activities. Six-year-olds love to read and look at books. They are very creative, and enjoy drawing and other various art activities. Six-year-olds typically cannot tell time, but have a greater sense of time especially in regard to birthdays and holidays.

Six-and-a-half-year-olds enjoy challenges and intellectual tasks. They are more aware of their environment and curious about how things work (Gesell Institute, 2011; Wood, 2007). They take pride in their work and most are able to read independently. Whereas 6-year-olds write primarily using only capital letters, 6½-year-olds are able to write using both capital and lower-case letters. They are able to decode unfamiliar words using context clues and their knowledge of phonics (Petty, 2010). They are able to count by twos, fives, and tens, can identify familiar money, and are beginning to comprehend simple addition, subtraction, and fractions. Six-year-olds are also able to identify the seasons and days of the week. They have a more realistic understanding of space, and increased capacity for visual perception and organization, distinguishing and creating visual patterns out of random or disordered stimuli (Davies, 2011).

Most 6-year-olds in the United States are in the first grade, and school becomes increasingly important and a more central focus for the 6-year-old (Petty, 2010; Wood, 2007). Six-year-olds enjoy completing assignments, paying more attention to the process than the product, as demonstrated in sloppy or work of variable quality. They often show great interest in completing their work *first* or doing the *most* work among their peers. Six-year-olds are deeply affected by encouragement and affirmation, and likewise by condemnation from teachers and other authority figures. The 6-year-old is highly sensitive to criticism and often responds to correction with an emotional outburst or sulking withdrawal. Teacher's verbal and nonverbal expressions all have a great effect on the burgeoning mind and emotions of the 6-year-old child. The child is intensely curious and receptive to learning, and is more acutely aware of others' perceptions of him or her.

> Six-year-olds work well within busy and noisy environments.

Six-year-olds become increasingly aware of others' evaluation of their skills and competencies (Davies, 2011; Wood, 2007). They also recognize their own gaps in knowledge and the superior abilities of older children and adults. First graders often approach the task of learning new concepts and skills with seriousness and intensity, but will often exorcise the stresses of expanding their cognitive abilities and adapting to highly structured learning environments in the form of boundless energy and activity at recess and emotional volatility at home.

WORLDVIEW/EGO DEVELOPMENT

Six-year-olds and 6½-year-olds begin developing self-evaluation in four main areas, including academic competence, social competence, physical competence, and physical appearance (Berk, 2007). The child's self-concept and self-esteem reflect how successful and confident he or she feels in each of these areas. At the age of 6, children face the challenge of developing what

Kimberly M. Jayne

Erikson described as a sense of "industry or inferiority" (Erikson, 1963). Children with a sense of *industry* view themselves as capable of doing things well and have confidence in themselves. Children with a sense of *inferiority* believe that whatever they do will go badly, and tend to have low self-confidence and self-esteem.

A 6-year-old's sense of industry or inferiority is going to be developed primarily in the context of their relationships with parents and teachers (Elkind, 2006; Erikson, 1963). If parents and teachers complain frequently about what the child does, comment on the child's every mistake, or fail to acknowledge the child's successes and strengths, the child may begin to see himself or herself as inferior. Children who are encouraged to develop their capabilities, who experience the confidence that others have in them, and whose achievements are recognized will develop a sense of their own competence and industry. Children who experience few academic or behavioral successes may have such a strong sense of inferiority that they develop a "learned helplessness" and further disengage from learning or relationships. Six-year-olds will look for approval and praise from parents and teachers, and can easily be crushed be criticism or disapproval.

In applying Loevinger's (1976) ego development model, 6-year-olds are typically in the "self-protective" stage of ego development. During this stage, children develop greater self-control of impulses and an understanding that there are rules that must be followed. They are able to understand and anticipate that there are positive and negative consequences for their behavior. The primary concern of the self-protective child is to get his or her needs met and to keep from getting caught. The self-protective child can regulate his or her own thoughts, feelings, and behavior in order to get his or her needs met and to avoid punishment. Although they understand the concept of blame in this stage, 6-year-olds tend to externalize blame to others and avoid taking responsibility for wrongdoing. While this may seem selfish at times, the 6-year-old is taking the necessary developmental steps toward following rules and understanding the consequences of his or her behaviors.

Racial/Ethnic Identity Development

The 6-year-old is becoming more aware of similarities and differences between himself or herself and others. Most 6-year-olds tend to play and make friends that look like them and have similar cultural or social attributes (Davies, 2011; Wood, 2007). Six-year-olds are able to identify racial labels based on physical features and characteristics, and are more likely to associate socially constructed positive attributes with the ethnic or racial majority and more negative attributes with the ethnic or racial minority, regardless of their own racial identity (Davies, 2011; Swanson, Cunningham, Youngblood, & Spencer, 2009). Prejudice based on stereotypes decreases, however, as a result of personal experiences that defy and challenge stereotypes. Owing to their increased interest in group play and group membership, 6-year-olds become more aware of race and culture as these impact upon peer acceptance and relationships.

Transitions into the school context heighten the 6-year-old's awareness of race and ethnicity because he or she is exposed to cultural frameworks beyond his or her primary family unit. Children learn which social categories are important by observing their social environments, and identifying patterns and social rules based on their observations and experiences (Winkler, 2009). As they become more aware of similarities and differences between themselves and others, 6-year-olds' understanding of their own race and ethnicity may impact on their self-esteem as they begin to implicitly understand related issues of social privilege and power. Whereas in-group bias or favoritism toward groups of which they are members is present in early childhood, by the age of 6 children show a bias toward socially privileged groups regardless of their own race or ethnicity. However, the 6-year-old's increased ability to understand the perspectives of others also allows him or her to see multiple dimensions of identity and to compare stereotypes to personal experience (Davies, 2011). Because of the increased influence of acceptance by authority figures and peers on a child's self-esteem at this stage, minority children face increased risks of either devaluing or rejecting their minority identities, internalizing stereotypes, or giving up on academic or extracurricular pursuits based on a belief that they will not be evaluated fairly or will experience discrimination.

88

SOCIAL DEVELOPMENT

Six-year-olds are competitive, and want to be the best and the first at everything (Gesell Institute, 2011; Wood, 2007). When they lose a game, they will often cry or become angry, and they often invent their own rules. They can be bossy and can tease, and they tend to express themselves very dramatically. Six-year-olds may lie to avoid blame or punishment and often find it hard to admit when they have done something wrong or to apologize to others. Admitting failure or wrongdoing threatens the 6-year-old's sometimes fragile self-esteem and developing identity as capable and competent.

> Six-year-olds may lie, cheat, or change rules of games in order to win or be the best.

Six-year-olds value friendships and tend to select friends who are similar to themselves in terms of age, sex, race, ethnicity, and socioeconomic status (Berk, 2007; Gesell Institute, 2011). They often make friends easily and enjoy playing in groups (Petty, 2010). Sometimes, 6-year-olds can be verbally and physically aggressive toward their friends, and they are often competitive and argumentative. When playing games, they may cheat or change the rules to win, or they may be bossy in order to get their own way (Gesell Institute, 2011; Wood, 2007). There will often be conflict around competition, and hurt feelings and tears when one child loses. Six-year-olds are often rough and loud in their play, wrestling, chasing, and screaming. They are much more interested in, and sometimes critical of, their friends' behaviors than they were when they were 5. While they do not avoid playing with children of the opposite sex, 6-year-olds may begin to start grouping by sex in their play, and become more aware and solid in their sense of gender roles.

Six-year-olds are gregarious, and enjoy conversations with peers and adults (Petty, 2010). In their communication and language development, 6-year-olds have become more masterful in their use of grammar and syntax, and have an ever-expanding vocabulary. They are also more skillful at solving problems through verbal communication rather than through action. This increased capacity for verbal communication is often reflected in less physical aggression and impulsive behavior. They are more avid storytellers, and are eager to ask questions and find answers. While some may find the rapid and intense inquiry of the 6-year-old exhausting at times, asking questions is a major tool for learning and communication at this stage of development.

> Six-year-olds have a much larger receptive vocabulary (i.e. words that they understand) than expressive vocabulary (i.e. words that they say).

With teachers, 6-year-olds are often affectionate and friendly (Gesell Institute, 2011; Wood, 2007). They may behave "perfectly" at school and want to do well academically. Six-year-olds often conform to teachers' expectations and are eager to please in the school environment. They may even get angry when parents recommend an alternate way of doing homework or propose alternate rules to those of their teachers. As they grow into 6½-year-olds, children become more humorous and talkative. They can be very warm and affectionate toward others, and often enjoy being with, and are enjoyed by, their parents, teachers, and friends.

RELATIONSHIP DEVELOPMENT

Six-year-olds are anxious to do well and seek approval from others. Any failure, however slight, can be very hard for them to accept (Gesell Institute, 2011; Sprenger, 2008; Wood, 2007). While they are becoming more independent and mature, 6-year-olds may seem insecure and have high emotional needs. They are emotionally sensitive and vulnerable. While they still see themselves as the center of their worlds, they have developed abilities to recognize that other people can have different thoughts and feelings from their own (Berk, 2007).

At the age of 6, the child's focus has shifted away from the primary caregiver to the self, and he or she may begin to seek more independence from parents. Six-year-olds often have fears and anxieties about parents getting sick or dying (Ames & Ilg, 1979). Relationships with parents are characterized by conflict and ambivalence, moving from "I love you" to "I hate you" rapidly and without warning. Six-year-olds still love and need their parents even as they struggle toward independence. Six-year-olds seek the time and attention of both parents, and fear disapproval. Often, the 6-year-old will behave better for the less patient or demanding parent and will behave worst with the primary caregiver. This push-and-pull dynamic can be challenging for parents and 6-year-olds alike.

With siblings, 6-year-olds may be combative and competitive at times. Six-year-olds tend to respect older siblings, but can fluctuate from being bossy and aggressive to being kind and nurturing toward younger siblings (Davies, 2011; Gesell Institute, 2011; Wood, 2007). Six-year-olds will be especially sensitive to comparisons made between them and their siblings, and may become more conflicted or competitive with siblings if they feel that they do not measure up. Peers are becoming more and more important to the 6-year-old, and more energy is devoted to gaining peer acceptance and developing social relationships beyond the home environment.

> Sensitive to comparison with siblings, 6-year-olds may become more competitive or aggressive if they feel inadequate.

DEVELOPMENT IN THE AGE OF TECHNOLOGY

Technology and media exposure are increasing realities for children of all ages (Rideout, 2013). The average 6-year-old knows more about digital technology and is more tech savvy than the average 45-year-old adult (Ofcom, 2014). Children are exposed to technology at a very early age, and this has potential impact on their brain and social development. The American Academy of Pediatrics (AAP, 2013) recommends that children over the age of 2 spend no more than two hours a day using screens, including televisions, computers, tablets, video games, or smartphones, and that "screen time" should be devoted to high-quality content (AAP, 2013). The AAP further recommends that parents exclude televisions and Internet-connected devices from children's bedrooms, monitor what media children are accessing and using, including social media platforms, and view media with their children to provide guidance and model discernment. It is important for parents to consider their individual child's sensitivity to certain types of media and how exposure to drama, violence, strong emotional content, or other genres of media may impact on their unique child. Several studies have shown that screen time increases the risk of obesity, may cause sleep disruptions for children aged 6–12, decreases focus and attention, negatively impacts on academic performance and engagement, decreases empathic responding and social skills, and impedes executive functioning (AAP, 2013; Campaign for a Commercial-Free Childhood, 2014).

One of the keys to helping children to develop a healthy relationship with technology is modeling appropriate behavior, and providing interaction and guidance while children are using different forms of technology and media. Because play and social interaction are so critical for a child's development at the age of 6, it is important that children have substantial opportunities for imaginative and fantasy play, interaction with adults and peers, physical activity, and exposure to nontechnological toys and materials that promote creativity and self-directed play.

BEST PRACTICES FOR COUNSELING/THERAPY

Although 6-year-olds may be challenging for many parents owing to their quickly changing moods, stubborn determination, and emotional sensitivity, counseling is not necessary for every tantrum-throwing, defiant 6-year-old. Parents and caregivers should consider bringing their 6-year-olds to counseling if:

- the child has significant behavior problems at school, or struggles to learn or succeed in school because of low self-esteem;
- the child has difficulties relating to peers and regularly withdraws from children his or her age, or is consistently aggressive and violent toward peers;
- there is disconnect in the child–parent relationship, marked by primarily negative interactions between the parent and child or emotional distance;
- the child experiences a significant loss or change in his or her environment and has difficulty adjusting to the change, such as a divorce or the loss of a parent;
- the child seems overly anxious or sad compared to other children his or her age; or
- the child experiences a traumatic event, neglect, or physical, sexual, or emotional abuse.

Child-centered play therapy (CCPT) Child-centered play therapy (CCPT) is the most developmentally appropriate intervention for 6-year-olds. Six-year-olds communicate their thoughts, feelings, and experiences through play, and while they are verbose, they still need freedom to express themselves actively and symbolically through play (Landreth, 2012; Ray, 2011). Six-year-olds develop their sense of self primarily in the context of relationships with parents, caregivers, teachers, and peers. In CCPT, the play therapist provides a safe, accepting, and empathic environment in which the child can express himself or herself freely, learn how to self-regulate, and follow limits. Because 6-year-olds are so sensitive to criticism and have a strong need for approval from others, allowing the child to lead the play session and to choose in what direction to go allows him or her to develop a more internalized locus of evaluation and a stronger sense of industry. In addition, as 6-year-olds navigate the challenges of their experiences in the playroom, the experience of being valued and accepted by the play therapist provides the child with the freedom and space in which to reach his or her full potential and to achieve developmental milestones. Child-centered play therapy is more effective with regular parent consultations in which the therapist communicates with parents about their ongoing concerns, discusses the child's progress in and out of therapy, and provides developmental knowledge, parent education, and parenting skills that are specific to the individual person and needs of the child.

Filial therapy   Filial therapy is also an appropriate intervention for 6-year-olds, especially if the presenting concern is related to the parent–child relationship, for example when there has been a disruption or disconnect in the parent–child relationship, or there are issues related to authoritarian or inconsistent discipline, or the child seems to have low self-esteem and self-confidence. Filial therapy – specifically child–parent relationship therapy (CPRT) – is a modality of therapy in which the therapist teaches the child's parent or primary caregiver the basic attitudes and skills of child-centered play therapy (Landreth & Bratton, 2006). Parents then use the skills with their child during a weekly, 30-minute play session. Child–parent relationship therapy provides parents with a different framework and ways of responding to a child that can help to foster a child's development of self-confidence, self-esteem, and self-control. If the child's needs are being met through increased empathy and connection with his or her parents, consistency, and discipline strategies that communicate acceptance to the child, while providing boundaries and teaching appropriate behavior, he or she will no longer try to get those needs met through misbehavior. Additionally, the parent will be able to respond to the child's emotionality and defiance in ways that foster the child's ability to self-regulate and develop self-control.

Parent–child interaction therapy (PCIT)   Parent–child interaction therapy (PCIT) is a structured approach aiming to improve parent–child relationships and to change parent–child interactions, specifically with young children who display problematic externalizing behaviors and defiance. Parents are taught specific skills with which to strengthen the parent–child bond and to support prosocial behaviors by means of both child-directed and parent-directed interactions, with live coaching from a trained mental health professional. It is an appropriate intervention for 6-year-olds who demonstrate oppositional behaviors that are outside the range of typical development. Parent–child interaction therapy incorporates the use of "time outs," which may intensify defiant or emotional reactions from children who have insecure attachment or traumatic attachment histories. It may not be appropriate for parents with limited contact with their child, parents with serious emotional or mental health challenges, parents who are hearing impaired or who have expressive or receptive language deficits, abusive parents, or parents with substance abuse issues.

When considering a filial, CPRT, or PCIT intervention, it is important to identify whether it is appropriate not only for the child's needs, but also for the parent. If the parent does not have the emotional, mental, or physical resources to learn the attitudes and skills necessary to provide a safe and accepting environment for the child, or if the child's behavior or experiences are too intense for the parent to respond to effectively, filial therapy is not an appropriate intervention. In many cases, working with the child in individual play therapy with parent consultations can lay the groundwork for future filial therapy when both the child and the parent are ready. Parents may also benefit from individual counseling to address their own emotional and psychological needs, or to learn parenting skills to support their parental competence and efficacy.

Couples or family counseling may also be appropriate if significant conflict or parenting differences persist in the partner relationship, or if the child's behavior is reflective of chronic stress or dysfunctional dynamics within the family system. When family therapy involves young children, it is essential to incorporate play, expressive arts, sand tray, and other nonverbal modalities that allow children to fully participate and communicate in the therapeutic process. Consideration should be given to the developmental needs of all family members.

Gestalt play therapy   Gestalt play therapy is another appropriate individual therapeutic approach for 6-year-olds. It incorporates play, expressive techniques, games, storytelling, and sand tray play, which allow children to express their thoughts and emotions, aiming to promote self-understanding through experiences within a safe and supportive environment. Gestalt play therapists often incorporate both nondirective and directive strategies. When employing more directive techniques with 6-year-olds, therapists should provide gentle prompts and provide freedom for the 6-year-old to choose how he or she wants to engage in the activity, to avoid approval-seeking behavior from the child or the child's perception of incompetence or inferiority.

Adlerian play therapy (AdPT)   Adlerian play therapy (AdPT) is another approach that can be used with children as young as 6. However, it should be applied with caution, because of the more directive nature of the approach. A 6-year-old may interpret the Adlerian therapist's directiveness in therapy as criticism or disapproval: If the Adlerian therapist directs the child to help him or her to clean the playroom at the end of the play session, for example, the 6-year-old may think that the therapist disapproves of him or her being messy or playing with certain toys. A discouraged child who has a strong sense of inferiority may also struggle with feeling competent in activities directed by the therapist, such as family drawings or collaborative puppet shows, and may compare his or her naturally inferior abilities to those of the therapist, or disengage from the activity or therapeutic relationship to avoid a sense of failure. Strengths of the Adlerian approach include its emphasis on encouragement and esteem-building, both of which may be helpful to the 6-year-old as he or she seeks to develop a strong sense of industry. Because 6-year-olds are primarily in the self-protective stage of ego development, they may not demonstrate high social interest: an important marker of mental health in Adlerian theory. Therefore the Adlerian therapist may need to assess other dimensions of the child's overall well-being and progress in therapy.

Working with Parents, Teachers, and Caregivers

Even though 6-year-olds can be hard to handle at times, it is important for parents, teachers, and caregivers to remember how emotionally sensitive and vulnerable they are. When setting limits, parents should remember that the 6-year-old is very sensitive to criticism and correction. Parents should set consistent limits and be cautious to send a clear message of acceptance toward the child, even if behavior is inappropriate, for example "I know you're really angry, but I'm not for kicking." Parents should also avoid statements that connect behavior with the child's character or value, such as "You're being mean," "Be a good girl," or "Don't be such a brat." Parents may need to be reminded that 6-year-olds are growing and changing rapidly, and are often overwhelmed by all of the new things that they are learning and their own conflicting feelings. Criticism or correction at every turn will promote a 6-year-old's sense of inferiority. It is more effective to help 6-year-olds to build on their successes by emphasizing their strengths and handling accidents, mistakes, and misbehavior gently.

Six-year-olds thrive with consistency and predictability in their routines and environments. While 6-year-olds may delight in new experiences and adventures, they thrive best in a consistent environment in which they feel safe and secure and know what to expect. Routines are especially helpful to the 6-year-old and his or her parent at mealtimes and bedtimes. Establishing a morning routine to help to reduce conflict before children are heading out the door to school each day and developing routines for getting dressed, brushing teeth, bath time, and bedtime will give 6-year-olds a sense of order and structure in their world, and will decrease emotional and behavioral disruptions.

It is easy to get into a power struggle with a stubborn 6-year-old who is striving toward greater self-dependence. Parents are encouraged to keep their cool and try to disengage from power struggles by setting clear and consistent limits, and by giving 6-year-olds choices that meet the child's need for a sense of control and independence. Parents are encouraged to present choices that they find acceptable, such as "You can choose to wear the pink dress or you can choose to wear the purple dress." Giving children choices helps them to experience a sense of control and to learn personal responsibility. Six-year-olds will be overwhelmed by unlimited choices or options, but will welcome the opportunity to choose between two or three options. Parents can make choices a part of snack time, story time, playtime, or bath time, among other things.

Six-year-olds will often look for and need approval and praise from parents, teachers, and caregivers. Parents can help their 6-year-old to develop a strong sense of competence and self-esteem by using encouraging statements and by focusing on the child's efforts in addition to his or her achievements.

Parents can encourage their 6-year-old's curiosity, imagination, and enthusiasm for life and learning by providing lots of time for him or her to enjoy unstructured play indoors and outside. When 6-year-olds are learning new skills, such as climbing the monkey bars or putting together a puzzle, parents can support their child's efforts with encouraging statements, a loving presence, and a helping hand when needed. Six-year-olds will also benefit from one-on-one time with parents, and still need lots of hugs and high fives.

CONCLUSION

The 6-year-old child is in a constant process of expansion and growth as he or she transitions from early childhood to middle childhood, and may often seem as if he or she has a foot in both worlds. Exuberant, eager to learn, gregarious, and full of energy, the 6-year-old can be a delightful companion. Their struggles to gain independence and desires to maintain connection with parents, teachers, and peers can make 6-year-olds seem a bit unpredictable and emotional at times. Eager to please and sensitive to the world around them, the 6-year-old is receptive and sometimes overstimulated by all of the new skills that they are mastering, new relationships that they are navigating, and new experiences that shape their daily lives. At this stage in development, growth is rapid, and it is best supported in an environment of consistency, empathy, and regard for the 6-year-old's sometimes intense and tumultuous evolution.

REFERENCES

Aamodt, S., & Wang, S. (2011). *Welcome to your child's brain: How the mind grows from conception to college.* New York, NY: Bloombury.

American Academy of Pediatrics (AAP). (2005). *Sexual behaviors in children.* Elk Grove, IL: AAP.

American Academy of Pediatrics (AAP). (2013). Policy statement: Children, adolescents, and the media. *Pediatrics, 132*(5), 958–961.

Ames, L. B., & Ilg, F. L. (1979). *Your 6-year-old: Loving and defiant.* New York, NY: Dell.

Berk, L. E. (2007). *Development through the lifespan* (4th ed.) Boston, MA: Allyn & Bacon.

Campaign for a Commercial-Free Childhood. (2014). Selected research on screen time and children. Retrieved from http://www.commercialfreechildhood.org/sites/default/files/kidsandscreens_0.pdf

Davies, D. (2011). *Child development: A practitioner's guide* (3rd ed.). New York, NY: Guilford.

Elkind, D. E. (2006). *The hurried child: Growing up too fast too soon.* Cambridge, MA: De Capo.

Erikson, E. (1963). *Childhood and society.* New York, NY: Norton.

Gesell Institute of Child Development. (2011). *Gesell Developmental Observation–Revised examiner's manual.* New Haven, CT: Gesell Institute.

Greenspan, S. (1998). *Playground politics: Understanding the emotional life of your school-age child.* Reading, MA: Perseus.

Kestly, T. (2014). *The interpersonal neurobiology of play.* New York, NY: Norton.

Landreth, G. L. (2012). *Play therapy: The art of the relationship* (3rd ed.). New York, NY: Routledge.

Landreth, G. L., & Bratton, S. C. (2006). *Child–parent relationship therapy (CPRT): A 10-session filial therapy model.* New York, NY: Routledge.

Loevinger, J. (1976). *Ego development.* San Francisco, CA: Jossey-Bass.

Madaras, L., & Madaras, A. (2007). *What's happening to my body: Book for boys.* New York, NY: Newmarket.

Ofcom. (2014). Children and parents: Media use and attitudes report 2014. Retrieved from http://stakeholders.ofcom.org.uk/binaries/research/media-literacy/media-use-attitudes-14/Childrens_2014_Report.pdf

Petty, K. (2010). *Developmental milestones of young children.* St. Paul, MN: Redleaf Press.

Piaget, J., & Inhelder, B. (1969). *The psychology of the child.* New York, NY: Basic Books.

Ray, D. (2011). *Advanced play therapy: Essential conditions, knowledge, and skills for child practice.* New York, NY: Routledge.

Rideout, V. (2013). *Zero to eight: Children's media use in America 2013.* San Francisco, CA: Common Sense Media.

Siegel, D. J., & Bryson, T. P. (2011). *The whole-brain child: Twelve revolutionary strategies to nurture your child's developing mind.* New York, NY: Delacorte Press.

Sprenger, M. (2008). *The developing brain: Birth to age eight.* Thousand Oaks, CA: Corwin Press.

Swanson, D. P., Cunningham, M., Youngblood, J., & Spencer, M. B. (2009). Racial identity development during childhood. In H. A. Neville, B. M. Tynes, & S. Utsey (Eds.), *Handbook of African American psychology* (pp. 269–281). Thousand Oaks, CA: Sage.

Weis, D. L. (1998). Interpersonal heterosexual behaviors. In P. Koch & D. L. Weis (Eds.), *Sexuality in America: Understanding our sexual values and behavior* (pp. 91–105). New York, NY: Continuum.

Winkler, E. N. (2009). Children are not colorblind: How young children learn race. *PACE: Practical Approaches for Continuing Education, 3*(3), 1–8.

Wood, C. (2007). *Yardsticks* (3rd ed.). Turners Falls, MA: Northeast Foundation for Children.

8

THE EXTRAORDINARY 7-YEAR-OLD

Hayley L. Stulmaker

Source: Used with permission from Shutterstock

Sasha, a typical 7-year-old, complains all of the time. She comes home from school almost every day saying that the teacher is so unfair. She works extremely hard at school and needs a new eraser every week because of her fastidiousness when completing assignments. Doug, a 7-year-old boy in Sasha's class, goes home every night excited to spend time with his father. He is nurturing to his siblings, but he says that his 6-year-old sister is always getting more attention. At night, Doug incessantly worries that the house is going to burn down.

Seven-year-olds begin to turn inward, appearing much calmer and quieter than their 6-year-old selves. Typically, 7-year-olds are moody and seem sad with no apparent reason. Seven-year-olds tend to worry about the weighty things in life, such as wars, tornadoes, money, etc. They have heightened levels of awareness of these events and begin to bear the burdens that come with them. Seven-year-olds tend to believe that the world is unfairly stacked against them.

Although 7-year-olds bear more burdens, they can think in a concrete manner, generally want to follow rules, and believe what they are told without questioning deeper meaning. Seven-year-olds are good listeners and generally well behaved. They are typically good students and like to read or be read to. They enjoy the challenges presented at school, but they are perfectionistic in their work. They will agonize over sharpening a pencil properly and will constantly revise their work so as to live up to self-imposed standards. These qualities make 7-year-olds appear to be better students, but they may display struggles in the classroom when there are transitions and express feelings of frustration.

Seven-year-olds are learning more about themselves, developing their identity, and constantly taking in information. They are watchful of the world around them, soaking in as much information as possible. They want to learn from their world and process their experiences internally. They are trying to form their own identity by means of a heightened awareness of others and comparison of those others to their view of themselves.

There are definite strengths and challenges related to this age. On the one hand, 7-year-olds are quieter and more reserved, making them easier to be around. They are relationally driven, and enjoy spending time with parents and teachers. On the other hand, 7-year-olds complain a great deal. They constantly seem sad and believe that everyone is "out to get them" at some time or another. They need lots of sympathy and understanding during these times, otherwise they will internalize a sense of rejection.

BRAIN DEVELOPMENT

At the age of 7, brain development seems to be influenced heavily by a combination of environmental and biological factors (Sprenger, 2008). Seven-year-olds are at an age at which nature and nurture play a huge role in their development. They are still developing within their biological patterns – but their environment becomes more important in shaping who they are and thus in influencing their brain development. Seven-year-old children experience large shifts in mood, becoming more sensitive and serious compared to their 6-year-old selves. These shifts can be explained by neurology and the many changes that are taking place in the brain.

Seven-year-old children experience an increase of the synaptic density in the frontal lobes, allowing for more receptivity in that area of the brain. Synapses are the "connector pieces" of neurons, which facilitate communication throughout the brain. An increase in synaptic density makes it easier for neurons to connect and increases processing of the information that is sent through those parts of the brain. The synapses in the frontal lobes are therefore more prepared to connect with other synapses, strengthening the pathways between the frontal lobes and the limbic system. Children are thus primed for learning and solidifying knowledge at this age. As a result, 7-year-olds have better impulse control, greater levels of independence, and a heightened ability to plan, and accept responsibility more easily (Sprenger, 2008).

Glucose, a basic source of energy for the brain, continues to be produced at high levels in 7-year-olds (Kagan & Herschkowitz, 2005). This increase in glucose, and therefore energy, is extremely important in helping the cortex to expand. The cortex is the part of the brain that is the end receptor for information. It can be thought of as a central information hub for sensory, motor, and muscle movement. The cortex takes in information, for example when someone's foot is stepped on, pain is felt in the foot, and the person understands the source of the pain. The surface of the cortex increases during the seventh year, allowing children to strengthen their abilities and speeds of processing sensory information (Davies, 2011; Sprenger, 2008).

Dopamine, a neurotransmitter that contributes to goal setting and attainment, is increased in 7-year olds. The heightened levels of dopamine allow 7-year-olds to be able to plan out goals and reach them more easily. Additionally, dopamine will improve their levels of motivation and attention (Berk, 2006; Kagan & Herschkowitz, 2005; Sprenger, 2008). This increase in dopamine tends to play out in the form of 7-year-olds not wanting to stop an activity once they have started and forgetting even to break for the restroom (Ames & Haber, 1985; Wood, 2007).

Seven-year-olds develop a greater amount of emotional language as a result of growth in Broca's area in the right hemisphere. This growth allows 7-year-olds to begin to understand irony and sarcasm, but this understanding comes with a warning: Most 7-year-olds do not outwardly display their senses of humor, and may not respond to irony and sarcasm consistently (Sprenger, 2008; Wood, 2007).

Myelination, an increasing in speed of signals being communicated, occurs in the posterior corpus callosum, which connects the left and right hemispheres of the brain. The posterior corpus callosum connects the temporal and parietal lobes, controlling behavior, sensory localization, and body movement, respectively. The strengthening of the connection between these two parts in the brain helps children to process more quickly across these sections of the brain (Davies, 2011; Sprenger, 2008). Children become more integrated in terms of their abilities to use both the right and left hemispheres simultaneously.

Essentially, most of the brain development of 7-year-olds is geared toward increasing interconnectedness among the various parts of the brain, which leads to enhanced processing and abilities. It is important to keep these changes in mind when considering the other types of development that will now be explained further.

> A 7-year-old's increased dopamine levels intensifies his or her attention span, sometimes resulting in him or her forgetting to take bathroom breaks.

PHYSICAL DEVELOPMENT

In terms of physical development, 7-year-old boys are slightly larger than 7-year-old girls (Davies, 2011). Seven-year-olds are developing their motor skills, both fine and gross. Additionally, 7-year-olds are solidifying their gender development, understanding the permanency that comes with their genitals. Moreover, there is a shift toward privacy in the area of sexual development as compared with 6-year-olds.

Motor Skills

Seven-year-olds are still mastering both fine and gross motor skills; they have, however, advanced from their earlier years. The quality of their motor skills is influenced by their cognitive and physical development, creating more stability in motor skills, yet there are areas that are still growing. They are working toward further frontal lobe development to engage in more complex activities, but they have generally good motor control (Sylwester, 2007; Sprenger, 2008).

Seven-year-olds plan their movements and practice skills, enhancing motor development. Their motor skills seem to be more mature, as evidenced by their ability to play physical games. Posture in 7-year-olds becomes tenser and more upright. They have well-established hand–eye coordination, allowing them to engage and participate in many active activities. Because of their improved coordination, 7-year-olds enjoy drawing and writing, although their perfectionistic tendencies may sometimes get in the way of that enjoyment. Seven-year-olds have a certain level of depth perception and are aware of direction in distance. They can jump, leap, swim, and ride bicycles and scooters. They continue to plan and practice these activities throughout their seventh year (Davies, 2011; Greenspan, 1993; Sprenger, 2008). Seven-year-olds display increased visual concentration, focusing on small visual details and needing extra time to copy from classroom boards (Wood, 2007).

> Because of intense visual concentration, 7-year-olds need to be encouraged to take breaks when working in school and at home.

GENDER AND SEXUAL DEVELOPMENT

Children are able to understand the permanency of gender at around the age of 3 or 4; however, by the age of 7, children make the connection between gender and genital differences. This awareness of genital differences creates an air of unchangeable identity for children as they realize that they are a boy or girl. Boys no longer think that, because they are wearing a pink bow, they may be mistaken for a girl or that a girl can become a boy simply by putting on a baseball cap; instead, they realize that they are physically and permanently one gender (Davies, 2011;

Kohlberg, 1987). As a result, if a 7-year-old is struggling with gender identity issues, he or she is likely to be emotionally affected by this lack of clarity and will need additional adult support.

Along with a recognition of the permanency of gender comes a child's identification of and preference for his or her own gender. Children take on the thought that the "I am" is what they value and reject other things. They have a "sour grapes" mentality: "I can't be a mom, so I don't want to be; I'll just be a dad instead." Seven-year-olds identify with same-sex parents because of this valuing of what is similar. Children tend to like themselves and therefore like other people who are similar to them. Boys begin identifying more with dad than mom at this stage, as they try to determine their own identity as a boy (Davies, 2011; Kohlberg, 1987).

> Seven-year-olds who used to be closer to their opposite-sex parent start switching to feeling closer to their same-sex parent.

Children's sexual curiosity and sexual behavior decreases between the ages of 6 and 7. They do not outwardly ask questions about sex – although that does not necessarily mean that their curiosity has completely diminished; rather, children seem to be more discrete about their wonderings and tend to be more self-conscious with their bodies, insisting on more privacy when they may be exposed (Ames & Haber, 1985).

Children in permissive cultures engage in systematic masturbation between the ages of 6 and 8. It seems as though children begin masturbating unconsciously early in life, see that it is pleasure producing, and continue doing so. This masturbating is not necessarily sexual in nature, but it is enjoyable; however, not much research has been done on this topic as a result of its nature and the potential risks involved in investigating childhood sexual behavior (Francoeur, Koch, & Weis, 1998).

Most research that has been conducted on childhood sexuality has been reflective research, asking participants to remember their childhood and sexual experiences. When adult males were asked about their early sexual memories, many recalled their first pleasurable erection as occurring at ages between 6 and 9. Further, almost all boys are able to orgasm without ejaculation around the ages of 7–10. Between the ages of 6 and 10, boys and girls have reported becoming sexually aroused when thinking about sexual events. Finally, in cultures in which children observe adult sexual relations, children as young as 6 or 7 will begin engaging in sexual behaviors (Francoeur et al., 1998).

Although children seem to engage in masturbation, they do not seem to understand the concept of sex and reproduction. Seven-year-olds understand that mommy and daddy are needed to make a baby, and they may know about the egg and the sperm; however, they have not completely pieced all of these things together. They tend to cling to their earlier thoughts of mommy and daddy kissing to make babies, instead of digesting the information fully and comprehensively (Greenspan, 1993).

> Seven-year-olds begin to be more self-conscious, needing more privacy regarding their bodies.

From the scarce amount of research, it appears that 7-year-olds have sexually stimulating experiences, including masturbation, which may be increased with greater exposure to sexual activities. However, children do not seem to understand the act of sex and how it relates to reproduction. Seven-year-olds' covert behavior related to sexual development is expected, given the withdrawn and internalizing behaviors that are seen across domains at this age.

COGNITIVE DEVELOPMENT

Many theorists touch on cognitive development in various capacities. They tend to describe development in terms of groups of age ranges, instead of per year. The following primary theorists' ideas regarding 7-year-olds will hopefully prove beneficial when working with this age group.

Cognitive development cannot be discussed without mention of Jean Piaget, who published extensively on the topic and is viewed as a cognitive development guru. According to his theory, 7-year-olds are in the "concrete operation" stage of cognitive development. They are able to understand logical and linear processes, reciprocity, generalizability, reversibility, inclusion, and conservation. They can now hold more information, including three-step directions (Ames & Haber, 1985; Sprenger, 2008). They can use their own reasoning to make deductions and can more fully understand their worlds; however, their logic is applied at face value and is not reflected on further (Davies, 2011; Fowler, 1981; Kohlberg, 1987; Piaget & Inhelder, 1969).

As a result of this new logical thinking, 7-year-olds can construct a reality that is orderly and predictable. They understand the principles of reversibility – that a mini candy bar is smaller than a regular-sized candy bar, but the mini candy bar can be the larger candy when compared to an M&M – and can give explanations of objects and their purposes. They have an increased sense of reasonableness in making deductions about events (Sprenger, 2008; Wood, 2007). They begin to use classification and can put things in temporal order, understanding that events occur as related sequences. Once children's lives appear to be more predictable, they are able to see the differences between themselves and others, and they acknowledge differing viewpoints; however, this accomplishment is best performed in the presence of people with whom children are familiar (Fowler, 1981; Ivey, 1986; Piaget & Inhelder, 1969). This ability to categorize helps children with gender development and overall identity development.

According to Robert Kegan (1979), 7-year-olds are transitioning from fantasizing about things that are not real, such as Superman or being a fairy princess, to fantasizing about things that are real, such as becoming a doctor. They are able to determine that others exist and the world does not revolve around them. Seven-year-olds begin to live in a private world that they have not fully known before as they continue to discover their separateness from everything else. Each child begins to develop a personality or general way of feeling that is unique to him or her and held constant because of his or her abilities to conserve information (Kohlberg, 1987).

Seven-year-old children can differentiate their cognitions from their physical bodies. With this distinction comes an awareness of the concept of the mind and how children are able to start the beginning stages of metacognition: thinking about thinking. Another interesting aspect of 7-year-olds is that they are aware that dreams are their own thoughts and can be controlled to some degree (Davies, 2011; Kohlberg, 1987).

Seven-year-olds improve their use of language and change their patterns of speech. They have an understanding of the syntax and grammar of their native language, and begin to understand figures of speech (Davies, 2011). Furthermore, Vygotsky (1978) observed that children at around the age of 7 stop outwardly narrating stories and instead begin to engage in private narrating techniques. He termed this narrating "self-directed speech" and believed that it became inner speech. He attributed this change to the function of speech, and to 7-year-olds' ability to discern between regulative speech, such as self-directed speech, and communication or expression. Instead of being their own personal broadcasters, children will now refrain from saying everything that they do and will keep those thoughts in their heads. Piaget (1926) also observed this phenomenon – but he attributed the change to be a diminishing of egocentrism (Davies, 2011; Kohlberg, 1987; Piaget, 1926).

Physical properties in addition to space and time are concepts that become clearer to 7-year-olds. The organization of the calendar makes more sense to children based on their understanding of numbers as symbols (Davies, 2011). The ability to think in a more complex way produces a fascination with time (Petty, 2010; Sprenger, 2008; Wood, 2007). Additionally, 7-year-olds have a better understanding of space around other people and their orientations to the world (Davies, 2011).

Overall, 7-year-olds can think logically, concretely, and linearly. They are able to take another person's perspective and view themselves as a constant entity. However, 7-year-olds lack the ability to think abstractly and make meaning out of events. They are confined to the reality that they experience; yet they are able to make the distinction between what is real and what is fantasy (Greenspan, 1993).

> Seven-year-olds can start using logic, but they still interpret information at face value.

Moral Development

Kohlberg was one of the leading theorists on moral development (Kohlberg, 1987). He identified levels and stages of moral progress throughout development. Kohlberg's model included three broad levels of development, then broke each level down into two stages to distinguish slight changes in development within each level. Seven-year-olds fall in the second stage of the first level, "preconventional," during which they strive to be good. They believe that they should follow rules to meet their needs, but they also value fairness in rules. Children at this age understand that what is good for one child may not be good for another. They truly believe in the "eye for an eye" principle. Additionally, 7-year-olds have a heightened understanding of others, based on their newly diminished egocentrism. This awareness of others helps them to understand other people and their feelings, meaning that they sometimes realize that their actions have an effect on others as well as themselves. Seven-year-olds begin to balance their own self-interests with the interests of others and with societal pressure to follow rules (Davies, 2011). Seven-year-olds strive to be ethical and fair in many facets of their lives (Fowler, 1981; Kohlberg, 1987; Reddy, 2010).

Piaget (1932) made reference to a stage of moral development called "morality of cooperation". He reiterated the notion that 7-year-olds have a deep respect for rules, but he argued that they view rules as fixed external mores as opposed to an overarching display of values. Further, Piaget asserted that children will conform to the rules and view them as unchangeable rather than question them. Although cognitive development is needed for moral development, moral development also incorporates a social development aspect, creating the need for children to understand what is socially acceptable (Kohlberg, 1987).

WORLDVIEW/EGO DEVELOPMENT

Faith Development

According to Fowler (1981), 7-year-olds are in the second stage of faith development: the "mythic-literal" faith stage. These children have moved into concrete operational thought and are therefore able to use narratives to create meaning by means of their understanding of the reversibility of thought, their adopting of the perspectives of others, and their understanding of cause-and-effect relationships. They begin to use these skills to create stories to make meaning of their experiences. Children in this stage create meaning out of stories, but they do not analyze them or think about them critically, as is appropriate based on their level of cognitive development. Children also do not generalize greater meaning from the stories and apply them to the meaning in life: A child who did so would be engaging with a very abstract concept for a child of this age.

This way of thinking and making meaning applies to a child's conception of a higher power, in that he or she will believe that the higher power can understand his or her perspectives. The 7-year-old sees a higher power as being compassionate and fair. Children in this stage tend to assume the beliefs of their communities without question, internalizing the literal interpretations and attitudes of these beliefs. Because 7-year-olds will view religious stories as very literal, they may become overly righteous or may internalize a sense of wholehearted badness based on their views of their actions. They will attribute negative experiences or bad events occurring as something willed by a higher power as punishment: If a storm blows a tree over in the yard and crushes a 7-year-old's bike, for example, he or she may believe that he or she has been punished for not spelling words correctly earlier that day (Ames & Haber, 1985; Fowler, 1981; Kohlberg, 1987).

Seven-year-olds' faith development is closely tied to their cognitive development. Western children are susceptible to believing in many Judeo-Christian principles, because the stories appeal to their held beliefs and values regarding fairness. Additionally, they do not examine information critically, but ingest the information that is given to them. Seven-year-olds are very literal in their thinking without much discernment, causing them possibly to overly apply religious concepts to their lives.

Personality and Ego Development

Seven-year-olds are taking this introspective time to understand their own personalities and more about themselves. Some 7-year-olds talk to themselves in the mirror as they try to figure out who they are, both physically and internally. This age group will spend time observing the outside world and then ponder what they have observed to determine their own sense of self.

Seven-year-olds have a sense of independence, but at the same time cling to what is familiar. They become aware of themselves as distinct persons with unique qualities. During this time of identity searching, they are less selfish, but almost entirely self-absorbed (Ames & Haber, 1985). Different theorists have created models to try to describe this act of soul searching for people throughout the lifespan and the characteristics that accompany each phase of development.

In Loevinger's (1976) ego development model, 7-year-olds may be categorized as "self-protective". Although Loevinger would argue against placing ages within stages, a typical 7-year-old would possess most of the qualities found in this stage. That child is able to anticipate rewards and therefore will act accordingly. Children in this stage tend to be vulnerable as they try to navigate and control their impulses, with a mantra of "Don't get caught." Typical 7-year-olds will attempt to find external places of blame or parts of themselves that they can disown, such as "my teacher wasn't fair," or "my eyes weren't working well enough to see the board" (Kirshner, 1988).

According to Erikson (1956), 7-year-olds will be facing the crisis of *industry vs. inferiority*. Children are learning either to produce as part of a greater cooperative whole or to feel inferior and inadequate. Children must use their physical and intellectual abilities to find a way in which to work in groups and regulate their own emotions, which is aptly timed considering their brain development at this age. Children who are in this stage of development focus on the end product, not on the process of completing a task. They will look to please others in order to get recognition and a sense of mastery. If they fail at this task, they will believe that they are not good enough and will become more isolated (Kohlberg, 1987).

Seven-year-olds are still struggling with who they are and their roles in the world. They are constantly processing their environments and their internal experiences to help them to build their own sense of self. They compare themselves to others in order to develop their own sense of self (Davies, 2011). Hopefully, children will meet this age successfully, with help of a guiding leader such as a parent or teacher, and will develop a sense of competency. It is important for influential people in 7-year-olds' lives to use encouragement to foster this sense of competency and to facilitate further development.

> Some 7-year-olds may repeat observations or behaviors over and over until someone stops them (Gesell Institute, 2011).

Racial/Ethnic Identity Development

Seven-year-old children are beginning to identify people who are similar and different from themselves, beginning racial/ethnic identity development (Davies, 2011). Seven-year-olds are entering into the concrete operational stage, which allows the ability to process racial-ethnic identity (Aboud, 1988). Children who are in this cognitive stage of development begin engaging in behaviors that are consistent with those of their racial or ethnic groups (Cameron, Alvarez, Ruble, & Fuligni, 2001; Kohlberg, 1987). As previously mentioned, 7-year-olds start identifying with children who are the same gender, which is also true of children who are of the same race (Davies, 2011). They also begin to classify ingroup from outgroup membership, based on behaviors, traits, norms, and values (Quintana & Segura-Herrera, 2003).

> Seven-year-olds may seem to be developing racist attitudes in that they display a preference for children who are similar to them. However, that preference is based on the child forming his or her own identity, not on a hatred or dislike for people who are different from him or her.

Racial/ethnic identity development is a more complex process than noticing similarities and differences between the self and others (Corenblum & Armstrong, 2012). The ability to think abstractly is necessary for ethnic identity, because ethnicity is not always something that can be seen directly; it is therefore difficult for 7-year-olds to have developed an understanding of ethnic identity or ethnic development (Rogers et al., 2012). Furthermore, 7-year-olds may identify as being similar to or different from another person, but they lack the understanding of the deeper meaning behind identifying with a specific race or ethnicity.

EMOTIONAL DEVELOPMENT

Seven-year-olds turn inward to learn about themselves. They are more serious and more sensitive than they were at the age of 6, and are constantly reflecting on their worlds. They believe that many things are not fair and that people are inherently against them. They seem to be living a life of contradictions: of enjoying feeling miserable. Seven-year-olds worry, are easily disappointed, plan, and develop fears that were not previously issues, such as being afraid of the dark. They cry easily, although they tend to try to hide their tears because of embarrassment. They begin thinking about themselves as they gain independence and determine who they are (Gesell Institute, 2011; Sprenger, 2008).

Seven-year-olds tend to persevere in the face of challenges and thoroughly try to complete projects once they have started them. They tend to be perfectionistic in their work and attempt tasks many times until they are good enough or stopped. Erasers are extremely important to most 7-year-olds, so that they can redo their work to their own imposed level of satisfaction. They tend to have high self-imposed standards and have inner conflicts over their accomplishments (Gesell Institute, 2011).

> Owing to their perfectionistic tendencies, 7-year-olds often erase and redo their work. They may also become frustrated if not provided enough time in which to complete a task.

Seven-year-olds change from being impulsive to having impulses that they are able to control (Kohlberg, 1987). They have developed greater strategies for emotional regulation (Davies, 2011). Seven-year-olds have a tendency to get wrapped up in tasks that they find enjoyable and show great levels of control. Seven-year-olds are constantly controlling their temper, voice, thoughts, and body, leading to quick fatigue. This control also contributes to the warmth, trust, and intimate relationships that 7-year-olds form with peers and adults (Greenspan, 1993; Sprenger, 2008; Wood, 2007).

SOCIAL DEVELOPMENT

Children become more emotionally stable as a result of the relationships that they form at this age. They assert themselves in relationships, but also cope with not getting their way within the relationship (Greenspan, 1993). Instead of focusing on beating peers in play, they try to come to a mutual understanding to better form relationships and to understand other children. Play becomes more social than egocentric, with children adhering to the rules instead of cheating to win. When something goes wrong during play, 7-year-olds tend to leave instead of causing a scene. Seven-year-olds are comfortable with losing on occasion, but they like to keep playing until they win (Davies, 2011; Gesell Institute, 2011).

Seven-year-olds are constantly comparing themselves to others in forming their own identities. Tattling on other children seems to decrease, but they seem to remain very concerned with other children's level of "goodness" or "badness." They want other people to like them and worry about how they are perceived by other children, leading to a tendency to withdraw rather than confront (Gesell Institute, 2011). This is also the age at which some boys and girls play together, but boys begin to discriminate against playing with girls (Ames & Haber, 1985).

Selmen and Byrne (1974) proposed stages of social cognition, which describe the way in which children relate to people through their abilities to differentiate between themselves and others, and to adopt someone else's perspective. Seven-year-olds fall in Selmen's first stage, which describes them as able to differentiate themselves from one another in terms of thoughts, physical characteristics, and behaviors. They believe that people's perspectives are subjective and their own perception tends to be linear. They start to recognize cause and effect, and the impact that one thing can have on another. This plays out in relationships, with children recognizing how someone's actions occur, yet not fully grasping the concept of reciprocity within relationships, allowing them to think relationships are one-sided (Kohlberg, 1987).

Greenspan (1997) argued that 7-year-olds are able to play differently with peers based on their firmer grasp of reality, their sense of their potential, their continued engagement in fantasy, and a keener awareness of social perceptions and responses (Greenspan, 1997). Seven-year-olds have friends, but would rather play with one friend at a time, and they spend a larger amount of time playing alone (Sprenger, 2008). Children recognize that there is a hierarchy that exists socially and they learn to monitor other children's reactions in order to determine where they stand in the social ranks. Seven-year-olds are able to explain who is the best speller, the most popular, the most athletic, and so on, and describe where they fall in the rank. As children build relationships, they use them to evaluate themselves.

Seven-year-olds tend to be fairly independent, but they do have a very sensitive nature (Sprenger, 2008). True empathy begins to occur at this age, because children can adopt another person's perspective. Seven-year-olds are able to define themselves as different from others and are therefore able to give up a portion of themselves to feel as though they are experiencing what someone else might be feeling (Greenspan, 1997). They are sensitive to others, while also generalizing their observations. Thus if one 7-year-old sees another 7-year-old being mean, the first 7-year-old may believe that everyone is mean (Sprenger, 2008). This use of empathy may contribute to the strength of the bonds found among children this age.

> Seven-year-olds enjoy playing and working alone. Seven is a common age at which a child becomes a collector (Petty, 2010).

RELATIONSHIP DEVELOPMENT

Seven-year-olds, although isolated, enjoy relationships and continue to build more complex relationships. They create a triangulation of relationships instead of relationships between only themselves and one other person. Children can see differences in people, such as caregivers or friends, and are able to use this differentiation to their advantage. They can recognize that certain people meet their needs more than others at times, instead of creating blanket generalizations, such as "All adults will let me down." This recognition can help the parent–child relationship run more smoothly because of the child's ability to be more forgiving in light of knowing that his or her needs will be met (Greenspan, 1993).

Seven-year-olds' relationships with their parents are less demanding and more relaxed. They want their parents to sympathize with them and help to alleviate their fears. Seven-year-olds will not fight aggressively with caretakers anymore, but they will use attitude such as "why should I?" and stand in the room with a sad expression (Ames & Haber, 1985).

Children at 7 years of age may align more with one parent than another. They really enjoy doing things with their chosen parent and value that parent's opinion of them. Seven-year-olds look up to parental figures at this age and even go as far as to quote their parents' advice, even though they may complain immensely (Ames & Haber, 1985).

Seven-year-olds tend to fight less with siblings, opting to withdraw instead of staying to fight when conflict arises. Their level of tattling dies down with this change in conflict style. They are protective of baby siblings and look up to older siblings. The real trouble occurs with younger siblings who are close in age: Seven-year-olds tend to tease these siblings. Seven-year-olds also view life as unfair compared to their similarly aged siblings and believe that parents treat other siblings differently from how they are treated themselves. The 7-year-old will sometimes be dramatic, declaring "Nobody likes me," or "I might as well be dead" (Ames & Haber, 1985; Wood, 2007).

Seven-year-olds value their families as a whole. They enjoy family outings and quality time that is spent with all family members together. Seven-year-olds have calmed down and behave better in public. They tend to have strong feelings for, and relationships with, their families, but they struggle to find their place in the family, both physically and emotionally: They will fight for a position in the car or at the dinner table. Seven-year-olds want to feel important and be significant contributors to the family dynamics (Ames & Haber, 1985).

Teachers are very important to 7-year-olds. They value proximity and will attempt to get close to their teachers when possible. Seven-year-olds thrive on the personal relationships that are created with teachers and want to ensure that they have enough one-on-one time with them. Because 7-year-olds think that most things are unfair in life, they will tend to take any mishap as a sign of rejection and will often complain to their parents about their teachers (Ames & Haber, 1985; Sprenger, 2008).

DEVELOPMENT IN THE AGE OF TECHNOLOGY

Many have debated the use of technology in regards to development for children. Armstrong and Casement (2000) argued that computers used in the classroom deprive learners of the sensory experiences that are crucial in development. Furthermore, Cordes and Miller (2000) described problems with emotional, social, and moral development as a result of utilizing technology. Implications regarding cognitive development have been noted as well (Clements & Sarama, 2003). Although none of these authors mention 7-year-olds particularly, they are referring to school-age children. These claims, paired with the understanding that 7-year-old brains are solidifying and strengthening connections, support decreased use of technology for development.

However, more recent claims have been made regarding the benefits of technology, including digital literacy and improving social interactions, although these benefits have been documented primarily with preschool children (Yelland, 2011). Plowman and McPake (2013) recommend that, when using technology in the classroom, teachers should recognize children's individual preferences. They advocate that technology can help to broaden children's ability to access knowledge and to develop ways in which to communicate. It therefore seems that a balance between learning through technology and other types of learning and engaging is important for 7-year-olds.

BEST PRACTICES IN COUNSELING/THERAPY

When Counseling/Therapy Is Indicated

Many of the behavioral and affective characteristics that drive parents to initiate counseling for their children are typically normal behaviors in 7-year-olds. For children of other ages, these behaviors may be indicative of potential mental health concerns. However, 7-year-olds who become more withdrawn, quiet, and perfectionistic are not children who need to be seen in counseling based on those facts alone. Because these qualities are normal for 7-year-olds, but not typically desired, it is therefore difficult to know exactly when to refer to counseling and when to decide that children are going through a crucial developmental stage that will pass with time.

Certain behaviors or characteristics are indicative of a need for mental health interventions, separate from typically developing children. The following are scenarios in which counseling may be appropriate and beneficial in helping children to improve their mental health. However, there is an important caveat to be shared here: All children have individual differences, meaning that these generalizations may not be accurate for each individual child. Typically developing children may engage in the following behaviors – but the degree to which these behaviors cause impairment should be considered within the context of a complete developmental history of the child at ages prior to 7.

Seven-year-olds who engage in conflict through aggression are not necessarily acting in a developmentally appropriate manner. Because 7-year-olds tend to internalize their emotions, they typically do not lash out in a physically aggressive manner. They also tend to disengage from conflict quickly, preferring to withdraw to their rooms or places of their own. Seven-year-olds who aggressively fight back or provoke others to engage in conflict are not typical. Seven-year-olds may complain about people or say that things are not fair, but they will do little more than sulk in addition to these verbalizations.

Seven-year-olds will go through periods of moodiness frequently, appearing to be in an overall state of being underwhelmed. However, if 7-year-olds are constantly showing signs of depression, especially outwardly such as excessive crying, displaying irritation that is not situational, and are lacking in friends, it may be helpful to refer to counseling. Seven-year-olds may not have many friends or play in large groups, but they usually have one or more friends; hence counseling may be indicated if social needs are not being met.

Developmentally Appropriate Approaches

If some of these behaviors are noted, it may be a good idea to begin counseling. It is important to select an appropriate type of intervention from among the many that are listed in the literature and used in practice. Based on developmental understanding of 7-year-olds, the following few interventions have been selected as likely to be the most appropriate. Each has unique elements that contribute to the overall mental health of the child. They may all serve different purposes, which is why it is important to choose with careful intent.

Child-centered play therapy (CCPT)   Child-centered play therapy (CCPT) is a common approach used with children. As described in other chapters, CCPT is a way of working with children that focuses on the relationship between child and therapist as the healing therapeutic factor. Seven-year-olds are very relationally dependent: Although they seem withdrawn at times, they truly value adult and peer relationships. Incorporating an intervention that calls for a significant relationship with an adult as the healing factor seems a logical choice for children at this age.

Child-centered play therapy focuses on building a child's self-esteem and self-concept through visceral experiences, which is crucial at this age. Seven-year-olds are trying to build their own identities through mastery, internal processing, and comparison to others. If a child is struggling with these tasks, he or she may benefit from engaging in a relationship with a therapist as the child attempts to determine who he or she is and to accept himself or herself for it. Child-centered play therapy allows children to engage in an internal process, through its nondirective nature, with the support of an accepting and understanding therapist.

Child-centered *group* play therapy may help 7-year-olds to practice the social skills that they are learning to integrate, in addition to helping them to form personal identity. It is important to have only two 7-year-old children in groups, because of their inclination to be closest with only one other child at a time. When trying to put together a group, it is crucial to attempt to find very similar children to be in group. Seven-year-olds try to compare themselves to one another, so finding children who share many characteristics and are seemingly equal can help with identity formation. Seven-year-olds have also developed empathy and can recognize others' points of view, suggesting that they can be healing to one another. Group should be used only if children are struggling with social interaction; otherwise, they would benefit more from one-on-one attention in working through their struggles.

Adlerian play therapy (AdPT)   Another potentially helpful modality of counseling is Adlerian play therapy (AdPT). Adlerian play therapy focuses on promoting significance in children's lives through encouragement. As 7-year-olds develop, they are attempting to find a place in their families – both literally and figuratively. Seven-year-olds want to mark out a space for themselves at the dinner table, but they also want to be loved and accepted as unique within the family. In AdPT, children are encouraged to reach their potential and to avoid unsuccessful behaviors.

An Adlerian play therapist will foster ad child's sense of superiority and help him or her to strive toward a sense of belonging. The therapist will attempt to discover how the child functions, and wants to help that child to find an adaptive role within his or her family that will be fulfilling and rewarding. This can be helpful with 7-year-olds because they struggle to find their place. Seven-year-olds also have the cognitive ability to understand and apply Adlerian concepts to themselves. Adlerian play therapists work on a cognitive level with children, rather than a visceral level, which appears to be appropriate to a 7-year-old's cognitive development, albeit that their cognitive abilities remain limited.

Jungian play therapy   Jungian play therapy is another popular type of play therapy, involving sand play: a symbolic means of expression. Seven-year-olds are unable to think abstractly; however, they may indirectly benefit from a Jungian perspective. Jungian play therapy involves heavy participation from parents, which could be very helpful in working with 7-year-olds because of their proximity to their parents. Seven-year-olds would be able to create scenes in a sand tray, but they would not be able to derive meaning other then what is concretely presented. This intervention may help therapists to collect concrete information from the child's perspective in order to share it with parents to gear future interventions or consultations.

Along with these interventions, it may be helpful to include parents or teachers in treatment given the significance of these relationships for 7-year-olds.

Parents may participate in *child–parent relationship therapy* (CPRT) to strengthen their bonds with their child. If children are struggling to relate to their same-sex parent, having that parent participate in CPRT may be beneficial to help to bridge the gap. If the opposite-sex parent is feeling left out, CPRT may be helpful in teaching the parent to respond with a better communication style and in educating parents about development. Child–parent relationship therapy with an opposite-sex parent may not be as successful because of gender identification at this age, but the change in response patterns may help the two to retain more of their relationship.

Many teacher training programs have been designed to intervene on a broader level to reach more children and to help teachers to function with classroom management. A few suggestions for models are *child–teacher relationship training* (CTRT) (Helker & Ray, 2009), *relationship enhancement for learner and teacher* (RELATe) (Ray, Muro, & Schumann, 2004), or *positive discipline* (Nelsen, Lott, & Glenn, 2013).

Child–teacher relationship training and RELATe are models that align with a child-centered philosophy, and are similar to CPRT. A note of caution with using these models is that spending time with one child individually may create jealousy and tension throughout the classroom, and that these models generally need support from administrative staff. If the models may not be implemented in full, it is therefore suggested that teaching relationship-building skills and how to apply them in the classroom as a whole is the priority, ahead of the individual sessions.

Positive discipline, meanwhile, is an Adlerian model for teachers, which focuses on understanding students' behaviors, and using encouragement and cooperative problem solving to change the classroom environment rather than targeting specific individuals. Teachers use "classroom meetings" as a time in each day to work through classroom concerns, involving all students in the class. This time may be difficult to drive toward a consensus because 7-year-olds are focused heavily on fairness and each individual child may perceive what is fair differently.

Working with Parents, Caregivers, and Teachers

This age group may be challenging for caregivers and teachers because of the moodiness and complaining, but 7-year-olds also strongly value their relationships. Sometimes, it can be challenging to keep the positive characteristics in mind and to see past the struggles when children are complaining constantly. What follows are some hints, tips, and reminders for working with this age group.

For parents in particular, 7-year-olds will begin to align with their same-sex parent. It is important to remember that this is normal and for the opposite-sex parent to try not to feel hurt: Just because a 7-year-old boy is now closer to his dad than his mom does not mean that he has stopped loving her or seeing her as important; rather, he is now trying to build his own identity as a male.

Seven-year-olds value predictability and consistency because of their many worries (Sprenger, 2008). They tend to work hard to get things exactly right and do not like to be interrupted. They will continue to worry unless they are satisfied with what they are doing. It is therefore important to allow for extra time to transition or complete tasks. Along with time for completion of activities, it is important to allow some time for breaks in between tasks. Seven-year-olds fatigue easily because of the focus and energy that they spend in their tasks.

Because of the value of fairness in 7-year-olds, it will be helpful to make a conscious effort to be fair when working with them. Although it is impossible always to be fair – and 7-year-olds will probably always find some way in which to make a situation appear unfair – it is good for adults to be aware of this quality and try to prevent situations, if at all possible. For example, if a child gets permission to go to the water fountain before another child, letting the second child go first next time establishes an environment of equity.

When giving a task to a 7-year-old, it will be more successful to give instructions in three steps or fewer. More than three steps at a time challenges the focus of a 7-year-old. Instead of asking them to take the dishes to the sink, wash them, dry them, *and* put them in the cupboard, reducing directions to only three will help with completion – after which more directions can then be given. This will help 7-year-olds to stay focused and to remember to complete all three steps.

Lastly, although 7-year-olds do not enjoy the task of doing chores, assigning them chores or tasks is a helpful way in which to build their self-esteem and feelings of significance (Sprenger, 2008). Knowing that they have a task for which others are depending on them can be rewarding for 7-year-olds, as long as they are not consumed with ensuring that the task is completed perfectly. The process of performing an important task helps 7-year-olds to build their identities and to view themselves as worthy.

CONCLUSION

Seven-year-olds turn inward to develop their own identities. They are moody, sulky, and private during this year. Their complaints are inspired by a need for close relationships and valuing the experience of being close to others. They compare themselves to others, processing their experiences internally, as they begin to develop who they truly are. On the surface, this age may seem difficult; however, 7-year-olds display many loving qualities and they are starting to develop more adult-like cognitive abilities. Seven-year-olds who are operating outside of developmental norms may benefit from interventions geared toward developing their self-concept or strengthening their relationships with key people in their lives.

REFERENCES

Aboud, F. E. (1988). *Children and prejudice.* New York, NY: Blackwell.

Ames, L. B., & Haber, C. C. (1985). *Your 7-year-old: Life in a minor key.* New York, NY: Dell.

Armstrong, A., & Casement, C. (2000). *The child and the machine: How computers put our children's education at risk.* Beltsville, MD: Robins Lane Press.

Berk, L. (2006). *Child development* (7th ed.). New York, NY: Pearson.

Cameron, J., Alvarez, J., Ruble, D., & Fuligni, A. (2001). Children's lay theories about ingroups and outgroups: Reconceptualizing research on prejudice. *Personality and Social Psychology Review, 5*(2), 118–128.

Clements, D. H., & Sarama, J. (2003). Young children and technology: What does the research say? *Young Children, 58*(6), 34–40.

Cordes, C., & Miller, E. (Eds.). (2000). *Fool's gold: A critical look at computers in childhood.* College Park, MD: Alliance for Childhood.

Corenblum, B., & Armstrong, H. D. (2012). Racial-ethnic identity development in children in a racial-ethnic minority group. *Canadian Journal of Behavioural Science, 44*(2), 124–137.

Davies, D. (2011). *Child development: A practitioner's guide* (3rd ed.). New York, NY: Guilford.

Erikson, E. H. (1956). The problem of ego identity. *Psychological Issues, 1,* 101–171.

Fowler, J. W. (1981). *Stages of faith: The psychology of human development and the quest for meaning.* New York, NY: HarperCollins.

Francoeur, R. T., Koch, P. B., & Weis, D. L. (Eds.). (1998). *Sexuality in America: Understanding our sexual values and behavior.* New York, NY: Continuum.

Gesell Institute of Child Development. (2011). *Gesell Developmental Observation–Revised examiner's manual.* New Haven, CT: Gesell Institute.

Greenspan, S. I. (1993). *Playground politics: Understanding the emotional life of your school-age child.* Reading, MA: Addison-Wesley.

Greenspan, S. I. (1997). *The growth of the mind – and the endangered origins of intelligence.* Reading, MA: Addison-Wesley.

Helker, W. P., & Ray, D. C. (2009). Impact of child–teacher relationship training on teachers' and aides' use of relationship building skills and the effects on student classroom behavior. *International Journal of Play Therapy, 18*(2), 70–83.

Ivey, A. E. (1986). *Developmental therapy: Theory into practice.* San Francisco, CA: Jossey-Bass.

Kagan, J., & Herschkowitz, N. (2005). *A young mind in a growing brain.* Mahwah, NJ: Lawrence Erlbaum.

Kegan, R. (1979). The evolving self: A process conception of ego psychology. *The Counseling Psychologist, 8*(2), 5–34.

Kirshner, L. A. (1988). Implications of Loevinger's theory of ego development for time-limited psychotherapy. *Psychotherapy, 25*(2), 220–226.

Kohlberg, L. (1987). *Child psychology and childhood education: A cognitive-developmental view.* New York, NY: Longman.

Loevinger, J. (1976). *Ego development.* San Francisco, CA: Jossey-Bass.

Nelsen, J., Lott, L., & Glenn, S. (2013). *Positive discipline in the classroom: Developing mutual respect, cooperation, and responsibility in your classroom* (4th ed., rev'd). New York, NY: Three Rivers Press.

Petty, K. (2010). *Developmental milestones of young children.* St. Paul, MN: Redleaf Press.

Piaget, J. (1926). *The language and thought of the child.* New York, NY: Harcourt Brace.

Piaget, J. (1932). *The moral judgment of the child.* New York, NY: Free Press.

Piaget, J., & Inhelder, B. (1969). *The psychology of the child.* New York, NY: Basic Books.

Plowman, L., & McPake, J. (2013). Seven myths about young children and technology. *Childhood Education, 89*(1), 27–33.

Quintana, S., & Segura-Herrera, T. (2003). Developmental transformation of self and identity in the context of oppression. *Self and Identity, 2,* 269–285.

Ray, D., Muro, J., & Schumann, B. (2004). Implementing play therapy in the schools: Lessons learned. *International Journal of Play Therapy, 13*(1), 79–100.

Rogers, L. O., Zosuls, K. M., Halim, M. L., Ruble, D., Hughes, D., & Fuligni, A. (2012). Meaning making in middle childhood: An exploration of the meaning of ethnic identity. *Cultural Diversity and Ethnic Minority Psychology, 18*(2), 99–108.

Selman, R., & Byrne, D. (1974). A structural-developmental analysis of role-taking in middle childhood. *Child Development, 45,* 803–806.

Sprenger, M. (2008). The 7-year-old brain. In *The developing brain: Birth to age eight* (pp. 87–99). Thousand Oaks, CA: Corwin Press.

Sylwester, R. (2007). *The adolescent brain.* Thousand Oaks, CA: Corwin Press.

Vygotsky, L. S. (1978). Interaction between learning and development. In M. Gauvain & M. Cole. (Eds.). *Readings on the development of children* (2nd ed., pp. 29–36). New York, NY: W. H. Freeman & Co.

Wood, C. (2007). *Yardsticks* (3rd ed.). Turners Falls, MA: Northeast Foundation for Children.

Yelland, N. (2011). Reconceptualising play and learning in the lives of young children. *Australian Journal of Early Childhood, 36*(2), 4–12.

9

THE EXTRAORDINARY 8-YEAR-OLD

Sinem Akay

Most 8-year-old children are pleasant to be around and more outgoing than they have ever been before (Gesell Institute, 2011; Sprenger, 2008). Even though they like observing and evaluating others, they are most observant and critical of their own behaviors. Children in this age group adore their caregivers and they are curious about conversations between their caregivers. They especially want to hear what their caregivers say about them, hoping to hear some praise that will help them to develop positive self-perceptions.

Eight-year-old children may appear to be emotionally fragile, because they get their feelings hurt easily by criticism or even constructive feedback (Sprenger, 2008). However, these children tend to feel good about themselves in general. They seek positive reinforcement for their efforts and accomplishments by saying things such as "I better do this project again – it's not good enough." They hope to hear positive statements from their caregivers, but they are cognitively capable of developing an awareness that their caregivers may sometimes be too busy to focus on them. Eight-year-olds can also distinguish real compliments from false ones. When 8-year-olds are unable to achieve or produce at a desired level and quickly, they will become defeated and self-critical (Wood, 2007).

Typical 8-year-olds tend to be highly worried about pleasing their caregivers (Sprenger, 2008). Girls, especially, enjoy being around their mothers and want to have a close relationship with them. On the other hand, they tend to criticize their caregivers easily. This combination of seeking closeness and being critical leads to complicated relationships between caregivers and their 8-year-old children.

Children in this age group usually enjoy going to school and have been referred to as "school-agers" (Petty, 2010, p. 67; Sprenger, 2008). They do not like missing anything that is going on in their classrooms and among their peer groups. Compared to younger children, 8-year-olds are less forgetful and more responsible with school work. However, the majority of them find third grade very difficult because they are given fewer directions by the teachers.

BRAIN DEVELOPMENT

Neurological advancements in middle childhood, between the ages of 8 and 12, overlap with the perceptual, cognitive, and motor development of children (Blume & Zembar, 2007). In early childhood, children create interconnection between the parts of the brain that facilitate the communication of different areas with one another. This preparation helps the brains of 8-year-olds to become ready to take on new challenges.

By the end of their eighth year, children's brains have reached 90 percent of their adult weight (Kagan & Herskowitz, 2005). Children develop their auditory cortex between the ages of 5 and 11, which improves their speech and sensory–motor integration (Blume & Zembar, 2007). Between the ages of 4 and 10, development of the left temporal lobe increases children's proficiency in speaking, understanding, reading, and writing language. It is for this reason that the learning of multiple languages is easiest during this period as compared to other periods of life.

Development of the corpus callosum between the ages of 5 and 18 enables increased speed of neural transmission between hemispheres, and improves motor coordination, selective attention, creativity, and complicated cognitive tasks (Blume & Zembar, 2007). An 8-year-old may show an increased ability to play chess with his or her father as a part of his or her improvement in complicated cognitive tasks; this same child may also show increased motor coordination by becoming a better soccer player. In addition, with the development of the corpus callosum, children gain skills that require holistic procession, such as reading.

Eight-year-olds begin to develop organizational skills for memory (Berk, 2006). In order to store material in long-term memory, children first need to organize the information. At this period of their lives, many skills have become automatic for children, such as reading and writing. This automatic processing ability makes it possible for the brain to concentrate on the development of memory.

PHYSICAL DEVELOPMENT

> Eight-year-olds are generally healthier than they were at age 6 and 7, contracting fewer childhood illnesses (Petty, 2010).

Children start to slow down in their physical growth at around the age of 8, and wide differences are seen between children in height and weight (Papalia, Olds, & Feldman, 2006). Fat tissue gradually increases in girls around the age of 7 and in boys around the age of 8 (Blume & Zembar, 2007). Thus children in this age group, especially girls, need to be supported with physical activity and a balanced diet to maintain a healthy body weight.

Eight-year-olds show a peak in their activity levels and they may start to be more accident-prone (Blume & Zembar, 2007; Sprenger, 2008). High activity levels among this age group rarely correspond with the expectations of caregivers and teachers that the children will control their behaviors. Thus caregivers and teachers need to provide outlets for acceptable release of energy rather than criticize children for their high levels of activity. Because middle-age children spend less time in free play and more time in structured activities, caregivers and teachers need to encourage them to exercise and to participate in sports.

Although 8-year-olds are capable of sitting still for longer time periods, sometimes up to 30 minutes, they need hands-on activities and a balanced schedule of vigorous and quiet activities throughout the day (Petty, 2010). Because 8-year-olds have a high energy level, they like to do things in a hurry; hence simple directions work more effectively (Gesell Institute, 2011; Wood, 2007). Eight-year-olds are exploratory by nature, with both their bodies and minds.

Throughout middle childhood, children show growth in their jaws, teeth, and faces (Blume & Zembar, 2007; Papalia et al., 2006). Eight-years-olds are in the process of replacing approximately 20 baby teeth, lost over the last couple of years, with 32 permanent ones. Most children complete this process around the age of 12.

Gross and Fine Motor Skills

Although physical growth rate slows, middle-age children continue improving in their gross motor skills (Blume & Zembar, 2007). With increased opportunities to participate in school activities, children will develop more specific and integrated motor skills. Children convert their gross motor skills to a variety of sports, such as transferring their running and jumping skills into basketball, balance and coordination into skating and hockey, and strength and flexibility into gymnastics. They benefit most from outdoor play as a result of their energy levels. Eight-year-olds can now visually focus on objects both near and far away (Wood, 2007). Middle childhood also comes with improvements in fine motor skills that support handwriting, sewing, and playing musical instruments. School-age girls tend to have more advanced fine motor skills as compared to boys. By the age of 8, children typically have an adult pencil grip, are able to draw in detail, and have clear handwriting.

Perceptual Motor Skills

Perceptual motor abilities are those skills that require combining sensory and motor systems (Blume & Zembar, 2007). They are the skills with which we integrate small and large muscle groups, such as eye–hand and eye–head coordination. Skiing, gymnastics, writing, and tying shoes are some examples of these abilities. Between early and middle childhood, children show major changes in their perceptual motor skills. School-age children rely more on visual information, which is a shift from their reliance on touch and taste in preschool years. When they regulate their motor behaviors, they can use information that comes from multiple senses rather than only one sense. As an example, middle-age children become better at playing soccer, because they can use information from their eyes, ears, and legs. Between the ages of 7 and 8, children develop the skills with which to correctly label the two sides of their body as "right" and "left."

> Most 8-year-olds do not need close supervision while they perform their daily routines, such as taking a bath, brushing their teeth, and getting dressed up (aboutparenting, n.d.).

> Physical and play activities in which 8-year-old children have engaged at earlier ages start to turn into physical skills and athleticism (PBSparents, n.d.).

GENDER AND SEXUAL DEVELOPMENT

Eight-year-old children are usually curious about sexuality and they are very interested in their bodies, as well as others' bodies, such as how their bodies work and where babies come from (Sciaraffa & Randolph, 2011). Touching and exploring their private parts and occasional masturbation are developmentally normal behaviors for this age group. However, mimicking adult-like sexual behavior and/or involving other children to their sexual behaviors by means of coercion are signs of emotional problems that need to be addressed by professionals.

If sexuality is a taboo in their family environments, 8-year-olds may seek information from their peer groups to satisfy their curiosity. To help children to gain accurate knowledge about sexuality, caregivers can use different activities to bring up this subject (Sciaraffa & Randolph, 2011). Activities such as reading books that address gender, pregnancy, and genital body parts can facilitate both auditory and visual learning.

COGNITIVE DEVELOPMENT

Cognition involves a series of intellectual functioning, such as thinking, reasoning, memory, decision making, and problem solving (Blume & Zembar, 2007). School-age children show a gradual increase in logical thinking, in ability to learn through conversing with others, in learning strategies, and in memory. Eight-year-olds love to learn and socialize at the same time.

According to Piaget and Inhelder (1969), school-age children are within the "concrete operational" stage in their development (Piaget & Inhelder, 1969). Children show cognitive shifts from a dependency on rigid and self-centered thought process toward a dependency on operations. In his cognitive developmental theory, Piaget distinguished children in the concrete operational stage from those in the "preoperational period" in terms of their improved skills in logic and organization.

One of the abilities that school-age children develop is "decentration", which is the ability to focus on several features of a task at a time (Piaget & Inhelder, 1969). In a task in which they are asked if there is the same amount of water in each glass, preoperational children will consider only one dimension of the glass, such as height, while a concrete operational child can consider more than one dimension when solving the problem: width or depth of the glass in addition to its height.

Children in the concrete operational stage can go through a series of mental actions and they can reverse the process (Piaget & Inhelder, 1969). The ability to reverse can be seen in mathematics: The 8-year-old child can understand that subtraction is the reverse process of addition, just as division is the reverse process of multiplication. Another cognitive skill of children who

111

have reached the concrete operations stage is to use classes and subclasses to make categorizations (Piaget & Inhelder, 1969). School-age children mostly enjoy collecting objects and they can sort their collections into different categories. They can group collector cards according to several features, such as by the power of characters, then by their skills, and then by their types.

"Seriation" is another ability that children in concrete operational stage gain (Piaget & Inhelder, 1969). This ability permits 8-year-old children to order items according to some dimension, such as length. School-age children also develop spatial reasoning skills that allow them to understand space, as well as to give people directions to get from one point to another. Seriation of length, weight, and volume emerge at different ages. Children between the ages of 7 and 8 can accomplish seriation of length, but seriation of weight and volume tends to occur between the ages of 9 and 12.

Children in the concrete operational stage develop an understanding of transformation, which allows conservation skills to develop (Piaget & Inhelder, 1969). Understanding transformation includes the ability to understand how an object can change some physical qualities while others stay the same, such as a round clay ball being squished into a different shape of clay. An 8-year-old child has the capacity to integrate a series of events into a whole and realize that the flat piece of clay in front of him or her is the clay ball that was on the table before his or her sibling started playing with it. Improvement of conservation tasks can be evidenced by the fact that most 8-year-old children can reason that if water is poured back into the original container, the amount of liquid will stay the same.

The ability of school-age children to understand causality also differs from that of preschool children. Children at the concrete operational stage, including 8-year-olds, have increased ability to understand the cause-and-effect relationship, and experiments become an area of interest. They frequently ask questions starting with "why" and "how" to understand the reasons behind the events. If an 8-year-old boy sees that his mom's favorite vase is in pieces on the floor and the cat is standing where the vase used to be, for example, he can make the connection between these clues and understand what caused the vase to be broken.

Concrete operational thinking is limited in some ways, because it depends on the concrete experiences of the child (Frost, Worthham, & Reifel, 2001). Eight-year-old children cannot apply logical thinking to the experiences in abstract contexts. Transferring logical thinking from a familiar context to less familiar context is not possible at the concrete operational stage. As an example, 8-year-old children who can classify specific types of collector card may not be able to sort cards by a given category without being familiar with the cards and their categories. Considering the limitations in concrete operational thinking, teachers and caregivers should adopt their educational instructions to the appropriate level of cognitive development by using manipulatives to explain problem solving (Rathus, 2006; Wood, 2007). As an example, when teaching an 8-year-old child about fractions, lecturing should be followed by allowing the child to divide concrete objects, such as plastic sticks or beans, into parts.

There are cultural and environmental differences in achieving concrete operational thinking (Blume & Zembar, 2007). Interest in a certain type of information and exposure to the topic will facilitate achievement in concrete operational thinking for that specific topic. As an

Eight-year-olds can read for pleasure and choose books that reflect their personal interest areas (PBSparents, n.d.).

example, many children in the United States have access to and extensive interest in video games, which enables them to apply concrete operational thinking skills to challenges in games. Achievement of cognitive tasks may, however, be delayed for children in cultures in which formal schooling starts after the age 7 if the tasks are presented in a traditional format (Blume & Zembar, 2007). For example, an 8-year-old Brazilian street vendor may have difficulty completing mathematical calculations on paper even though he or she can solve such problems in a short period of time if they are associated with money. Thus cultural differences do not intervene with the ability to use thought in learning for school-age children if they are presented in a more familiar, rather than traditional, format. Regardless of their environmental and cultural differences, however, children use similar logical and mental strategies to learn.

In terms of thinking strategies, school-age children have the ability to use selective attention, which involves being able to focus on only one task at a time while they are learning a subject at home or at school (Atkinson & Shiffrin, 1968). The capacity for selective attention develops as a result of cognitive inhibition, which requires ignoring both internal and external distractions. As an example, children can screen out external distractions such as noises in their classroom when they listen to the teacher and can keep their focus on the information. They can also ignore their own irrelevant thoughts and impulses, such as their urge to go to the playground instead of listening to the teacher's lecture. School-age children demonstrate the ability to use their selective attention skills for both problem solving and memorizing.

Middle-age children have the ability to use mnemonic strategies, which are specific strategies to memorize information (Atkinson & Shiffrin, 1968). One of these strategies is organization, which allows them to place materials into a logical order. Children also use rehearsal strategies by repeating the information in order to remember it. Children between the ages of 6 and 7 can engage in passive rehearsal by rehearsing a single item ("apple, apple, apple"), whereas 8-year-olds develop the ability to engage in active rehearsal by rehearsing more than one item ("apple, banana, orange"). In addition, they have the ability to use retrieval strategies to recall the information when they need to use it.

> Eight-year-old children frequently show black-or-white thinking, such as seeing things as good or bad, ugly or pretty, and right or wrong (MyHealth.Alberta.ca, n.d.).

Language Development

In the third grade, caregivers and teachers expect children to learn from their readings (Sprenger, 2008). However, not all 8-year-old children read at the same level, which needs to be a consideration for educators or caregivers who use books as learning materials for this age group. Eight-year-old children can easily use complex and compound sentences. They are expected to read with ease and write simple compositions. When they read aloud, 8-year-olds can control their rate, pitch, and volume.

Eight-year-olds enjoy language and like to speak rapidly, explaining ideas and events. They are capable of speaking about their emotions, strengths, and weaknesses, and they like when others talk to them and about them – but only when that talk is positive. They also enjoy exaggeration and drama in their speech, often using descriptive, slang, and humorous language (Gesell Institute, 2011; Petty, 2010; Wood, 2007).

WORLDVIEW/EGO DEVELOPMENT

Middle-age children go through major changes in their personalities (Frost et al., 2001). Family relationships continue to have an important impact on children's ego development, while peer relationships and school achievement become significant influences on personality development. Eight-year-olds gain personal competencies by participating in activities, developing emotional self-regulation, and acquiring a deeper sense of who they are and what they are capable of achieving (Blume & Zembar, 2007).

According to Erikson (1963), children go through four stages in personality development until their adolescence: *trust vs. mistrust* (infancy), *autonomy vs. shame and doubt* (toddlerhood), *initiative vs. guilt* (early childhood), and *industry vs. inferiority* (middle childhood) (Erikson, 1963). The primary psychosocial task of an 8-year-old child is to achieve a sense of *industry*, which is characterized by the skill to work on a task and to continue to focus on it for an extended period of time. If children are not sufficiently encouraged to gain industry, they will develop a sense of *inferiority*. Eight-year-old children spend a large amount of time on developing skills and becoming more competent in different tasks. They feel driven to engage in activities in which they are competent rather than activities in which they do not show talent. Children in this age group want to demonstrate to themselves and others that they are competent and that they have skills of which they are proud. As they explore their potential by initiating activities and competencies, 8-year-olds may develop a sense of inferiority if they fail, needing adult encouragement when they do not perform well (Wood, 2007). They are in need of adult protection from excessive self-criticism or from trying too much at once (Gesell Institute, 2011).

Kohlberg's model describes the moral reasoning level of 8-year-olds as at the "preconventional" level, in which many children are still egocentric (Berk, 2006; Rathus, 2006). According to the

Most 8-year-olds enjoy helping their parents around the house (Boots, n.d.). Giving them opportunities to help with chores such as cooking or fixing the sink can strengthen the child–parent relationship, as well as improve the child's self-esteem.

model, children at this age group are usually between stages of "punishment and obedience" and "individual, purpose, and exchange". In the "punishment and obedience" morality stage, children base their moral judgments on adult rules. They use punishment and obedience to figure out how they need to behave: "How can I avoid punishment?" At this stage of moral development, children may engage in negative behaviors when they believe that there will be no punishment or consequence, such as hitting a baby brother when there is no caretaker around. As 8-year-old children move to the "individual, purpose, and exchange" morality stage, they begin to engage in exchanges with others to get their needs met in return: "What's in it for me?" As an example, children may share their toys (exchange) to make friends (meeting social needs).

Racial/Ethnic Identity Development

Similar to differences in the onset of puberty or the growth of cognitive skills, racial identity development looks different in every child, progressing through stages of racial classification abilities (Byrd, 2012). Racial development theory proposes that children will actively construct their worlds using both external and internal experiences and information. Most 8-year-olds are in the preconceptual level of understanding racial classification, indicating that they understand that racial differences are not only based on skin color, but also characteristics based on heredity or biology. They can also understand differences between people based on social characteristics, such as lifestyles and speech. Some 8-year-olds enter the conceptual stage, in which case they show the ability to identify flexibility in categorization of race. Children who are in the conceptual stage start to understand the superficiality of focusing on skin color for racial classification and pay more attention to biological or social dimensions. They are more flexible in their understanding of racial categories, recognizing that it is difficult to categorize based on a single dimension.

EMOTIONAL DEVELOPMENT

Eight-year-olds show some typical characteristics in their emotional development (Sprenger, 2008). They can articulate their feelings more easily than younger children. They may be sensitive and they tend to dramatize. Caregivers and teachers may experience 8-year-olds as resistant to the rules at first, but will find that children eventually obey them. Although they can be rude, demanding, and bossy from time to time, 8-year-olds are usually affectionate, helpful, outgoing, and curious. They are particularly interested in fairness, owing to the concrete nature of their cognitive abilities.

Eight-year-olds can be very impatient. Waiting for special events such as birthdays can be frustrating (GreatKids, n.d.).

In middle childhood, children develop the ability to understand their own emotional states, to accurately interpret their emotional experiences with others, and to exercise control over their feelings (Blume & Zembar, 2007; Petty, 2010). Emotional self-regulation tasks include managing negative emotions and directing the focus on positive goals. For example, children at this stage of emotional development can avoid frustration by staying away from arguments and conflicts with their caregivers, and they may seek rewarding experiences (such as getting their caregivers' positive attention) by helping them out.

Hormones start to become ready for puberty for some 8-year-olds, especially for girls (Sprenger, 2008). Hence children at the age of 8 may display some emotional reactions that others do not expect. They desire to have some privacy in their lives and, for most children at this age group, it is important to have a personal space at home and school. Caregivers and teachers can help children with their needs by providing them a locked drawer or a locker.

SOCIAL DEVELOPMENT

Social development among 8-years-olds includes gaining a better understanding of interpersonal relationships, improving concepts of friendship, and guiding social interactions with moral reasoning (Blume & Zembar, 2007). Children's mental representations related to interpersonal relationships and adopting other's perspectives impact on their decision making; yet they seek approval from both adults and peers. Eight-year-olds enjoy groups and group activities.

Most children in early childhood are egocentric, and they fail to make a distinction between their own perspectives and those of others (Selman, 2003). However, children between the ages of 6 and 8 start to acquire the capacity for social informational role-taking, which requires a child to understand that others' perspectives may defer from his or her own. On the other hand, the child is still unable to focus on more than one perspective at a time. Eight-year-olds start to gain awareness of others' emotions and intentions in addition to their own (Selman, 2003). They seek cues from others to guide their own behaviors. They gain the ability to use reciprocal role-taking, which includes putting themselves in someone else's shoes, and being able to reflect on others' intentions and behaviors.

According to Greenspan (1993), 8-year-olds become more aware of their roles in their peer groups and they have increased willingness to participate in these groups. They tend to spend most of their times around their friends. Children at this age maintain their close relationships with their family members, but they also tend to compete with their siblings. When they compete with others, they can go through competitions without overreacting or avoiding. They gain the ability to verbalize their emotions to others, and their ability to self-regulate helps them to experience disappointment without becoming aggressive or withdrawn.

> Peer pressure highly impacts on 8-year-olds' social interactions (aboutparenting, n.d.). It is important for caregivers to talk with their children about peer pressure and to encourage them to make good judgments.

RELATIONSHIP DEVELOPMENT

Eight-year-olds become heavily involved with their peers, and these peer groups become an additional support to their family support (Rathus, 2006). Children attribute great importance to acceptance among friends, which is reflected in their interactions with peers. Eight-year-olds make friends easily and they can establish good two-way relationships (Sprenger, 2008). They may also develop same-sex close friendships.

Peer groups among school-age children have unwritten rules for membership. Being different from other members of the group may cause exclusion from the group. Differences in physical and personality characteristics, manner of dress, and socioeconomic status, as well as aggressive behaviors, are the most common reasons why 7- and 8-year-olds may be rejected by their peers (Dodge, 1983). To be accepted by groups, children work on developing a variety of physical and intellectual skills, such as performing tricks on their bikes, learning jokes and stories to tell others, and using slang expressions (Berk, 1997).

Children learn social rules and the importance of obeying them from their peers, as well as their caregivers and teachers (Rathus, 2006). Peer culture may, however, have some different rules from the social rules of adults: Adults may expect children to inform teachers about others' misbehaviors, but in peer groups this "ratting" behavior will be punished by exclusion from the group.

Adults are still significant figures in the lives of 8-year-olds. They seek approval from parents and teachers, while at the same time establishing independence. Criticism from adults is especially difficult for 8-year-olds and they will often hesitate to come to an adult to talk about feeling hurt once they have been criticized. Hence parents and teachers need to be attuned to the emotional consequences of their words and actions for a typical 8-year-old.

DEVELOPMENT IN THE AGE OF TECHNOLOGY

New technologies in this era are changing the way in which children play and learn. Technological progress requires a better understanding of the way in which technology impacts on childhood development. Technological gadgets such as computers, tablets, and smartphones can have both positive and negative impacts on children's social development (Brown, Winsor, & Blake, 2012). In the 21st century, 8-year-old children learn expectations of society and the ways in which to build relationships with others both by means of face-to-face interactions with people and by playing on their computers or tablets with their peers. Providing children with technological tools with time limits can help them to benefit from both ways of socializing with others – but if caregivers do not set limits on the time for which children use technology, it may prevent them from developing face-to-face socialization skills.

Another important point about the use of technology for 8-year-olds is online safety. Considering that children at this age group start to become interested in sexuality, caregivers need to exercise parental controls on electronic devices to prevent their children's exposure to inappropriate sexual materials online. Caregivers can visit websites, such as http://www.netsmartz.org/InternetSafety to learn about the ways in which they can protect their children from harmful online materials.

BEST PRACTICES IN COUNSELING/THERAPY

Most children who are younger than 10 have only limited ability, if any, to use abstract reasoning or verbal processing of their thoughts and emotions (Piaget, 1962). Many therapists therefore prefer to use play in their therapy to communicate more effectively with children. This section of the chapter is therefore mainly focused on major play therapy approaches.

As discussed in the first section of the chapter, 8-year-olds want to be around their caregivers, and they seek caregivers' positive feedback and reinforcement. Like other school-age children, teachers are also an important part of 8-year-olds' lives. Considering the significant impact of caregivers and teachers on the development of 8-year-olds, this section includes suggestions about parent and teacher involvement in the therapy process.

Child-centered play therapy (CCPT)   Child-centered play therapy (CCPT) is widely practiced with children below the age of 10 (Landreth, 2012). Because these children have only limited abilities to reason abstractly, toys and play materials help them to communicate their feelings and thoughts; thus, like the other age groups, 8-years-olds can benefit from CCPT. Child-centered play therapy is also suited to children from different cultures and backgrounds. Child-centered play therapists provide empathy, genuineness, and understanding to every child, regardless of his or her culture, background, or presenting concern (Ray, 2011).

Adlerian play therapy (AdPT)   According to Adlerian therapists, every child strives to gain belonging and significance in his or her family environment (Adler, 1929). Children observe their family members and family atmosphere to figure out ways in which they can fit into that environment. Through observations, they come to conclusions about themselves, others, and the world. It is especially important for 8-year-olds to receive positive reinforcement and encouragement from those in their environment if they are to develop healthy self-perceptions. One of the main focuses of Adlerian play therapy (AdPT) is to provide encouragement to children during therapy sessions, as well as teaching caregivers and teachers the ways in which to reinforce positive self-perception at home and at school.

Adlerian play therapists believe that, by the time a child is 7 years old, he or she has completed the development of the organized rules, or "lifestyles," which the child will use as a cognitive blueprint for his or her behaviors (Kottman, 1997). Adlerian play therapists help children to modify their lifestyles and to learn healthier ways in which to feel significant in their environments. Considering that 8-year-old children have recently completed their lifestyle developments, it will be easier for Adlerian play therapists to work with them on modifying their dysfunctional lifestyles so that they become healthier ones.

Cognitive-behavioral play therapy (CBPT)   The cognitive-behavioral play therapy (CBPT) approach is based on behavioral and cognitive theories of personality development, maladjustment, and therapeutic interventions (Knell, 1997). Because 8-year-old children have improved ability to think logically, to learn through conversing with others, and to use learning strategies and memory, their cognitive flexibility and sophistication will allow them to use their cognitive skills in the therapy process. Cognitive-behavioral play therapists encourage children to work on their distorted thoughts and to achieve behavioral change by addressing issues related to control, mastery, and responsibility. Children and therapists work together to establish goals, to decide on activities, and to choose play materials. In contrast with nondirective play therapy approaches, CBPT includes teaching new skills to children in session. An 8-year-old's ability to learn from conversations and hands-on activities makes it easier for him or her to learn new skills in therapy as compared to younger children.

Filial therapy   Filial therapy is a play therapy approach that involves working directly with caregivers (Guerney, 1997). It has also given rise to a specific ten-week working intervention known as child–parent relationship therapy (CPRT) (Landreth & Bratton, 2006). The filial model of working with caregivers is based on Carl Rogers' (1951) person-centered theory and Virginia Axline's (1947) child-centered play therapy model (Axline, 1947; Rogers, 1951). It is an intervention that can be helpful for any age group, including 8-year-old children, because it focuses on facilitating improved parenting skills, and a better relationship between children and their caregivers. Eight-year-old children try to establish independence, but they still highly value their caregivers' approval. Considering the emotionally sensitive, but also independent nature, of this age group, filial therapy can help caregivers to learn ways in which to interact with and discipline 8-year-old children without getting in power struggles or damaging the child–parent relationship.

Systematic training for effective parenting (STEP)   The systematic training for effective parenting (STEP) model is designed to help caregivers to communicate with their children more effectively (Dinkmeyer & McKay, 1976). The model is based on the Adlerian perspective of therapy. Social equality among caregivers and children, mutual respect, and encouraging children are some of its basic tenets. Therapists facilitate caregivers' understanding of children's goals in misbehaving, as well as teaching caregivers discipline methods that promote responsibility and problem-solving skills. Considering that, because 8-year-olds work on developing industry, they can be critical of others and test limits, STEP can help caregivers to learn how to discipline their children by teaching egalitarian relationships and taking responsibility for their actions. Thus STEP focuses on helping children to become healthy adults without caregivers resorting to criticism and other harsh disciplinary methods, which may negatively impact on an emotionally fragile 8-year-old's self-perception.

Caregivers and healthcare professionals can visit http://www.steppublishers.com for more information about STEP books and training.

Positive discipline   Another caregiver training model that is based on Adlerian theory is positive discipline (Nelsen, 1996). Positive discipline teaches caregivers to approach their children with respect and kindness rather than punishment. The intervention focuses on skills such as bridging gaps in communication, avoiding power struggles, encouraging rather than praising, focusing on strengths, and holding children accountable for their behavioral decisions. Eight-year-olds strive to have a sense of belonging in their families, but also want to practice independence using their newly developed cognitive and motor skills. Caregivers who use positive discipline methods can help their children to learn ways in which to build healthy relationships and to have self-discipline without losing their independence or self-respect. Teachers can also benefit from positive discipline in classroom settings.

Caregivers, teachers, and healthcare professionals can find more information on positive discipline online at http://www.positivediscipline.com

Considerations for Therapy

Regardless of his or her age, every child engages in acting-out behaviors from time to time (Doft & Aria, 1992). Stressors in children's lives can explain their occasional behavioral or emotional issues, and one isolated problem rarely indicates treatment. However, children need to learn self-control, establish a better understanding of societal rules, and gain the ability to take others' perspectives into account as they grow older. Thus some behaviors may become a bigger concern with older children compared to younger ones, especially if they are persistent. It is important to evaluate the need for therapy considering external stressors, a child's developmental level, and the persistency of issues.

Some typical behaviors may be a concern for some caregivers and teachers of 8-years-olds, such as sensitivity to judgment, a tendency to dramatize negative situations, a high level of physical activity, curiosity about sexuality, and occasional masturbation. It is important to remember that these behaviors are developmentally appropriate if they are not excessive and do not negatively impact on a child's everyday functioning.

Because young children do not have a clear understanding of the distinction between truth and fantasy, they tend to lie more than older children (Doft & Aria, 1992). However, after the age of 7, children typically have better control over their impulses and an improved understanding of negative interpersonal consequences of lying. Thus 8-year-old children who lie a great deal of the time may need some emotional support and therapy.

Stealing is also a common behavior among young children (Doft & Aria, 1992). Children below the age of 4 have difficulties differentiating between what belongs to them and what belongs to others. By the age of 6, the majority of children develop an understanding of others' properties. Hence an 8-year-old child with stealing behaviors may need therapy to deal with issues underlying his or her behavior.

Children may become upset with caregivers when they experience separation for even brief periods of time (Doft & Aria, 1992). This is a normal emotion that does not become a problem with most children. However, high separation anxiety in school-age children may need intervention because it interferes with the child's social development and daily functioning, with consequences such as missed school or a withdrawal from his or her social environment.

Bedwetting is a complicated issue that can be explained by biological or emotional factors, or both (Doft & Aria, 1992). Bedwetting should not be considered to be a problem until the age of 6. If it continues after the age of 6, children need to be seen by a physician first; then, if medical causes are ruled out, caregivers should seek therapy for their 8-year-old to help him or her with possible emotional problems or to help him or her to deal with self-concept issues related to bedwetting.

Another common problem among children is sleep problems (Doft & Aria, 1992). If 8-year-old children have difficulty soothing themselves to fall asleep, caregivers should consider consulting a therapist. In addition, persistent night terrors and nightmares can be signs of emotional difficulties, which also may require therapy.

CONCLUSION

Having 8-year-old children at home or in class can be fun, but sometimes challenging, for caregivers and teachers. Trying to achieve a sense of industry, but being emotionally sensitive, can make life difficult for 8-year-olds. However, with the support and understanding of caregivers and teachers, children in this age group can thrive in their social and emotional development. These children can also bloom in their cognitive abilities given the appropriate tools and approaches with which to facilitate the best learning conditions for them.

It is important that caregivers and teachers remember those behaviors that are normal for 8-year-olds to exhibit, such as being active, having difficulty sitting still for long periods of time, and being interested in sexuality. Additionally, 8-year-olds can benefit from the use of technology, but it is the responsibility of caregivers and teachers to limit the time spent with these tools and to exercise control over the materials that children can access online. If caregivers and teachers are supportive of their healthy development, 8-year-olds can be very pleasant to be around.

In summary, 8-year-old children go through significant milestones in their psychological, biological, and social development. Thus caregivers and teachers have the important task of creating environments that promote optimal growth for 8-year-old children who are at a very significant point in their development.

REFERENCES

aboutparenting. (n.d.). Child development: Your 8 year old child. Retrieved from http://childparenting. about.com/od/physicalemotionalgrowth/tp/ Child-Development-Your-Eight-Year-Old-Child. htm

Adler, A. (1929). *The practice and theory of individual psychology* (Rev'd.). New York, NY: Harcourt Brace.

Atkinson, R. C., & Shiffrin, R. M. (1968). Human memory: A proposed system and its component processes. In K. W. S. Spence & J. T. Spence (Eds.), *The psychology of learning and motivation* (pp. 47–89). London: Academic Press.

Axline, V. (1947). *Play therapy*. Cambridge, MA: Houghton Mifflin.

Berk, L. (1997). *Child development* (4th ed.). Boston, MA: Allyn & Bacon.

Berk, L. (2006). *Child development* (7th ed.). New York, NY: Pearson.

Blume, L. B., & Zembar, M. J. (2007). *Middle childhood to middle adolescence: Development from ages 8 to 18*. Columbus, OH: Prentice Hall.

Boots. (n.d.). Children's health guide: Childhood milestones age 8. Retrieved from http://www.webmd.boots.com/children/guide/childhood-milestones-age-8

Brown, J., Winsor, D. L., & Blake, S. (2012). Technology and social-emotional development in the early childhood environments. In S. Blake (Ed.), *Child development and the use of technology: Perspectives, applications and experiences)*pp. 112–128). Hershey, PA: Information Science Reference.

Byrd, C. M. (2012). The measurement of racial/ethnic identity in children: A critical review. *Journal of Black Psychology, 38*(1), 3–31.

Dinkmeyer, D., & McKay, G. D. (1976). *The caregivers handbook: Systematic training for effective parenting*. Circle Pines, MN: American Guidance Service.

Dodge, K. A. (1983). Behavioral antecedents of peer social status. *Child Development, 54*(1), 1386–1399.

Doft, N., & Aria, B. (1992). *When your child needs help*. New York, NY: Harmony Books.

Erikson, E. H. (1963). *Childhood and society* (2nd ed.). New York, NY: Norton.

Frost, J. L., Worthham, S. C., & Reifel, S. (2001). *Play and child development*. Upper Saddle River, NJ: Merrill Prentice Hall.

Gesell Institute of Child Development. (2011). *Gesell Developmental Observation–Revised examiner's manual*. New Haven, CT: Gesell Institute.

GreatKids. (n.d.). Developmental milestones: Your 8-year-old child. Retrieved from http://www.greatschools.org/gk/articles/developmental-milestones-your-8-year-old-child/

Greenspan, S. I. (1993). *Playground politics: Understanding the emotional life of your school-age child*. Reading, MA: Addison-Wesley.

Guerney, L. (1997). Filial therapy. In K. J. O'Connor & L. D. Braverman. (Eds.), *Play therapy theory and practice: Comparing theories and techniques* (pp.131–160). Hoboken, NJ: John Wiley & Sons.

Kagan, J., & Herschkowitz, N. (2005). *A young mind in a growing brain*. Mahwah, NJ: Lawrence Erlbaum.

Knell, S. M. (1997). Cognitive-behavioral play therapy. In K. J. O'Connor & L. D. Braverman. (Eds.), *Play therapy theory and practice: Comparing theories and techniques* (pp. 79–100). Hoboken, NJ: John Wiley & Sons.

Kottman, T. (1997). Adlerian play therapy. In K. J. O'Connor & L. D. Braverman. (Eds.), *Play therapy theory and practice: Comparing theories and techniques* (pp. 310–341). Hoboken, NJ: John Wiley & Sons.

Landreth, G. L. (2012). *Play therapy: The art of the relationship*. New York, NY: Routledge.

Landreth, G. L., & Bratton, S. C. (2006). *Child–parent relationship therapy. (CPRT): A 10-session filial therapy model*. New York, NY: Routledge.

MyHealth.Alberta.ca. (n.d.). Milestones for 8-year-olds. Retrieved from https://myhealth.alberta.ca/health/Pages/conditions.aspx?hwid=ue5720

Nelsen, J. (1996). *Positive discipline*. New York, NY: Ballantine Books.

Papalia, D. E., Olds, S. W., & Feldman, R. D. (2006). *Human development*. New York, NY: McGraw-Hill Humanities Social.

PBSparents. (n.d.). Child development tracker. Retrieved from http://www.pbs.org/parents/child-development/

Petty, K. (2010). *Developmental milestones of young children*. St. Paul, MN: Redleaf Press.

Piaget, J. (1962). *Play, dreams, and imitation in childhood*. New York, NY: Norton.

Piaget, J., & Inhelder, B. (1969). *The psychology of the child*. New York, NY: Basic Books.

Rathus, S. A. (2006). *Childhood and adolescence: Voyages in development*. Belmont, CA: Thompson/Wadsworth.

Ray, D. C. (2011). *Advanced play therapy: Essential conditions, knowledge, and skills for child practice*. New York, NY: Taylor & Francis.

Rogers, C. R. (1951). *Child-centered therapy: Its current practice, implications, and theory*. Boston, MA: Houghton Mifflin.

Sciaraffa, M., & Randolph, T. (2011). Responding to the subject of sexuality in young children. *Young Children, 66*(4), 32–38.

Selman, R.L. (2003). *The promotion of social awareness*. New York, NY: Russell Sage Foundation.

Sprenger, M. (2008). *The developing brain: Birth to age 8*. Thousand Oaks, CA: Sage.

Wood, C. (2007). *Yardsticks* (3rd ed.). Turners Falls, MA: Northeast Foundation for Children.

Part IV

LATE CHILDHOOD

10

THE EXTRAORDINARY 9-YEAR-OLD

Brittany J. Wilson

Jake is a healthy, active, and industrious 9-year-old. His days are filled with tasks, which he boldly approaches as opportunities to demonstrate mastery in his environment. Jake is independent, self-motivated, and largely determined. Jake's mother frequently struggles with feeling rejected by him: After all, it was only one year ago that Jake appeared to be captivated by her, yet now he desires independence at every turn. Most of all, Jake is different from other 9-year-olds in his class, because individuality and variability are hallmarks of this age, often leaving parents and teachers confused and, at times, uncertain as to what to expect next. In fact, Jake's parents have come to understand his unpredictability as the single most predictable characteristic of this new and exciting stage in his development.

Nine-year-olds are fundamentally self-determined, self-motivated, and overall less warm toward the adults in their lives as compared to their 8-year-old selves. At times, 9-year-olds may appear detached and even disinterested in parents, particularly female caregivers, often leading to feelings of rejection. Although this is disconcerting for the adults in their lives, children at this age are quite content in moving away from the dependency that they once felt toward primary caretakers at age 8, and into a newfound sense of independence and autonomy (Gesell Institute, 2011).

Nine-year-olds tend to be very concrete and logical in their reasoning and ways of being. They pride themselves in figuring things out and in mastering everyday challenges, such as understanding how and why LEGO blocks fit together, as compared to previous years, in which the primary objective was praise for their creation. In fact, 9-year-olds often find themselves feeling frustrated and dissatisfied until they have successfully mastered a self-directed task. Nine-year-olds can even be interrupted while engaged in a task and return ready to pick up right where they left off: a particular developmental milestone for this age. They are self-starters and prefer to do things in their own ways, in their own time, and with far less direction from adults as compared to only a year ago (Gesell Institute, 2011). Additionally, a 9-year-old's persistent need for mastery is becoming an increasingly internal process as he or she seeks to prove his or her competencies to *himself or herself* rather than to others. Overall, "remarkably persistent," "impatient," and "unique" are terms that best characterize children at the age of 9.

> Nine-year-olds often begin to enjoy household chores and see them as further opportunities for mastery (Allen & Marotz, 2007).

BRAIN DEVELOPMENT

Children's brains are not fully developed or integrated until they reach their mid-20s. Integration allows children to use their whole brains in a coordinated way. Ideally, by the time people reach their mid-20s, their brains will be horizontally integrated, allowing the left-brain logic to work well with the right-brain emotions. Additionally, vertical integration should have taken place, which allows for the physically higher parts of the brain associated with thoughtful consideration to work well with the physically lower parts of the brain, associated with instinct and survival (Siegel, 2012). Although full brain integration is not expected until a person reaches his or her mid-20s, the 9-year-old's brain is actively developing and becoming increasingly integrated every day.

Over the past several years, researchers have concluded that experience plays a large role in molding the brain and promoting whole-brain integration. When children undergo an experience, neurons begin to fire. The brain has 100 billion neurons, even in childhood, with an average of 10,000 connections to other neurons (Siegel, 2012). When neurons fire together, they grow connections between them, referred to as "neural pathways," in a process known as "wiring." Over time, certain neural pathways can become rewired with new experiences. The wire and rewire process of the brain is what integration is all about. Children's experiences, either healthy or unhealthy, will create connections between different parts of the brain and affect the integration process. Children's brains are constantly being wired and rewired by their experiences. This process ultimately affects the overall structure of children's brains and subsequent mental processes, both in the present and throughout an individual's lifespan (Siegel, 2012).

The neurology taking place in the 9-year-old's brain can explain his or her constant seeking of novelty and mastery in the environment. The successful completion of a task (that is, mastery), supports the release of dopamine and other chemicals flowing through a child's frontal lobes. This dopamine release provides an instant sense of enjoyment, focus, and purpose (Badenoch, 2008). The often euphoric feeling produced by dopamine encourages children to persist in their frequent quests for mastery. Dopamine has also been shown to contribute to goal setting and attaining, explaining the 9-year-old's highly competitive and hardworking nature (Gesell Institute, 2011; Sprenger, 2008).

Increasing myelination in the 9-year-old's brain enables the signals going from one area of the brain to another to travel at an increasingly rapid rate. This improved interconnectedness in children's brains allows for several decreased behaviors associated with early childhood, such as outbursts, perseverance, inattention, and insistence on routines (Berger, 2005). Parents and caregivers often interpret this shift in the 9-year-old as an overall improvement in behavior and an increase in maturity.

The 9-year-old's brain is also becoming increasingly interconnected, particularly in the posterior corpus callosum, allowing for increased processing speed and further holistic integration (Sprenger, 2008). Nine-year-olds are in the process of rapid brain development, increased interconnectivity, and continued integration. The neurobiological effects of their developing brains can be recognized through their external behaviors. Armed with the knowledge of what is emerging in their children, caretakers and adults are better equipped to promote healthy brain development and to further understand the 9-year-old experience.

PHYSICAL DEVELOPMENT

The 9-year-old tends to be slower than he or she was just a year ago at the age of 8. Nine-year-olds make every effort to complete each task methodically to the best of their abilities. While 9-year-olds have typically slowed considerably compared to their younger selves, doing things "right" tends to be of increased importance at this age.

Extensive complaining is a key feature of the ninth year, specifically in relation to physical health. Although 9-year-olds are typically in excellent physical condition, somatic complaints become quite frequent. When they perceive a task to be overly challenging, it is common for 9-year-olds to complain of physical aches and pains, such as stomachaches, headaches, or grueling fatigue, in an effort to avoid feelings of failure. Such symptoms often occur in relation to a particular dislike or challenging task: If a 9-year-old feels incompetent or frustrated when attempting to play the piano, for example, he or she will commonly complain of debilitating physical pain in his or her fingers, preventing him or her from continuing to practice. Physical symptoms should not be ignored or taken lightly – but caretakers should be aware that such symptomology is often tied to emotionality within the child (Ames & Haber, 1990).

At 9 years old, children are better coordinated, are likely to push their physical limits, and tire easily. Additionally, they tend to look toward outlets to relieve their often anxious state. Such emotional releases include twisting hair, biting nails, or pursing lips to relieve tension (Wood, 2007).

Fine Motor Skills

At 9 years old, children's gross and fine motor skills have greatly improved. At this age, children tend to show more interest in details due to their increased ability for coordination and control. Nine-year-olds can typically master cursive handwriting and demonstrate full ability to copy from the board in class. Nine-year-olds benefit from practice with a variety of fine motor tasks, such as cutting, drawing, or painting, to further develop their fine motor skills. Children at this age are typically capable of producing neat and organized written assignments, and often create beautifully crafted artwork (Wood, 2007).

As a result of the increased myelination in the brain noted earlier in the chapter, 9-year-olds' motor abilities – particularly those connected with the coordination of both sides of the body and the performance of complex tasks – have greatly improved. Additionally, with the continued maturation of the corpus callosum during middle childhood, 9-year-olds are now capable of increased balance and are able to use both hands simultaneously, as well as independently, in a smooth manner (Berger, 2005; Gesell Institute, 2011).

> Nine-year-olds can eat at any time of day and are typically still hungry at mealtimes. They are much more willing to try new foods and often enjoy cooking (Allen & Marotz, 2007).

Gross Motor Skills

Nine-year-olds love to push their own physical limits, as well as the physical limits of others. Nine-year-old boys in particular love to roughhouse, and frequently engage in tumbling and wrestling games. Research indicates that there are direct benefits from children's active play, particularly the rough-and-tumble play, to their overall physical development. Additionally, active play demonstrates beneficial effects on children's emotional regulation and social interaction (Berger, 2005). Although this active and oftentimes rough play can be bothersome to parents and caregivers, the play of a 9-year-old lends itself to guidance rather than suppression. Nine is an ideal age for entering children into organized team sports as a way of permitting such active play through an appropriate modality, as well as satisfying their frequent needs for mastery and competition.

> Nine-year-olds frequently maintain activity levels that fluctuate between extremes of high intensity and almost nonexistent activity. They may virtually collapse following periods of intense play (Allen & Marotz, 2007).

The typical 9-year-old is considerably more skillful in motor performance than he or she was at earlier ages. Nine-year-olds demonstrate improved timing and coordination skills, and are generally better capable of physical control of their bodies. Although they may still have trouble staying within physical boundaries, 9-year-olds are far more capable in regards to physical coordination than they were aged 8 (Ames & Haber, 1990).

Visually, 9-year-olds prefer to hold things very close to their eyes. It is characteristic of 9-year-olds to put their heads close to their working points, to sit too close to the television, or to hold a book right up to their nose to read. Children of this age also frequently engage in open-eyed stares, which they are able to maintain for several minutes at a time without blinking. Often, this stare involves very little focus or attention on what the child is actually observing: a common frustration for teachers (Ames & Haber, 1990).

GENDER AND SEXUAL DEVELOPMENT

Overall, 9-year-olds tend to hold a mostly positive view of themselves. Both boys and girls are continuing to internalize the gender roles and expectations that they perceive from the environment. At this age, very little romantic or platonic interest in the opposite sex exists. In fact, an intense disinterest in and, at times, even a distain for the opposite sex are hallmarks of the 9-year-old. It is routine to see children at this age greatly segregated by gender at recess and in the cafeteria at school. Although some boy–girl attractions do exist at this age, they tend to result in very little social interaction (Ames & Haber, 1990).

By the age of 9, children tend to have a clear understanding of what sex is, as well as what it means to be in a romantic relationship. Nine-year-olds also readily recognize the feelings and sensations affiliated with the concept of love despite their relative disinterest in it (Rademakers, Laan, & Straver, 2012). Nine-year-olds have a general sense of curiosity about their bodies, and the many ways in which they are beginning to grow and change as they enter this prepubescent phase of development. It is not uncommon for some 9-year-old girls to begin menstruation. At the very least, girls this age begin asking questions about menstruation and the hormonal changes that they may be experiencing (Ames & Haber, 1990).

> Nine-year-olds show very little interest in personal hygiene. They often need reminders from caregivers to bathe, wash their hair, brush their teeth, and to put on new clothes (Allen & Marotz, 2007).

Although little interest in the opposite sex exists at this age, particularly if curiosity regarding reproduction was explained at the age of 8, 9-year-olds are quite interested in the details of their own sexual organs and functioning (Ames & Haber, 1990). Common to 9-year-olds is a seeking out of information regarding their sexuality from books, the media, and their same-sex peers. While there is a deep curiosity about sex, 9-year-olds also tend to be overly self-conscious about exposing their bodies to anyone. They commonly exclude younger siblings, peers, and parents when changing clothes, and have a profound appreciation and desire for privacy (Ilg, Ames, & Baker, 1981).

COGNITIVE DEVELOPMENT

According to Jean Piaget, the leading cognitive theorist to date, the ways in which children think and take in information from the world around them change across time and with experience. Piaget concluded that children vary in their thought processes depending on age and that such thought processes subsequently affect their behaviors (Berger, 2005). According to Piaget, 9-year-olds are in the midst of the "concrete operational" period of cognitive development, which ranges from ages 6 to 11. The concrete operational period is marked by very logical and rational thinking (Piaget & Inhelder, 1969). Children in concrete operational thought interpret experiences within their environment in a very objective manner. Cognitive processes in this period are causal in nature and are best understood as black-and-white thinking. An example is the 9-year-old's strong desire for mastery and heightened interest in science. At the age of 9, there is an answer for every question and a logical, linear thought process for every query. By applying their newfound logical abilities, 9-year-olds are better able to understand concepts such as conservation, number classification, and scientific logic (Berger, 2005; Piaget & Inhelder, 1969).

> Nine-year-olds tend to be better test takers as compared to their younger counterparts owing to their strong desire for mastery, coupled with their increasing ability for memorization (Gesell Institute, 2011).

When children reach the concrete operational period, they become decreasingly self-centered and better able to recognize the perspectives and feelings of others. When a 9-year-old believes that he or she has hurt or insulted someone, the 9-year-old can now rely on the rules of logic to correct his or her actions (Ames & Haber, 1990). This quality becomes increasingly important as children begin entering into meaningful friendships: a particularly impactful developmental milestone at the age of 9.

Nine-year-olds are able to apply simple logic, enabling them to arrive at conclusions, to reason deductively, and to classify information in a rational way (Gesell Institute, 2011; Wood, 2007). The once magical thinking of younger ages tends to dissipate by the age of 9, as an increasingly realistic viewpoint of the world and a decreased interest in fairytales, fables, and magic begin to emerge. This can be both relieving and unsettling for parents; however, explaining things in logical terms will best appeal to the 9-year-old's very concrete ways of thinking. Table 10.1 illustrates several examples of concepts primarily associated with the concrete operations stage of cognitive development.

Academic Functioning

By the age of 9, children are beginning to read to learn, rather than learn to read (Ames & Haber, 1990; Wood, 2007). Reading often accompanies the 9-year-old's fascination for learning and strong desire for understanding. Most children at this age enjoy reading silently and can begin

Table 10.1

Hallmarks of Concrete Operations

Term	Definition	Example
Conservation	The realization that if nothing is added or reduced, the amount stays the same regardless of any alterations to its appearance	Jeff understands that if he breaks a large clay ball into many smaller pieces, the total weight of the clay remains the same.
Multiple classification	The recognition that objects may belong to several groups or categories concurrently	Sally understands that a brown dog can belong to the larger category of "dogs," while simultaneously belonging to a smaller category of "brown dogs."
Deductive reasoning	The logical inference that something must be true given other correlated information already presented as true	Carlos concludes that if all birds have feathers and blue jays are birds, blue jays must have feathers too.

Source: Adapted from McDevitt and Ormrod (2002)

to master higher level books, including chaptered books. Reading errors tend to become less common as the 9-year-old's vocabulary becomes increasingly expansive (Ames & Haber, 1990). With regards to mathematical abilities, 9-year-olds begin working almost exclusively with word problems and often become extremely critical of themselves. Additionally, computation of money, the use of decimals, and knowledge of multiplication tables become progressively fluid at this age (Wood, 2007).

Nine-year-olds take great pride in attention to detail and often place increased value on the product of a task, rather than on the process or expended effort. They often search hard for explanations of facts, making scientific exploration of particular excitement. Additionally, by the age of 9, children typically master print and become capable of cursive writing. Because they take a great sense of pride in their work, handwriting at this age tends to be neat and legible. Overall, 9-year-olds tend to enjoy intellectual tasks, making math and science classes of particular interest (Ames & Haber, 1990; Wood, 2007). However, 9-year-olds will often struggle with test taking, a common event at this age, due to their perfectionism and avoidance of being wrong. They need support and practice in test taking if they are to remain encouraged. Finally, 9-year-olds tend to learn better on their own as compared to their younger and older counterparts (Wood, 2007).

Moral Development

Kohlberg (1927) developed a model of moral reasoning that he linked to specific developmental periods across the lifespan, as did Piaget in his model of cognitive development. According to Kohlberg, it is actually the *way* in which people reason, rather than the moral conclusion that they reach, which ultimately determines their stage of moral development (Berger, 2005). Additionally, Kohlberg believed that children will continue to advance in their moral reasoning and move up the hierarchy with continued life experiences and advancing age.

According to Kohlberg, 9-year-olds tend to fall into the "conventional" level of moral reasoning, which is related to Piaget's concrete operational thought in that it refers to current, observable, practices (Berger, 2005). The emphasis at this level is placed on social rules and comprised two stages: stage three and stage four, respectively. Kohlberg understood *stage three* as the "good girl," "nice boy," stage, often accompanied by behaviors that are societally proper and behaviors that are pleasing to others. At this stage, social approval is the goal and is of higher value than most external rewards. *Stage four* is understood as the "law and order stage," at which "proper" behavior is defined as being a dutiful citizen and obeying the laws and rules of society. Kohlberg believed that the majority of 9-year-olds engage in conventional moral reasoning and fall into one of these two stages (Berger, 2005; Kohlberg, 1927).

An example of Kohlberg's conventional level of moral reasoning might be asking a 9-year-old why it would be important to return a stranger's wallet if they were to find one on the ground. Most 9-year-olds would answer with something similar to "because my Mom/Dad told me that's the right thing to do," or "because it's against the law to keep a wallet that's not mine." This demonstrates the 9-year-old's strong desire for approval and to follow the rules of society.

Moreover, an appreciation for the rights and feelings of others is beginning to develop in 9-year-olds. They can now more readily empathize with others in a way that was not possible during earlier developmental periods. The once egocentric nature of the young child is beginning to dissolve and a regard for that which is valued by parents, caretakers, siblings, and peers is beginning to emerge. Furthermore, a respect for the rules of society is prized by most 9-year-olds: It is very common to see children at this age consumed with following the rules at school. Nine-year-olds often speak up if they observe someone else breaking a rule in an effort to gain the approval of their teachers, parents, or peers (Allen & Marotz, 2007).

WORLDVIEW/EGO DEVELOPMENT

Most 9-year-olds hold very positive perspectives of themselves, as well as of their families. In fact, many 9-year-olds describe an almost magical and uniquely special perspective on their families. Parents of 9-year-olds often report a marked change in the child for the better: They describe their 9-year-old as less tense, more independent, more self-sufficient, and overall in better equilibrium compared with how he or she presented at the age of 8 (Gesell Institute, 2011). The majority of 9-year-olds feel very secure within themselves and are confident in their own abilities. Children of this age tend to busy themselves with their personal concerns and are far less dependent on others to meet their needs compared to 8-year-olds. The self-concept of 9-year-olds is no longer tied to their parents' perspectives as the child begins to identify himself or herself as distinct from caretakers (Berger, 2005). In general, 9-year-olds are quite dependable and trustworthy. They are ambitious in terms of the demands that they place on themselves and they desire a strong sense of personal success. Given 9-year-olds' increasing capacity to set their mind to a task and see it through, they are generally satisfied with both themselves and their accomplishments.

According to Erik Erikson's stages of psychosocial development, 9-year-olds are facing the crisis of *industry vs. inferiority*. In this particular stage of ego development, children are busily attempting to master the abilities valued by their families and cultures (Berger, 2005). In line with 9-year-olds' cognitive stage of development, they evaluate themselves according to very concrete, black-and-white thinking. At 9 years old, children generally understand themselves as competent, productive, capable, and knowledgeable, given their successful mastery over tasks in their environments. If they cannot master tasks, however, they suddenly understand themselves as incompetent, failing, or even unintelligent. If children begin to understand themselves to be inferior, they could lose trust in their innate abilities and may become riddled with self-doubt (Ames & Haber, 1990).

Applying Loevinger's theory of ego development, 9-year-olds could be categorized in between the "self-protective" and "conformist" stages of development. A child's understanding of societal and familial rules, and a willingness to abide by such rules, are hallmarks of the self-protective stage. However, such adherence to rules is for the child's own satisfaction and advantage, rather than for the good of society (Loevinger, 1976). Blame is also identified as a hallmark of this stage, because children are quick to protect themselves and to project any wrongdoing on to others, making the self-protective stage very opportunistic by nature.

Most 9-year-olds have moved from the self-protective stage to the conformist stage of ego development. A child's movement into this developmental stage is significant and is characterized by an identification of personal welfare with that of the group – typically, a peer group. Unlike the previous stage, a child in the conformist stage obeys rules because he or she is accepted by the group, not simply to avoid punishment as he or she did in previous stages. To children in this stage, the group, and their acceptance within the group, is hugely impactful to their overall feelings of self-worth (Loevinger, 1976).

Racial/Ethnic Identity Development

Limited research exists examining the racial and ethnic identity development of children. To date, the vast majority of racial identity development models include adolescents and adults, but fail to incorporate children (García Coll & Marks, 2009). It is not uncommon for adults to overlook the important role that a child's racial and ethnic identity plays in his or her overall positive development. However, research demonstrates an innate drive in children to detect both ingroup and between-group differences among themselves and others within their environment, beginning at an early age (Quintana & McKown, 2008). Ethnic identity development is an integral component of a child's overall development, and carries social and emotional implications across the individual's lifespan.

Children have an innate motivation to better understand their own membership of a social group (Quintana & McKown, 2008). Nine-year-olds in particular are in the midst of defining themselves based upon group membership and demonstrate a heightened awareness of group differences (Greenspan, 1993; Loevinger, 1976). By the age of 9, many children are aware of the ethnic, racial, and cultural groups to which they belong. They are also becoming increasingly familiar with many customs and traditions associated with their own ethnic and/or cultural groups. Additionally, by the age of 9, children are better able to understand the permanency of ethnic group membership and begin to identify themselves as cultural beings. It is not at all uncommon for a 9-year-old to boldly announce the physical differences between himself or herself and a classmate with regards to race, ethnicity, or culture: a typical component of racial identity development at this age.

EMOTIONAL DEVELOPMENT

Emotions are best understood as a child's affective response to an occurrence in the environment, and include feelings, both physiological and psychological, about these events. This differs from a child's temperament, or his or her fundamental ways of responding to emotional events. Children's temperaments are at least in part a function of genetics and are largely unique to the individual child (McDevitt & Ormrod, 2002). Both emotions and temperament are heavily influential in a child's emotional development. Nine-year-olds tend to worry about everything, from their own worlds to the outside world, leading to the perception that they can sometimes seem "neurotic" (Gesell Institute, 2011, p. 43).

Nine-year-olds gradually learn to regulate their emotions as they begin to develop coping strategies for the breadth of emotionally significant events taking place in their lives. Additionally, 9-year-olds are better able to organize their thoughts and emotions into communications with those around them. They are becoming increasingly capable of sharing their feelings with friends, family, and caregivers (Ray, 2011). Emotions are a fluid and consistent part of the 9-year-old's experience. While some emotions may manifest more internally, such as feelings of depression and anxiety or social withdrawal, others may manifest externally, such as aggressive behaviors or problems with attention.

Greenspan (1993) believed that all children move through distinctive emotional phases at each stage of development, which they must master if optimal emotional growth is to occur. Greenspan viewed the emotional growth of a child as unique in comparison to other measures of development, such as physical, cognitive, and behavioral. Each stage of emotional development, according to Greenspan, builds on the previous one and carries the child forward into the next stage. Greenspan asserted that 9-year-olds fall into the developmental phase of "The world is other kids," which spans the ages 8 to 10 (Greenspan, 1993).

Children in this stage are moving away from the family-oriented phase of development and immerse themselves in peer relationships. Nine-year-olds define themselves in terms of the ways in which their peers view them, as opposed to the ways in which their parents view them:

an often jolting transformation for the caregivers in their lives. Nine-year-olds' self –images begin formulating around the group to which they see themselves as belonging. An overreliance on external evaluation also begins to emerge at this age (Greenspan, 1993). Naturally, this can lead to children's positive or negative self-evaluations, depending on the role that they see themselves as fulfilling within their groups. If children are able to successfully navigate this new stage, by 9½ they begin to enter into an increasingly balanced state in which they are better able to match external realities with their own internal ideals (Greenspan, 1993).

SOCIAL DEVELOPMENT

Nine-year-olds' strong desires for relationships play a large role in their social functioning. They are generally eager to please, wish to be liked by both peers and adults, and love to be chosen to participate in activities (Ames & Haber, 1990). Nine-year-olds are able to work in groups, but tend to spend a considerable amount of time disagreeing about facts, rules, and directions, as opposed to working on the actual task assigned (Wood, 2007).

In regards to peer relationships, 9-year-olds have a strong preference for same-sex friendships and have very little interest in socializing with the opposite gender. Formations of cliques are beginning to emerge, because 9-year-olds tend to be overly critical of both themselves and others. Additionally, 9-year-olds can be quite self-conscious and sensitive to criticism, particularly from adults (Ames & Haber, 1990). An adult's sarcastic sense of humor could be devastating to a 9-year-old, who will be quick to internalize any type of disapproval, whether real, implied, or even imagined. Because they experience exaggerated internalized emotions at the age of 9, children will magnify both criticism and praise; hence adult interactions may have inflated consequences (Wood, 2007).

Nine-year-olds' heightened sensitivity to failure also greatly contributes to the degree of self-criticism that they often experience. It is not uncommon for 9-year-olds to burst into tears at the very thought of failing themselves or of failing another significant person in their lives. By the age of 10, children are becoming increasingly calm and accepting of both themselves and others. An emergent sense of relief is often experienced by parents and teachers as they observe the child moving toward a newfound sense of self-acceptance by the end of 9½.

RELATIONSHIP DEVELOPMENT

A hallmark of the age of 9 is a sudden moving on from the overreliance on maternal figures that is common to 8-year-olds and the emergence of autonomy and independence. Nine-year-olds begin to detach from their mothers as peer relationships begin to play an increasingly essential role in their lives (Ilg et al., 1981). This observed disinterest in maternal relationships is often unsettling to parents, particularly to mothers, but is actually quite typical and a mark of healthy development.

Along with decreased interest regarding maternal relationships comes decreased argumentative behaviors. At the age of 8, any type of attention – even negative attention – is sought after, which is no longer the case at the age of 9. Nine-year-olds are very capable of solitude and are overall less involved, less demanding, and less challenging compared to their 8-year-old selves. Nine-year-olds both want and need independence from their parents if optimal healthy development is to occur (Gesell Institute, 2011).

> Nine-year-olds like to work with a partner of their choice, who will typically be of the same gender. This is also the age at which children begin forming social groups or cliques (Allen & Marotz, 2007).

At 9 years old, sibling relationships are becoming increasingly valued and important. Perhaps for the first time since young childhood, children at this age are returning to a fascination with, and appreciation of, their siblings. Older siblings are perceived as people to be admired, while younger siblings are often protected and even nurtured by 9-year-olds (Ames & Haber, 1990). Owing in part to a growing sense of responsibility, helping to take care of younger siblings is often an exciting task. Holistically, 9-year-olds are in a stage of striving for independence from parents, becoming closer with siblings, and strengthening relationships with peers. While 9-year-olds can be very social, they are also quite comfortable with solitude. This age group is full of individuality and unique personalities.

DEVELOPMENT IN THE AGE OF TECHNOLOGY

Children are growing up in a rapidly evolving and expansive society. Technological advances have become a fundamental component of such evolvement, undoubtedly influencing children's development. Personal computers, smartphones, and tablets have become commonplace in children's homes and in classrooms across the country. In fact, several primary and secondary school systems now emphasize the development of a technology-integrated curriculun to guide children's learning processes (Hsin, Li, & Tsai, 2014).

By the age of 9, many children have become somewhat mesmerized by technology and use it regularly in daily life. Substantial exposure to computers, smartphones, video games, and social media is typical of this age. Nine-year-olds, social beings that they are, often derive great satisfaction and fulfillment in playing video games with friends or conversing via social media. As a result of the independent and self-directed nature of 9-year-olds, they are likely to contest any attempts at parental monitoring or restriction of their use of technology.

Nine-year-olds frequently become engrossed in a task, such as playing a video game or app, which may intrigue them for hours at a time. They will often lose track of time or even forget to eat a meal as a result. Once interrupted or asked to stop, 9-year-olds will often become impatient to return to the game or task as soon as possible (Elkind, 1994). This may lead to feelings of frustration for parents and an inclination to restrict the usage of electronic devices. Gaining a sense of mastery is a highly common and necessary developmental milestone for this age. Frustrating as it may be, 9-year-olds are bound to spend hours at a time completing self-initiated tasks, including tasks associated with some form of technology.

Although all children grow and mature at differing rates, many social networking sites establish minimum age requirements, typically exceeding the age of 9, in response to the emotional readiness of young children for such content. In fact, one of the most popular social networking sites, Facebook, requires its users to be a minimum age of 13. Nonetheless, 9-year-olds frequently look to social networking outlets as a primary means of communication and socialization with peers. As the surfacing importance of popularity begins to collide with the anxiety inherent to the 9-year-old's experience, a resulting reliance upon social media outlets could ensue. Yet despite this growing interest in such sites, the appropriateness of particular social media outlets may simply exceed the developmental maturity of many 9-year-olds.

> As an emphasis on popularity begins to develop, 9-year-olds often begin to admire and even idolize older children, including older siblings (Gesell Institute, 2011).

The subject of children and technology remains widely debated among parents, teachers, and healthcare professionals. While many have come to view technology as an exciting aspect of childhood development, with many potential benefits to learning, others remain largely concerned about the possible implications of a technologically driven society on children's social and emotional health (Elkind, 2001). Research exists indicating many potential learning and social benefits to the use of technology with children (Hsin et al., 2014). However, other research supports the notion that technology may place demands on children to grow up too fast, too soon (Elkind, 2001). In a culture in which technology appears to permeate everything, parents and caregivers are left with a challenging decision regarding how much or how little their children will be permitted to engage in the technological advancements of society.

BEST PRACTICES FOR COUNSELING/THERAPY

When Counseling/Therapy Is Indicated

Because of the very individualistic nature of 9-year-olds, identifying typical and atypical behaviors, in efforts to generalize when counseling may be indicated, is a difficult task. Often, the parents of 9-year-olds observe their child frantically worrying, frequently troubled, and depending far less on caretakers for comfort and support, and quickly rush him or her to a counselor for help. While counseling may always be beneficial, it may not be completely necessary for these behaviors, because they are actually quite typical and represent normative developmental patterns in 9-year-olds. Parents and caretakers should keep in mind that, according to the stages of development outlined by the Gesell Institute (2011), 9-year-olds are inwardized–outwardized, troubled, and neurotic by nature. While these behaviors and attitudes may be less than ideal for some parents and caretakers, they are not particularly troublesome to a child's overall emotional well-being when within normal bounds. Additionally, it is helpful for parents to remember that this crucial developmental period is fleeting and typically passes with time.

However, certain behaviors and attitudes could exist that are more troubling and which should be closely monitored by parents, teachers, and caretakers of 9-year-olds. It is important to keep in mind that each 9-year-old is unique and should be considered within the context of his or her environment, circumstances, and distinctive personality. Additionally, the degree of a child's behaviors is an important consideration: Children who have experienced any type of abuse, neglect, or trauma may experience more extreme versions of otherwise typical behaviors.

Nine-year-olds are in a period of self-discovery and independence. They are generally self-contained and self-sufficient (Gesell Institute, 2011). However, there may be times at which a 9-year-old becomes overly contained, or even withdrawn. This becomes particularly worrisome if he or she begins to withdraw from his or her peers, because it would be atypical for a 9-year-old to isolate himself or herself from social circles on a regular basis. Perhaps even more bothersome is a 9-year-old who does not have any friends at all: While 9-year-olds are capable of solitude and often enjoy independent space for task mastery, a healthily functioning 9-year-old draws great satisfaction from regular social interaction.

Nine-year-olds are known for their worrisome and often neurotic attitudes. It is not uncommon for children at this age to fear the worst in any given situation, despite all logic and past experiences. Again, while this is likely to be of concern to parents, these anxious behaviors are characteristic of the 9-year-old experience. However, if 9-year-olds begin experiencing debilitating levels of worried or anxious behaviors, to the extent that they interfere with school or social life, it may be helpful for parents to contact a therapist. Frequent or persistent nightmares, especially when leading to increased anxiety and worry, may also indicate the needs to seek counseling services.

The extent to which 9-year-olds engage in peer relationships is a strong marker of emotional health: Children this age should be engaged socially. The formation of social groups and the exclusion of opposite-sex children are characteristic of this age group. Nine-year-olds who withdraw socially, who are overly involved or attached to children of the opposite gender, or who appear very uncomfortable around peers may be likely to benefit from counseling, because these may be signs of deeper emotional struggles.

Developmentally Appropriate Approaches

Because of the developmental and relational needs of 9-year-olds, activity therapy continues to emerge as an increasingly appropriate modality. As discussed, 9-year-olds are cognitively operating from concrete operations, making abstract thought and reasoning abilities somewhat limited. However, at the age of 9, children are gradually moving toward more abstract thinking. As a consequence, 9-year-olds tend to label *toys* in the *play*rooms as overly immature and may even be insulted if brought into a playroom; in an *activity* room, however, there are more age-appropriate activities in which they can engage if they so choose.

Materials in activity rooms may include woodworking stations, a wide variety of arts and crafts materials, baking ingredients and ovens, and even games. These materials and activities allow 9-year-olds to express themselves in a multitude of ways, while also feeling valued and accepted by the therapist. Nine-year-olds can begin to express themselves through various media in ways in which they feel most understood. How directive or nondirective the therapist is in an activity room depends greatly upon the theoretical orientation of the counselor, because activity therapy allows for a great deal of variation in therapeutic approach.

Child-centered activity play therapy (CCAPT) In terms of specific intervention types, child-centered activity play therapy (CCAPT) offers a balanced approach, allowing children the opportunity to use certain materials, such as crafts and games, to express themselves concretely, while also allowing for more abstract thought in verbally processing feelings and emotions with a counselor.

Whereas, in play therapy, the modality of play becomes the language through which the child's meaning is interpreted, 9-year-olds have the actual verbal and cognitive ability to utilize language in a way that younger children do not (Landreth, 2012). For this reason, counselors often prefer CCAPT for 9-year-olds. Additionally, it offers children a nondirective environment, much like child-centered play therapy (CCPT), in an increasingly developmentally appropriate way.

Cognitive-behavioral therapy (CBT)   In addition to CCAPT, increasingly directive approaches such as cognitive-behavioral therapy (CBT) may also be efficacious at this age. Due to 9-year-olds' cognitive capacities for logical and rationale thinking, CBT has demonstrated effectiveness with children and adolescents for a host of emotional concerns, including anxiety, depression, aggression, and social stressors (Kazdin, 2003). Cognitive-behavioral therapy typically consists of helping children first to identify and recognize symptoms of distress, then to challenge cognitions or beliefs around such stressors, altering distorted beliefs and self-talk, and finally to evaluate the newfound course of action (Kazdin, 2003). Additionally, CBT becomes preferable at this age as compared to behavioral interventions alone because 9-year-olds place a decreased value on rewards and punishments, and an increased value on social and group norms.

Group activity therapy   Group activity therapy can be another extremely beneficial modality for 9-year-olds because of their strong desire for peer relationships and social approval. Group activity therapy provides a relational connection vital for the 9-year-old's growth and can meet his or her developmental needs of a sense of belonging (Ray, 2011). Much like individual activity therapy, group activity therapy typically involves a concrete expression through which more abstract meaning is discovered. For example, there are several expressive art group activities in which 9-year-olds may be given a very specific and concrete prompt, such as "make an animal from clay that represents you," through which more abstract meaning can subsequently be made by means of processing. Unique to group activity therapy, is the added bonus of children engaging socially with one another and gaining increased awareness as a result of their social interactions. Appropriate forms of self-expression and peer interactions, in the presence of a trained therapist, can be extremely beneficial for 9-year-olds.

Working with Parents, Caregivers, and Teachers

Although 9-year-olds can be challenging by nature, these struggles are not permanent and are crucial developmental markers for children. However, knowing this does not make the day-to-day life of caretakers any easier or less frustrating. Perhaps the most imperative thing to keep in mind during this time is the importance of maintaining a strong parent–child relationship. Although it may be challenging, the following are some helpful tips to remember.

Specific to parents – particularly mothers – is the difficulty involved when 9-year olds detach from their parents, and move increasingly toward peer support and relationships. Although it would be easy to internalize such behaviors, parents should remember this in no way implies that their 9-year-old loves them any less; in fact, just the opposite is true. Nine-year-olds are moving into preadolescence, a time during which they will need the support of their parents more than ever, despite their apparent disinterest in parental relationships at the age of 9. While 9-year-olds are prone to excessive complaining and it may seem extreme at times, parents taking time to validate their child's feelings will help him or her to feel valued and understood by the important people in his or her life.

Nine-year-olds also have a tendency to perceive the world around them as unfair. This can be exhausting to parents and teachers. While their perceptions may seem skewed, it is important to keep in mind that a 9-year-old's perception is his or her reality. Although absolute equality is impossible to achieve, efforts should be made to make things as fair as possible, both at home and at school. This is particularly true when 9-year-olds are working in groups, as a result of their growing sense of peer importance and group solidarity (Wood, 2007).

Lastly, it is important for parents and caretakers to remember that all relationships are accompanied by occasional ruptures. But focusing on the rupture itself is not nearly as important as focusing on its repair. Nine-year-olds are forgiving, and care deeply about feeling connected and bonded to their parents and other important figures in their lives. Parents may seek to better understand the ways in which their own behaviors and emotions could lead to a rupture in the parent–child relationship, to initiate the process of repair with their children (Siegel & Hartzell, 2004). While 9-year-olds are likely to respond to the repair process, they are not very likely to initiate it on their own.

CONCLUSION

Like all developmental stages, the ninth year in a child's life marks a period of unique challenges, as well as many new and exciting discoveries. Nine-year-olds constantly seek out opportunities for mastery in their environments. They are quick to surrender a task if they feel as though failure may ensue, making encouragement and support from the adults in their lives of primary importance. Perhaps the most significant developmental hallmark of the age of 9 is a newly emerging emphasis and priority placed on same-sex peer relationships. This too can be challenging for caregivers, because they no longer seem to be the object of their 9-year-old's admiration. Parents and caregivers should, however, keep in mind that 9-year-olds continue to rely on parental support as much now, if not more than they did in the past, even if they show it less. As 9-year-olds continue to mature and gradually approach the prepubescent years, their reliance on parents for guidance and support will only continue to increase.

REFERENCES

Allen, K. E., & Marotz, L. R. (2007). *Developmental profiles: Pre-birth through twelve.* Clifton Park, NY: Thompson Delmar Learning.

Ames, L. B, & Haber, C. C. (1990). *Your 9-year-old: Thoughtful and mysterious.* New York, NY: Dell.

Badenoch, B. (2008). *Being a brain-wise therapist: A practical guide to interpersonal neurobiology.* New York, NY: W. W. Norton & Co.

Berger, K. S. (2005). *The developing person through childhood and adolescence.* New York, NY: Worth.

Elkind, D. (1994). *A sympathetic understanding of the child: Birth to sixteen.* Needham Heights, MA: Allyn & Bacon.

Elkind, D. (2001). *The hurried child: Growing up too fast too soon.* Cambridge, MA: Perseus.

García Coll, C., & Marks, A. K. (Eds.). (2009). *Immigrant stories: Ethnicity and academics in middle childhood.* Oxford: Oxford University Press.

Gesell Institute of Child Development. (2011). *Gesell Developmental Observation–Revised examiner's manual.* New Haven, CT: Gesell Institute.

Greenspan, S. I. (1993). *Playground politics: Understanding the emotional life of your school-age child.* New York, NY: Addison-Wesley.

Hsin, C. T., Li, M. C., & Tsai, C. C. (2014). The influence of young children's use of technology on their learning: A review. *Educational Technology & Society, 17*(4), 85–99.

Ilg, F., Ames, L., & Baker, S. (1981). *Child behavior: The classic child care manual from the Gesell Institute of Human Development.* New York, NY: HarperPerennial.

Kazdin, A. E. (2003). Psychotherapy for children and adolescents. *Annual Review of Psychology, 54,* 253–276.

Kohlberg, L. (1927). *Child psychology and childhood education: A cognitive-developmental view.* New York, NY: Longman.

Landreth, G. L. (2012). *Play therapy: The art of the relationship* (3rd ed.). New York, NY: Routledge.

Loevinger, J. (1976). *Ego development: Concepts and theories.* San Francisco, CA: Jossey-Bass.

McDevitt, T. M., & Ormrod, J. E. (2002). *Child development and education.* Upper Saddle River, NJ: Merrill Prentice Hall.

Piaget, J., & Inhelder, B. (1969). *The psychology of the child.* New York, NY: Basic Books.

Quintana, S. M., & McKown, C. (2008). Introduction: Race, racism, and the developing child. In S. Quintana & C. McKown (Eds.), *Handbook of race, racism, and the developing child* (pp. 1–15). Hoboken, NJ: John Wiley & Sons.

Rademakers, J., Laan, M., & Straver, C. J. (2012). Studying children's sexuality from the child's perspective. In T. G. M. Sandfort & J. Rademakers. (Eds.), *Childhood sexuality: Normal sexual behavior and development* (pp. 49–60). New York, NY: Routledge.

Ray, D. C. (2011). *Advanced play therapy: Essential conditions, knowledge, and skills for child practice.* New York, NY: Routledge.

Siegel, D. J. (2012). *The developing mind: How relationships and the brain interact to shape who we are* (2nd ed.). New York: Guilford.

Siegel, D. J., & Hartzell, M. (2004). *Parenting from the inside out: How a deeper self-understanding can help you raise children who thrive.* New York, NY: Penguin.

Sprenger, M. (2008). *The developing brain: Birth to age eight.* Thousand Oaks, CA: Corwin Press.

Wood, C. (2007). *Children in the classroom ages 4–14* (3rd ed.). Turners Falls, MA: Northeast Foundation for Children.

The Extraordinary 10-Year-Old

Deborah Ojiambo and LaKaavia Taylor

Source: Used with permission from Shutterstock

At the age of 10, children reach a smooth and stable period of development. The complaints and worries of the 9-year-old dissipate, and a noticeable shift occurs in the flexibility, niceness, and satisfaction of the 10-year-old. The typical 10-year-old is happy, friendly, energetic, and loving. He or she enjoys and finds comfort in relationships with family, friends, and teachers. In particular, 10-year-olds typically enjoy family outings and peer activities (Gesell Institute, 2011; Wood, 2007).

Ten-year-olds recognize their abilities, and will engage in tasks to display and refine their competence. In completing and mastering tasks, 10-year-olds will display increased focus and sustained concentration. Often referred to as the "golden end" of childhood, 10-year-olds consolidate their learning from previous development to prepare for the upcoming challenges that lead into adolescence (Wood, 2007, p. 119). Ten-year-olds have greater self-control and regulation. They often use more socially appropriate ways of expressing their thoughts and emotions than in previous years (Davies, 2011). At times, they might have quick tempers, with a stronger emotional pull toward anger (Wood, 2007). However, they quickly stabilize and are typically forgiving: A 10-year-old boy might stomp his feet and shout when angry about something a parent has said, then shortly afterward, once calmed, express remorse or attempt to problem solve (Ames, Ilg, & Bakers, 1988; Wood, 2007).

Ten-year-olds also have a greater understanding of the social rules within their environments and how to respond to them. The moral sense of children matures at the age of 10. They have an increased sense of right, wrong, and fairness (Davies, 2011; Wood, 2007). Ten-year-olds also respond well to rules and instructions, for example a 10-year-old might tell a friend, "I'm not riding my bike across the street because mom says it's not okay."

BRAIN DEVELOPMENT

Older children experience spurts of brain growth throughout adolescence. The prefrontal cortex is one area of the brain that grows while a child is aged 10 (Sowell, Thompson, Tessner, & Toga, 2001; Toga, Thompson, & Sowell, 2006). As such, this area of the brain is one of the last regions to develop and mature (Berk, 2012). The prefrontal cortex is responsible for cognitive processes such as problem solving, memory, impulse control, consciousness, and movement (Berk, 2012). With increasing age, the prefrontal cortex allows for stronger executive functioning, achieved by means of myelination and synaptic connections (Sowell et al., 2001). These processes increase the speed and efficiency of brain processing. Thus myelination is associated with the cognitive and behavioral changes that occur in older childhood, such as increased memory and self-regulation (Sowell et al., 2004). However, the prefrontal cortex is not fully developed at the age of 10 and will continue to mature into adolescence through adulthood. Even with growth in the prefrontal region, 10-year-olds are therefore likely to experience struggles related to reasoning and impulse control.

> The prefrontal cortex of the brain is under construction at the age of 10, and responsible for improvements in memory and problem solving.

In early development, the left hemisphere is quite active and undergoes increased growth. However, between the ages of 8 and 10, primary brain growth occurs in the right hemisphere of the brain (Berk, 2012). The right hemisphere is particularly responsible for intuitive and experiential processes (Siegel & Bryson, 2011). This region of the brain helps children to experience emotions, to store personal memories, and to apply meaning to life events. Additionally, the right hemisphere of the brain is responsible for the maturation of spatial skills, such as drawing and identifying geometric shapes, at the age of 10 (Berk, 2012). The growth in this region of the brain is consistent with the age progression of cognitive abilities discussed later in this chapter.

Ten-year-olds are sensitive to the enriched environmental experiences that are necessary to support continued brain development (Siegel & Bryson, 2011; Toga et al., 2006). These experiences wire and rewire the brain, changing its physical structure. Specifically, when children have positive environmental experiences, these activate neurons through synaptic growth, increasing white matter in the brain (Broderick & Blewitt, 2010; Fields, 2005; Toga et al., 2006). White matter increases the speed of the myelination needed to help to increase the brain's processing of information (Fields, 2005). The increase is critical for learning because it influences mental capacities such as abstract reasoning and the perception of stimuli (Sowell et al., 2004). Therefore healthy brain development is based on how enriching experiences are for children, from the learning methods that they receive to the activities that they choose (Siegel & Bryson, 2011). Much of what children experience in their daily experiences will positively or negatively impact their brain development in some way.

PHYSICAL DEVELOPMENT

Physical growth occurs at the age of 10, and is associated with an increasing ability to make movements that require muscle strength and coordination resulting from large muscle growth (Santrock, 2014; Wood, 2007). Boys tend to develop muscle strength more quickly than girls. Despite large muscle growth, upper body strength is less developed in 10-year-olds (Wood, 2007). Thus frequent physical activity is necessary to support growth. By the age of 10, children have developed the necessary gross motor skills responsible for the increased balance, agility, and flexibility that allows physical movement with greater precision, such as running and kicking (Frost, Wortham, & Reifel, 2008; Santrock, 2014; Wood, 2007). Furthermore, 10-year-olds are more coordinated in their body motions: They are capable of making swift movements and changes in direction as they steer their bodies (Ames et al., 1988; Frost et al., 2008; Greenspan, 1993). Ten-year-olds typically enjoy organized sports activities, which provide opportunities for them to continue developing their motor skills. Their engagement in organized sports also reflects the changes in their cognitive and social development. Ten-year-olds are organized, structured, and logical, and desire to be accepted by peers. As a result, their play reflects a need for order and a need to belong (Hughes, 2010; Wood, 2007).

Ten-year-olds enjoy playing and engaging in activities requiring the mastery of skills and stamina (Ames et al., 1988; Frost et al., 2008). Outdoor free play, in particular, provides children with rigorous physical benefits, for example the opportunity to run, chase, climb, jump, and skip. Physical activity, healthy snacks, and times of rest are helpful for the 10-year-old's swiftly growing body (Wood, 2007). Despite the benefits of physical activity, however, 10-year-olds are more susceptible to unintentional physical injury (Charlesworth, Wood, & Viggiani, 2011). Specifically, playground and bicycle injuries are very common in older children. This frequency of injuries indicates an increased need for monitoring of physical activity and teaching children about physical safety.

> Ten-year-old boys in particular have increased susceptibility to unintentional injuries.

At the age of 10, fine motors skills in particular are strengthened. Specifically, hand–eye coordination for drawing and writing improves (Davies, 2011). Writing skills and speed increases. However, penmanship at this age tends to be sloppy as children integrate learned writing skills (Davies, 2011; Wood, 2007). A noticeable difference is displayed in art: Drawings in late childhood show improvement in detail, organization, and depth (Berk, 2013). Typically, older children demonstrate drawings that are realistic, with distant objects smaller than those that are near. Around the ages of 9 and 10, children also display accuracy when drawing three-dimensional figures. For example, 10-year-olds can typically draw a cube, with attention to overlaps, diagonal placement, and emerging lines. This is a difficult skill to learn in earlier development.

Pubescent changes influence physical development in preadolescence for girls and boys, as reviewed in Table 11.1. After the age of 9, the trend of body growth reverses (Berk, 2013). During puberty, girls physically develop and accumulate body fat more quickly than boys (Madaras & Madaras, 2007). Growing pains come and go between the age of 10 and 11. Typically, minor aches occur in areas such as the knees, thighs, groin, and back. During their tenth year, most girls are on the verge of a spurt in height growth. At the age of 10, boys and girls have similar heights, although the growth of boys takes a much slower pace. Owing to estrogen hormones, girls go through a slight softening and rounding at this age, particularly in the hip region. Also noticeable are changes in breast development. Girls aged 10–11 years old are clearly aware of their own breast development and might be concerned if they do not see signs of this growth process. The process of breast growth follows a normative pattern, but some girls develop more slowly or faster than others. Body hair will also increase in this period of development. Preadolescent girls may begin developing hair on their arms, legs, underarms, and pubic area as a result of increased hormones. On average, girls start their menstrual cycle at 12 years old, but the range of onset is 9–15.

By the age of 10, boys display slight changes in their physique, with minor rounding off and softening of body curves, particularly in the chest, chin, and neck areas (Ames et al., 1998; Madaras & Madaras, 2007). Boys appear to have narrower waists as their shoulders broaden in preadolescence. Additionally, boys tend to have larger calves, thighs, and upper arms as their muscle growth increases. Boys reach their height spurt later than girls, but tend to grow longer trunks, making them appear shorter.

Puberty for boys typically begins between the ages of 9 and 14. One of the first physical indicators of puberty includes changes in genitalia: The size increases and growth quickens, while pubic hair also appears. During their tenth year, some boys may experience increased and spontaneous erections. This increase is normal and a result of the body's adjustment to the increased production of hormones. Erections tend to gradually reduce as the hormones are stabilized. This process has the potential to cause embarrassment and uncertainty for boys.

Girls experience faster sexual and social development than boys, and as a result have heighted sexual awareness. In comparison to boys, girls tend to become more embarrassed when learning information about sex. However, they like reading books about sex and babies. Boys take in sex information casually and, like girls, are attracted to reading simple books explaining the growth process and birth of babies (Ames et al., 1988). As proposed by Greenspan (1993), children aged 10 need to understand the "facts of life," but as presented in a developmentally appropriate way (Greenspan, 1993).

Ten-year-olds view sex roles as defined by social or shared expectations and norms. At this age, the child's sex identity and values are largely determined by conformity to social roles, and this conformity to social roles has a heavy basis in the distinction by gender. As children become more aware of their bodies, sexual information, and sexual roles, some also become aware of same-sex attractions, typically between the ages of 10 and 12 (Davies, 2011). Ten-year-olds are actively receptive to learning; thus it is an effective time to provide education on the human body, sex, and childrearing, because they are less self- conscious about their bodies.

COGNITIVE DEVELOPMENT

According to Piaget's cognitive theory, 10-year-olds are in the "concrete operational" stage of development. This stage is characterized by use of logical, adaptive, and orderly thought processes applied to concrete experiences (Berk, 2012; Santrock, 2014). As mentioned earlier in the chapter, changes in the frontal cortex are correlated with cognitive advances for 10-year-olds (Broderick & Blewitt, 2010; Sowell et al., 2004). At the age of 10, children demonstrate an increased capacity for logical reasoning and its application in many circumstances (Broderick & Blewitt, 2010; Ray, 2011). Operating from the concrete operational stage, 10-year-olds will think and process mainly through issues that they have experienced personally. They use basic cognitive processes to think about familiar events. However, at 10, children often find it difficult to resolve problems that are unfamiliar to them (Broderick & Blewitt, 2010; Rice, 1992). Logic and concrete understanding are vital cognitive processes that 10-year-olds experience; thus they are still prone to learning through doing (Ray, 2011).

> Ten-year-olds think and process information using real objects.

The categorization skills of children drastically improve during this developmental age (Santrock, 2014). Ten-year-olds have the ability to classify objects and things, for example a 10-year-old girl might collect beads and group them based on size, texture, and use. This is a skill that is completely different from that in earlier childhood when young children classify objects in only one way. Ten-year-olds are also interested in collecting, classifying, and organizing for school-related tasks. They are careful with homework, and keen on form, structure, directions, and organization (Wood, 2007). By the age of 10, children enjoy learning pictorial material, and are very good at memorization and solving problems (Davies, 2011). Ten-year-olds can use organization strategies to help with memorization of facts. They are often receptive

Table 11.1

Gender Differences in Physical Development

Girls	Boys
More developed fine motor skills	More developed gross motor skills
Faster growth in height	Slow steady growth in height
Increased body fat and less muscle mass	More muscle mass and less body fat
Broadening of hips and waist	Broadening of shoulders
Maturation in female reproductive organs	Maturation in male reproductive organs
Development of breasts	Development of testes
Increase in body hair (e.g. pubic and underarm)	Increase in body hair (e.g. pubic and underarm)
Curiosity about sexual development	Curiosity about sexual development

to learning and can master a great deal of factual information, such as multiplication tables. At 10, children are able to focus attention, while suppressing distracting impulses, and they experience an increased processing speed (Davies, 2011). They enjoy listening to stories and telling their own.

Moral Development

At the age of 10, children's moral abilities expand and are further developed. Although Kohlberg (1987) did not clearly specify stages for 10-year-olds, it can be inferred that children aged 10 would be at the "conventional" level of moral reasoning. As suggested by Kohlberg, children at this stage are characterized by "being nice" and showing concern about other people. For example, in response to Paul's attempt to block Mary's entry into class, she may remark, "Paul is a troublemaker and unkind – he's not a good person." A key milestone at this stage is the child's ability to put himself or herself in the other person's place and see things from that person's perspective (Kohlberg, 1987). Children demonstrate this capacity for empathy and try to think of reasons for their decisions, in the context of being nice to others and wanting others to be nice to them (Kohlberg, 1987). The child has a need to be perceived as good by others and that need drives the child's behavior. Ten-year-olds are often truthful, and in the process of developing a mature sense of right and wrong (Wood, 2007).

Parental modeling has been noted as influencing the morality that children internalize (Davies, 2011). Ten-year-olds admire their parents and easily respond to parents' instructions without resentment. Additionally, Piaget and Kohlberg both posited that peer relations played an important role in the development of moral reasoning. Piaget reasoned that, within the peer group, children negotiated and resolved disagreements; thus creating changes in moral reasoning (Santrock, 2014). At 10, Piaget suggested, the child shows autonomous morality, which involves awareness that people create rules and laws, and that intentions and consequences need to be taken into consideration when making decisions (Santrock, 2014).

> The moral sense of 10-year-olds is influenced by the need to be good and fair to others.

WORLDVIEW/EGO DEVELOPMENT

A unity of personality that ties all experience together is referred to as the "ego," or "self." The self develops as a whole, including a unified combination of cognitive, moral, and psychosexual features of development (Kohlberg, 1987). Ego development includes the holistic development of the child, comprising thoughts, feelings, and behavior (Ray, 2011). Loevinger (1976) conceptualized ego development as the inner structure or personality used by an individual to synthesize and give meaning to his or her experiences (Loevinger, 1976). In applying Loevinger's ego development theory, it may be presumed that typical 10-year-olds fall into the "conformist" stage. Within this stage, 10-year-olds are most concerned with group identification, following the rules and norms of their identified groups.

> Ten-year-olds have the capability for self-control and to tolerate emotional ambivalence.

Ten-year-olds begin to perceive their own welfare as associated to that of the group. Belonging to an identified group creates a sense of security for 10-year-olds. At this age, their peer group defines their self-image – that is, they define themselves by means of their perception of how they fit into their peer group at school (Davies, 2011; Greenspan, 1993). Typical 10-year-olds therefore display compliance with recognized groups and follow group rules. Their decision making is influenced by what they perceive to be beneficial or moral for the group. As conformists and concrete thinkers, 10-year-olds tend to stick to clear rules, which are socially approved, and condemn vague or unusual conduct (Loevinger, 1976; Ray, 2011). At this age, since children's self-images are typically defined by the group, Greenspan (1993, p. 83) describes the 10-year-old as at an "all-or-nothing stage of life".

Ten-year-olds are much more confident and sure of themselves than they were when they were younger (Gesell Institute, 2011; Wood, 2007). They are more in touch with their thoughts than their feelings, although they generally display a general sense of well-being (Ames et al., 1988). Ten-year-olds are able to picture or describe their feelings, but because of their organizational ways of thinking, 10-year-olds communicate their emotions logically, prioritizing certain emotions and categorizing them (Greenspan, 1993). Additionally, they are in the process of developing inner personal beliefs and values. Their developing sense of self is based on their interactions with friends, family, and significant others.

Based on Erikson's (1980) psychosocial identity theory, 10-year-olds are in the *industry vs. inferiority* stage. According to Erikson, 10-year-olds and other children at this stage have a need to become competent and productive in mastering new skills, desire to learn and make things, and need to learn the social rules in society. Ten-year-olds have a need for industry, developing a sense of mastery by means of the successful performance of varied activities (Hughes, 2010). Thus they will increasingly be drawn to activities in which they believe themselves to be competent. They have developed an awareness that they are good at certain things and not good at other things. Success in industry helps the 10-year-old to begin narrowing and honing certain skills and abilities.

> Ten-year-olds define their self-images by means of group norms.

At the age of 10, children are progressing through faith development and can typically be categorized in Fowler's (1981) "mythic-literal" stage. Fowler proposed that, during this stage, children have the ability to narrate their experiences. This means that, in relation to faith, they have the capacity to give meaning to their experiences through stories. Thus meanings are conserved and expressed through stories. The mind of the child at this stage works through concrete operations; thus he or she uses symbols to express his or her literal understanding of issues or concepts. Fowler further proposed that, during this stage, children are able to construct the perspectives of others, including the perspective of a "higher power."

Racial/Ethnic Identity Development

Racial and ethnic identity is heavily studied for early childhood, adolescence, and adulthood (Cabrera & SRCS Ethnic and Racial Issues Committee, 2013; Coll & Marks, 2009). However, available research for racial identity development in older children is sparse. Despite the limited research, current studies indicate that racial and ethnic identity is a normative and critical construct for child development, particularly critical for children of minority groups (Ponterotto & Park-Taylor, 2007). The racial identity process in preadolescence greatly influences identity development later in life (Coll & Marks, 2009). Sociocognitive developmental models are useful for understanding racial and ethnic identity development in preadolescent children. These models cover the developmental processes of cognitive skills and social factors related to the development of racial attitudes and identification with an ethnic group (Corenblum & Armstrong, 2012).

The emergence of racial identity development begins around the age of 10 (Moore-Thomas & Watkinson, 2013). As preadolescents develop cognitively and interact in their social environments, their understanding of their ethnic identity matures (Blackmon & Vera, 2008). Through these avenues, preadolescents begin to construct ideas about their race and ethnic identity. Ten-year-olds will typically present with questions and explore aspects of racial identity. Generally, the ideas and thoughts at this developmental age become the precursors to the racial identity processes that will become salient in adolescence and early adulthood (Coll & Marks, 2009).

By the age of 10, older children understand that race remains stable and understand their membership of a particular ethnic and racial group (Coll & Marks, 2009). This factor is distinctly different in early childhood, when young children have only a limited cognitive capacity to understand that ethnicity is unchangeable (Blackmon & Vera, 2008). Understanding racial permanency is a matter of a child understanding his or her own perspective and sense of self in the world. The 10-year-old can now identify and articulate the cultural, hereditary, and social factors that attach him or her to a particular ethnic group. The specific perspectives that 10-year-olds develop about their ethnic and racial membership are greatly influenced by the messages received from their caregivers and other significant others in their lives (Charlesworth et al., 2011). A focus on ethnic history, pride, and cultural values increases the positive views of a child toward racial identity. Moore-Thomas and Watkinson (2013) explained that it is imperative to address negative racial stereotypes and assumptions, along with cultural pride, at this

Deborah Ojiambo and LaKaavia Taylor

age – particularly among minority groups. Ten-year-olds are less likely to apply and internalize negative messages if they have a positive understanding of their respective ethnic groups. Furthermore, neglecting to address aspects of ethnic pride and understanding may foster a negative view of ethnic and racial identity.

In this developmental period, it is very common for children to have peers who come from similar ethnic and racial backgrounds (Charlesworth et al., 2011). Quintana and Scull (2009) explained that this is likely to be because of children's preference for similarity and assumptions of such among ethnic group membership. Unlike in earlier developmental periods, 10-year-olds show more ingroup favoritism toward same-ethnicity peers (Berk, 2013). It is for this reason that there is a possibility of unintentional discrimination and biases. Unintentional biases are likely to be linked to lack of contact with racially and ethnically different groups; thus children in this age period will benefit from exposure to children of different racial and ethnic groups.

EMOTIONAL DEVELOPMENT

In late childhood, children experience changes in their emotional development. They make great strides in their emotional awareness, understanding, and regulation (Berk, 2013). One area of emotional growth is in the expression of self-conscious emotions such as shame, envy, and pride. As older children gain a greater sense of self, the expression of self-conscious emotions is linked to personal responsibility rather than parental influence. Additionally, emotions in older childhood become linked to individual achievement and morals. Ten-year-olds are typically happy, but they can be quick to anger – and just as quick to forgive (Wood, 2007).

Anger is the most common emotional expression at the age of 10.

Ten-year-olds have a better understanding of the social expectations and rules related to communicating and expressing their emotions. In comparison to early developmental stages, older children are able to better appraise situations using social rules to determine and justify the appropriate emotional responses (Berk, 2013; Davies, 2011). For example, a 10-year-old boy might mask his anger at a parent at the grocery store because he is aware that anger should not be expressed in a public setting, or a 10-year-old girl might not express dislike for a friend's picture to avoid embarrassing her friend in front of their peers. Ten-year-olds adapt their emotional responses to be more socially acceptable, rather than for the purpose of avoiding ridicule or punishment, as was their rationale when they were younger.

Emotional coping using cognitive control of emotions is stronger in preadolescence. At the age of 10, preadolescents display increased accuracy in their appraisal of stressful situations (Berk, 2012; Saarni, 2011). They exhibit greater improvements in their ability to reflect on their feelings and appraisal. In response to stressful situations, preadolescents often engage in coping strategies and solutions to deal with the experiences. They might use more "problem-centered" or "emotionally focused" strategies to cope with perceived negative events (Berk, 2012).

- *Problem-centered* coping involves assessing the situation to determine control of the outcome and the difficulty followed by a plan, for example a child might problem solve with support from a peer or adult for an upset friend.
- *Emotionally focused* coping involves using internal emotions to shift focus away from intense emotions related to the experience: A child who did not achieve a desired win in a spelling bee might suppress his or her sadness or distract from his or her disappointment by saying, "I'll get another try next season."

SOCIAL DEVELOPMENT

At the age of 10, children have developed social perspective taking and to show increased understanding of other people's viewpoints, social expectations, and social demands of situations (Ames et al., 1988; Davies, 2011). Jane, a 10-year-old at a religious service, might be bored during part of the event, but will restrain herself from loudly expressing her feelings; instead, she will wait, able to behave in a socially appropriate way. With heightened social perspective taking,

10-year-olds are also aware of the psychological qualities and intentions of others (Ames et al., 1988; Davies, 2011). Apart from understanding the motives of others, they now have a good grasp of the rules of social interactions. At the age of 10, they are also drawn toward peer relationships and have developed social skills though peer interactions. Ten-year-olds are friendly and outgoing, seeking to join clubs, teams, and group activities (Wood, 2007). They view friendships as relationships that provide mutual support; thus they work to resolve conflicts to remain friends (Davies, 2011).

> A hallmark of 10-year-olds is heightened assumption of social perspectives.

Boys tend to get along well with friends of the same sex. Some 10-year-old boys have one or two "best," or "trusted," friends; other boys have a group, all of whom they refer to as "friends." Despite having many friends, some boys prefer playing with one friend at a time. Girls experience more difficulty in their relationships, characterized sometimes with intensity, such as getting angry, cutting off communication, and reconnecting with friends (Ames et al., 1988). Girls have many same-sex friends and often have a best friend. For girls, relationships among these friends can be extremely intricate and characterized by intense emotions. In response to a friend who annoyed her, a 10-year-old girl might say, "We didn't talk for a few days – but then we started talking when Rose was a little nicer." Ten-year-old girls also emphasize secrets and the need to trust friends: A 10-year-old might say, "Even if Joy gets mad at me, I know she won't tell anyone anything about me. I trust her." Regarding opposite-sex friends, girls and boys show limited interest in each other as peer groups (Ames et al., 1988).

RELATIONSHIP DEVELOPMENT

Typically, 10-year-olds enjoy family and friends, and show lovable traits, and this eagerness is demonstrated by sharing things, which are important to them, such as class projects. They love their friends and are pleased when their friends can be trusted. In their relationships, they engage fully in peer groups and are quite aware of their roles in groups. Group initiatives and challenges are a great success at this age. Ten-year-olds are reasonably calm and show cooperative pursuits.

Ten-year-olds maintain nurturing relationships with parents and seek their help in navigating through peer relationships (Greenspan, 1993). Ten-year-olds tend to value their parents, recognizing the strengths of both mother and father. Ten-year-olds respond positively to parents' instructions, and still need a lot of supervision and direction (Ames et al., 1988). They do, however, show a relative decrease in intensity of attachment behavior as part of their normal developmental growth. Most 10-year-olds can tolerate short separations (that is, one week) from primary caregivers, but may have difficulty enduring long separations (that is, three weeks) (Mayseless, 2005). Although primary caregivers are still their main secure attachment figures, 10-year-olds are now able to seek support from peers when needed. There is a continued developmental process of children increasingly using peer relationships to meet some of their attachment needs, including some of the emotional security previously sought in the parent–child relationship (Davies, 2011; Mayless, 2005). Most 10-year-olds have difficulty relating to siblings, especially the younger ones. Although they are good at caring for or helping with young siblings, they can be competitive with siblings closer in age.

DEVELOPMENT IN THE AGE OF TECHNOLOGY

Technology today is changing the way in which people learn, communicate, and socialize. In fact, Taylor (2012) explained that technology is one the most powerful forces in society today. Because of the numerous technological advancements, technology consumes the everyday lives of Americans, from television to smartphones. In most families, children's exposure to technology occurs much earlier than it did for previous generations. There is a consequent rise in media and technology use by children (Strasburger, Jordan, & Donnerstein, 2010). Television viewing is the most frequent form of media used, followed by listening to music, using the computer, and playing video games. The Kaiser Foundation found that children between the ages of 8 and 10 spend about seven hours a day using noneducational media technology (Rideout, Foehr, & Roberts, 2010). This amount is considerably higher that the recommendation by the American Academy of Pediatrics (AAP, 2013) of no more than two hours a day of screen time for children.

Watching television impacts on preadolescent development. Children aged 6–12 often spend more time watching television than playing and engaging in other activities (Boyd & Bee, 2012). Ten-year-olds show decreased interest in cartoons, with an increased preference for adventure, comedies, and sitcoms (Comstock & Scharrer, 2007). This shift in preference is related to their increased cognitive capacities to understand and process more realistic content. However, preadolescents may occasionally struggle with distinguishing between reality and fantasy, because their cognitive processes are still evolving. Ten-year-olds are capable of handling action-oriented television and fantasy violence, without gore and extreme violence (Knorr, 2013). Preadolescents have difficulty processing and an increased risk of misinterpreting adult-oriented content (AACAP, 2011).

Excessive television viewing has negative influences on development, such as limiting the time that children spend socializing, studying, with family, and in physical activity (Boyd & Bee, 2012). Television only in moderation is therefore critical for development. Despite the negative influences of television, some benefits exist: Educational television positively impacts on behaviors and attitudes if targeted at concepts such as science, history, or racial tolerance. Additionally, age-appropriate television shows allow children to be exposed to socially acceptable methods of approaching problems and aspects of creativity. Parental monitoring, regulation, and discussion are thus necessary to help to ensure appropriate exposure and to reduce negative influences.

The Internet, whether on PC, laptop, or tablet, is commonly used by most children, whether at school or in their home environment, with about 60 percent of children using the Internet on a regular basis (Boyd & Bee, 2012). Many preadolescents use the Internet with some autonomy. Internet connections can be useful for preadolescents to complete homework assignments, research information, and engage in learning games. Additionally, social media can be used to connect with others and to entertain. However, the Internet exposes children to content and media that may not be developmentally appropriate. For parents of preadolescents, controlling and maintaining boundaries when allowing their children to browse the Internet can be challenging. Often, preadolescents do not realize the digital footprint that they leave behind, and may not understand the effects and risks of their actions. Further, with greater Internet and social media use, children are at increased risk of exposure to bullying (in the form of cyberbullying – that is, the use of electronic media to repeatedly harass, humiliate, and threaten others), harassment, and adult content. In recent years, cyberbullying has become prevalent, particularly through social media outlets (Sabella, 2009). Children therefore benefit from limited and monitored use of computer connections – and parents may even consider delaying social media connectivity until a child reaches adolescence, or may limit the child's use of social media to occur only with parental presence.

The influences of video gaming are similar to those other forms of technology – that is, they have both positive and negative influences on development. Video games provide children with the opportunity to engage in learning, with the most noted development being in spatial-cognitive abilities as a result of tracking, mentally manipulating, and planning different strategies within video games (Boyd & Bee, 2012; Paturel, 2014). The brain is affected as well when children play video games – but the focus of concern is on the risks of video game usage among children. Areas of concern include inappropriate lengths of time spent playing games, changes in mood, and decreased social contact (Paturel, 2014). Furthermore, video games containing violence are thought to influence the emotions of older children, particularly emotional hostility, with a consequent reduction in empathy. Increased and repetitive exposure to violence can be problematic for children, impacting on their behavioral and cognitive responses. Parents therefore benefit from being familiar with games played by their children and may even become players themselves to maintain a relevant connection with the child.

BEST PRACTICES IN COUNSELING/THERAPY

When Counseling/Therapy Is Indicated

As discussed in this chapter, 10-year-olds are generally well adjusted and happy, and have reached a period of stability. Counseling might be considered necessary when a 10-year-old has no friends, dislikes school, or displays emotional and social difficulties. Additionally, if a child does not express a sense of belonging in a recognized group, this might be an area of concern. At the age 10, children also have a need to experience a sense of mastery or competence; thus if they are struggling with finding areas of competence, they might need help.

Developmentally Appropriate Approaches

To optimally facilitate the therapeutic process with 10-year-olds, it is vital for counselors to establish inviting counseling environments with age-appropriate materials. Developmentally, 10-year-olds lack the cognitive ability and skills with which to fully benefit from therapies reliant only on verbal expression. As concrete operational children, their thinking and problem solving are easier for them when they use real events or symbols (Broderick & Blewitt, 2010). In the context of their learning process – learning by doing – effective counseling will offer a setting in which they can engage in activity and use symbolic expressive materials.

The materials selected for an activity room for 10-year-olds need to foster peer interaction, enhance creative expression, encourage the exploration of feelings, thoughts, and experiences, facilitate the expression of real-life concerns, and enhance children's development of problem-solving strategies (Bratton & Ferebee, 1999; Bratton, Ceballos, & Ferebee, 2009). Also, large, open space fits the needs of 10-year-olds, who benefit from physical challenges and movement (Bratton & Ferebee, 1999; Bratton, Ray, Edwards, & Landreth, 2009; Packman & Bratton, 2003; Sweeney, Baggerly, & Ray, 2014). The materials selected should also be culturally appropriate to the group with which the 10-year-old identifies (see Ojiambo & Bratton, 2014).

Activity play therapy provides concrete materials that allow 10-year-olds to make sense of their world or experiences through physical manipulation. As concrete operational children, 10-year-olds are developing abilities to think about symbols and meaning; hence children at this point still need concrete materials to facilitate their learning experiences (Broderick & Blewitt, 2010; Ray, 2011). Provision of concrete materials for 10-year-olds in the context of activity play therapy fosters their process of creating meaning of the world and responds to the developmental need of children at the concrete operations stage. Also, the appeal or structure of activity play therapy meets the 10-year-old's need to be competent and productive (Hughes, 2010; Wood, 2007).

> A hallmark for therapy with 10-year-olds is using expressive symbolic materials.

Activity play therapy can be facilitated using varied modalities, such as collage, sandtray play, modelling, drawing, and puppetry (Bratton & Ferebee, 1999; Bratton, Ceballos, & Ferebee, 2009; Oaklander, 1988). Also, modalities such as sandtray play enable 10-year-olds to easily use symbolic expression. Activity play therapy can also be provided in a group format, which provides further developmentally appropriate benefits for 10-year-olds. Research studies have indicated that group activity play therapy (GAPT) is an effective modality among preadolescents (Flahive & Ray, 2007; Ojiambo & Bratton, 2014; Packman & Bratton, 2003; Shen & Armstrong, 2008). Peers and relational expression are characteristic of 10-year-olds; thus they can benefit from group activity therapy, which provides 10-year-olds with both verbal and nonverbal options for developing relationships, and working through and resolving conflicts (Bratton & Ferebee, 1999; Bratton, Ceballos, & Ferebee, 2009).

Group counseling is another modality of choice for 10-year-olds, because at this age they are more responsive to change founded on group acceptance. Also, the group provides the relational connection that is vital for a 10-year-old's growth and meets his or her developmental need for a sense of belonging (Davies, 2011; Ray, 2011; Wood, 2007). As the 10-year-old interacts with peers, he or she is influenced by those peers' opinions, integrating these into his or her developing sense of self. Additionally, the group format provides 10-year-olds with an environment in which they can enhance the development of their social skills, learn self-control, confront difficulties, problem solve, and make decisions (Packman & Bratton, 2003).

Child-centered activity play therapy (CCAPT) Child-centered activity play therapy (CCAPT) can be a developmentally appropriate modality for 10-year-olds. It is conducted in an activity room, with materials that encourage the expression of all feelings and thoughts, and a wide range of personal and cultural experiences. In using the child-centered approach, therapists believe that they achieve a counseling relationship in which children experience genuineness, caring, and profound nonjudgmental understanding, which helps them to attain constructive change (Bratton, Ray et al., 2009; Landreth, 2012; Ray, 2011; Ray & Schottelkorb, 2009). This high level of relational interaction matches to the 10-year-old's need for developing relationships within a safe environment. The accepting relationship provided during CCAPT allows children to feel safe to examine experiences perceived as inconsistent with their self (Ray, 2011). Ten-year-olds are formulating their self-structures; thus CCAPT frees them to explore their emerging selves within an accepting safe environment, which nurtures the child's attitude of self-worth and self-acceptance (Ray, 2011; Ray & Schottelkorb, 2009; Sweeney et al., 2014). Because the 10-year-old feels positively regarded, he or she is able to behaviorally express and explore his or her feelings and thoughts through play and symbolic expression.

Cognitive-behavioral play therapy (CBPT) Cognitive-behavioral play therapy (CBPT) can also be considered developmentally appropriate for 10-year-olds. Cognitive-behavioral therapists/ theorists view cognitive distortions as the basis of human behavior and thought. In working with children, these distortions are perceived as maladaptive, and thus can lead to problematic behaviors or beliefs (Knell, 2009). The therapeutic process used by cognitive-behavioral play therapists while working with children to deal with these distortions integrates cognitive and behavioral approaches using play materials and activities (Knell, 2009). Using symbolic materials resonates with 10-year-olds, who are developing logical thinking abilities within concrete operations. Cognitive-behavioral therapy without play, however, may be of only limited use with 10-year-olds because of their continued need to learn by doing, with active manipulation of materials.

Within the CBPT philosophy, components highlighted include the establishing of goals, the use of therapy for education, the selection of play materials and activities, and praise and interpretations (Knell, 2009). The cognitive-behavioral play therapist works with the child in establishing goals, and selecting play materials and activities. By means of the materials and activities, a cognitive-behavioral play therapist will facilitate a child's identification and changing of maladaptive beliefs and thoughts, to enhance his or her personal understanding, ideally resulting in empowerment or improved functioning (Knell, 2009).

Some of the strategies used within CBPT are likely to resonate with 10-year-olds, such as roleplaying to identify adaptive and positive behavior. Cognitive-behavioral play therapists also employ forms of contingency management, such as worksheets for anger management, improvement of self-esteem, and reduction of anxiety (Knell, 2009). At the age of 10, children are able to solve logical problems using multiple strategies, and worksheets provide concrete materials that may facilitate that process. Geldard and Geldard (2002) provided examples of worksheets that can be used by cognitive-behavioral play therapists.

Praise and encouragement within the CBPT intervention may meet the 10-year-old's need for affirmation as he or she works toward a sense of mastery and competence (Knell, 1994, 2009). Educational strategies used in CBPT fit the 10-year-old's desire to learn – especially to learn information that may be presented in playful ways by means of stories, puppets, and materials. Because CBPT is presented as short, structured, directive, and problem focused, 10-year-olds may positively respond to the presentation of structure and direction (Knell, 2009).

Adlerian play therapy (AdPT) Adlerian play therapy (AdPT) is another activity therapy considered to be developmentally appropriate for 10-year-old children. Within Adlerian personality theory, some of the key features, such as the need to belong and to gain significance, resonate with the need of a 10-year-old to belong to a group (Kottman, 2009). While working through the phases of AdPT, play therapists use play and varied structured activities that engage 10-year-olds. Structured activities, such as asking questions, roleplaying, storytelling, bibliotherapy, using metaphors, and expressive arts, are utilized (Kottman, 2009). At the age of 10, children are in an ongoing process of self-understanding; thus these strategies, presented by Adlerian play therapists within a supportive relationship, help the child to make desired changes in his or her beliefs, feelings, and actions. At 10, children appreciate order and organization; hence the structure presented in AdPT is likely to resonate with 10-year-olds.

In the reorienting and re-educating phase of AdPT, therapists use strategies such as brainstorming, modeling, playing games, teaching new skills such as anger management, and sharing metaphors (Kottman, Bryant, Alexander, & Kroger, 2009). At the age of 10, children can comprehend the therapeutic process applied through these approaches and match it with their concrete operational thinking. A key component of the therapist's approach is using encouragement with children: The Adlerian play therapist encourages children within an environment that communicates unconditional acceptance, enhancing the child's feeling of capability and the process of gaining significance.

Adlerian play therapists also work with children to develop positive goals, known as the "Crucial 'C's" (Kottman, 2010). The play therapist facilitates the child's experience of being *connected* with others, feeling *capable*, feeling that he or she *counts*, and developing *courage*, all of which meet the social needs of a typical 10-year-old. Adlerian play therapists emphasize the concept of social embeddedness, which resonates with the 10-year-old's need to belong. Indeed, Kottman (2003) posited that therapists encourage social interest as they build a relationship with the child (Kottman, 2003).

Gestalt play therapy   Gestalt play therapy, developed by Oaklander (1988), is considered developmentally appropriate for 10-year-old children because of the experiential nature of its techniques. Carroll (2009) described the key concepts in Gestalt theory as including the view that children engage in a process of organismic self-regulation as they regulate behavior to meet the needs being experienced (Carroll, 2009). As a child interacts with his or her environment, he or she moves toward meeting his or her pressing organismic needs. Carroll further explained that the interaction of child with the environment, referred to as "contact" in Gestalt theory, is the pillar of the experience that facilitates development of the self, perceived as vital for a child's healthy functioning. At the age of 10, children are developing their sense of self, which resonates with the Gestalt focus on the self.

In working with children using Gestalt play therapy, the goal is help a child to re-establish healthy organismic self-regulation, to enhance his or her awareness of internal and external experiences, and to facilitate his or her use of the resources in the environment to get his or her needs met (Carroll, 2009). In working toward the attainment of therapeutic goals, Gestalt play therapists use play materials and activities in the context of a positive trusting relationship with the child and with significant others in child's life. Gestalt play therapy can be a particularly useful modality for 10-year-olds because of the experiential nature of the techniques: Such techniques as storytelling, poetry, symbol play, sandtray play, and drawing lend themselves to 10-year-olds' preferences and abilities (Carroll, 2009; Oaklander, 1988). Oaklander (1988) and Carroll (2009) presented detailed descriptions of using varied Gestalt child therapy techniques in working with children, including 10-year-olds.

Working with Parents, Teachers, and Caretakers

In working with parents or caretakers and teachers of 10-year-old children, consideration of developmentally responsive approaches is vital. Ten-year-olds respond positively to parents and maintain nurturing relationships. Using this potential for a stable relationship, parents and 10-year-olds might be responsive to principles from the child–parent relationship therapy (CPRT) model developed by Bratton, Landreth, Kellam, & Blackard (2006) to foster relationship building skills. Child–parent relationship therapy can be especially helpful for this age group when materials and activity sessions are modified to fit the developmental needs of an older child. At the age of 10, children might enjoy activities such as crafts, cooking, and board games. Child–parent relationship therapy provides opportunities for parents to offer relational attunement by means of reflective listening, self-esteem building, and appropriate encouragement responses.

The systematic training for effective parenting (STEP) program, developed by Dinkmeyer, McKay, and Dinkmeyer (1997), is a parent training program suitable for teachers and parents of 10-year-olds. It targets the social, behavioral, and academic factors that impact on the overall functioning of children – factors that are pertinent because the needs of 10-year-olds involve family relationships, mastery, and self-regulation. Parents are provided with positive discipline strategies with which to understand child's behavior, facilitate responsibility, and improve communication with the children at home and in the classroom. Program facilitators engage parents and teachers in roleplaying, group exercises, and outside activities to increase retention of skills and training content. The systematic training for effective *teaching* (STET) version of the STEP resource was developed allow teachers to engage 10-year-olds within groups and to enhance discipline (Dinkmeyer & McKay, 1980).

Parents and teachers might also use self-help books to support the development, relationships, and communication patterns with children. In *How to Talk So Kids Will Listen and Listen So Kids Will Talk* (Faber & Mazlish, 2004), the authors provide parents with practical ways in which to support and communicate with children so as to reduce parent–child relationship stress (Faber & Mazlish, 2004). In addition, the authors offer illustrations and specific examples to help parents to understand reflective responses, limits, and alternatives to punishment. This particular book might help parents of 10-year-olds value and understand the experiences of their children. *Between Parent and Child* (Ginott, Ginott, & Goddard, 2003), *Positive Discipline* (Nelsen, 2006), and *Positive Discipline in the Classroom* (Nelsen, Lott, & Glenn, 2000) are other self-help resources for parents and teachers of 10-year-olds who are showing increased moral reasoning and responsibility. These texts provide parents and teachers with practical strategies to facilitate self-discipline, problem solving, and compliance in the classroom and home environment.

Finally, there are resources available online that might help parents and teachers to meet the increasing technological needs of 10-year-olds. Russell Sabella's website, http://www.school-counselor.com is a helpful site for teachers working with children in developing responsible use of technology (Sabella, n.d.). Parents might also find the site https://www.commonsense-media.org useful for selecting age-appropriate media, such as books, movies, games, apps, and websites (Common Sense Media, n.d.a). The site also provides rating and reviews of different forms of media. Another related site is https://www.commonsenseeducation.org, which provides teachers with ratings and reviews of web-based learning models and curricula (Common Sense Media, n.d.b).

CONCLUSION

The tenth year is a smooth and stable period for children and parents. For 10-year-olds, peer, family, and teacher relationships hold great interest and importance. At this age, a child focuses on refining his or her academic skills and maintaining his or her social relationships. Noticeable maturation occurs in emotional and cognitive development, greatly influencing improvements in how children think, feel, and process information. These maturational changes allow for increased executive functioning and self-efficacy. Ten-year-olds additionally experience greater physical and pubescent changes that alter their body composition. As a result, children will need emotional and physical support to help them to navigate and understand these changes as they move toward independence and greater maturation.

REFERENCES

American Academy of Children and Adolescent Psychiatry (AACAP). (2011). Children and watching TV. *Facts for Families, 54*. Retrieved from http://www.aacap.org/App_Themes/AACAP/docs/facts_for_families/54_children_and_watching_tv.pdf

American Academy of Pediatrics (AAP). (2013). Policy statement: Children, adolescents, and the media. *Pediatrics, 132*(5), 958–961.

Ames, L. B., Ilg, F. L., & Baker, S. M. (1988). *Your ten-to-fourteen-year-old*. New York, NY: Dell.

Berk, L. (2012). *Child development* (9th ed.). Boston, MA: Pearson.

Berk, L. (2013). *Exploring lifespan development* (3rd ed.). Boston, MA: Pearson.

Blackmon, S. A., & Vera, E. M. (2008). Ethnic and racial identity development in children of color. In J. K. Asamen, M. L. Ellis, & G. L. Berry.

(Eds.), *The Sage handbook of child development, multiculturalism, and media* (pp. 47–61). Los Angeles, CA: Sage.

Boyd, D., & Bee, H. (2012). *Lifespan development* (6th ed.). Boston, MA: Pearson.

Bratton, S. C., & Ferebee, K. W. (1999). The use of structured expressive art activities in group activity therapy with preadolescents. In D. S. Sweeney & L. E. Homeyer. (Eds.), *The handbook of group play therapy: How to do it, how it works, whom it's best for* (pp. 192–214). San Francisco, CA: Jossey-Bass.

Bratton, S. C., Ceballos, P. L., & Ferebee, K. W. (2009). Integration of structured expressive activities within a humanistic group play therapy format for preadolescents. *Journal for Specialists in Group Work, 34*(3), 251–275.

Bratton, S. C., Landreth, G. L., Kellam, T., & Blackard, S. R. (2006). *Child–parent relationship therapy (CPRT) treatment manual.* New York, NY: Routledge.

Bratton, S. C., Ray, D. C., Edwards, N. A., & Landreth, G. (2009). Child-centered play therapy (CCPT): Theory, research, and practice. *Person-Centered and Experiential Psychotherapies, 8*(4), 266–281.

Broderick, P. C., & Blewitt, P. (2010). *The life span: Human development for helping professionals* (3rd ed.). Boston, MA: Pearson.

Cabrera, N., & SRCD Ethnic and Racial Issues Committee. (2013). Positive development of minority children. *Social Policy Report, 27*(2). Retrieved from http://www.srcd.org/sites/default/files/documents/washington/spr_272_final.pdf

Carroll, F. (2009). Gestalt play therapy. In K. O'Connor & L. Braverman. (Eds.), *Play therapy theory and practice: Comparing theories and techniques* (2nd ed., pp. 283–314). Hoboken, NJ: Wiley.

Charlesworth, L., Wood, J., & Viggiani, P. (2011). Middle childhood. In E. D. Hutchinson. (Ed.), *Dimensions of human behavior: The changing life course* (pp. 170–219). Thousand Oaks, CA: Sage.

Coll, G., & Marks, A. (2009). *Immigrant stories: Ethnicity and academics in middle childhood.* New York, NY: Oxford University Press.

Common Sense Media. (n.d.a). Reviews and age ratings: Best movies, books, apps, games for kids. Retrieved from https://www.commonsensemedia.org/

Common Sense Media. (n.d.b). Media and technology resources for educators. Retrieved from https://www.commonsensemedia.org/educators

Comstock, G., & Scharrer, E. (2007). *Media and the American child.* Burlington, MA: Academic Press.

Corenblum, B., & Armstrong, H. (2012). Racial-ethnic identity development in children in a racial-ethnic minority group. *Canadian Journal of Behavioural Science, 44*(2), 124–137.

Davies, D. (2011). *Child development: A practitioners' guide* (3rd ed.). New York, NY: Guilford.

Dinkmeyer, D., & McKay, G. (1980). *The STET: Systematic training for effective teaching – Teacher's handbook.* Circle Pines, MN: American Guidance Service.

Dinkmeyer, D., McKay, G., & Dinkmeyer, D. (1997). *The parent's handbook: Systematic training for effective parenting* (4th ed.). Fredericksburg, VA: STEP.

Erikson, E. (1980). *Identity and the life cycle.* New York, NY: Norton.

Faber, A., & Mazlish, E. (2004). *How to talk so kids will listen and listen so kids will talk.* New York, NY: HarperCollins.

Fields, R. (2005). Myelination: An overlooked mechanism of synaptic plasticity? *Neuroscientist, 11*(6), 528–531.

Flahive, M. W., & Ray, D. (2007). Effects of group sandtray therapy with preadolescents. *Journal for Specialists in Group Work, 32*(4), 362–382.

Fowler, J. (1981). *Stages of faith: The psychology of human development and the quest for meaning.* San Francisco, CA: Harper & Row.

Frost, J. L., Wortham, S. C., & Reifel, R. S. (2008). *Play and child development* (3rd ed.). Upper Saddle River, NJ: Pearson/Merrill Prentice Hall.

Geldard, K., & Geldard, D. (2002). *Counselling children: A practical introduction* (2nd ed.). London: Sage.

Gesell Institute of Child Development. (2011). *Gesell Developmental Observation–Revised examiner's manual.* New Haven, CT: Gesell Institute.

Ginott, H. G., Ginott, A., & Goddard, H. W. (2003). *Between parent and child.* New York, NY: Three Rivers Press.

Greenspan, S. (1993). *Playground politics: Understanding the emotional life of your school-age child.* Reading, MA: Addison-Wesley.

Hughes, F. P. (2010). *Children, play, and development* (4th ed.). San Francisco, CA: Sage.

Knell, S. M. (1994). Cognitive behavioral play therapy. In K. J. O'Connor & C. E. Schaefer (Eds.), *Handbook of play therapy: Advances and innovations, vol. 2* (pp. 111–142). New York: John Wiley & Sons.

Knell, S. M. (2009). Cognitive-behavioral play therapy. In K. O'Connor & L. D. Braverman (Eds.), *Play therapy theory and practice: Comparing theories and techniques* (2nd ed.) (pp. 203–236). Hoboken, NJ: John Wiley & Sons.

Knorr, C. (2013). Tips on how to deal with media violence [Web log]. February 13. Retrieved from https://www.commonsensemedia.org/blog/tips-on-how-to-deal-with-media-violence

Kohlberg, L. (1987). *Child psychology and childhood education: A cognitive-developmental view.* New York, NY: Longman.

Kottman, T. (2003). *Partners in play: An Adlerian approach to play therapy* (2nd ed.). Alexandria, VA: American Counseling Association.

Kottman, T. (2009). Adlerian play therapy. In K. O'Connor & L. Braverman. (Eds.), *Play therapy theory and practice: Comparing theories and techniques* (2nd ed., pp. 237–282). Hoboken, NJ: Wiley.

Kottman, T. (2010). *Play therapy: Basics and beyond* (2nd ed.). Alexandria, VA: American Counseling Association.

Kottman, T., Bryant, J., Alexander, J., & Kroger, S. (2009). Partners in the schools: Adlerian school counseling. In A. Vernon & T. Kottman. (Eds.), *Counseling theories: Practical applications with children and adolescents in school settings* (pp. 47–83). Denver, CO: Love.

Landreth, G. L. (2012). *Play therapy: The art of the relationship* (3rd ed.). New York: Routledge.

Loevinger, J. (1976). *Ego development*. San Francisco, CA: Jossey-Bass.

Madaras, L., & Madaras, A. (2007). *The "What's happening to my body?" book for girls* (3rd ed. rev'd). New York, NY: Newmarket Press.

Mayseless, O. (2005). Ontogeny of attachment in middle childhood: Conceptualization of normative changes. In K. A. Kerns & R. A. Richardson. (Eds.), *Attachment in middle childhood* (pp. 1–23). New York, NY: Guilford.

Moore-Thomas, C., & Watkinson, J. S. (2013). Conversations with children: Discussions about race and identity. In S. Grineski, J. Landsman, & R. Simmons. (Eds.), *Talking about race: Alleviating the fear* (pp. 93–101). Sterling, VA: Stylus.

Nelsen, J. E. (2006). *Positive discipline*. New York, NY: Ballantine Books.

Nelsen, J. E., Lott, L., & Glenn, S. (2000). *Positive discipline in the classroom: Developing mutual respect, cooperation, and responsibility in your classroom*. New York, NY: Three Rivers Press.

Oaklander, V. (1988). *Windows to our children*. Highland, NY: Gestalt Journal Press.

Ojiambo, D., & Bratton, S. (2014). Effects of group activity play therapy on problem behaviors of preadolescent Ugandan orphans. *Journal of Counseling & Development, 92*(3), 355–365.

Packman, J., & Bratton, S. C. (2003). A school-based group play/activity therapy intervention with learning disabled preadolescents exhibiting behavior problems. *International Journal of Play Therapy, 12*(2), 7–29.

Paturel, A. (2014). Game theory: How do video games affect the developing brains of children and teens? *Neurology Now, 10*(3), 32–36.

Ponterotto, J., & Park-Taylor, J. (2007). Racial and ethnic identity theory, measurement, and research in counseling psychology: Present status and future directions. *Journal of Counseling Psychology, 54*(3), 282–294.

Quintana, S. M., & Scull, N. C. (2009). Latino ethnic identity. In F. A. Villarreal, G. Carlo, J. M. Grau, M. Azmitia, N. J. Cabrera, & T. J. Chahin. (Eds.), *Handbook of US Latino psychology: Developmental and community-based perspectives* (pp. 81–98). Thousand Oaks, CA: Sage.

Ray, D. (2011). *Advanced play therapy: Essentials conditions, knowledge, and skills for child practice*. New York, NY: Taylor & Francis.

Ray, D. C., & Schottelkorb, A. A. (2009). Practical person-centered theory application in the schools. In A. Vernon & T. Kottman (Eds.), *Counseling theories: Practical applications with children and adolescents in school settings* (pp. 1–45). Denver, CO: Love.

Rice, F. P. (1992). *Human development: A life-span approach*. New York, NY: Macmillian.

Rideout, V., Foehr, U., & Roberts, D. (2010). Generation of M²: Media in the lives of 8 to 18-year-olds – A Kaiser foundation study. Retrieved from https://kaiserfamilyfoundation.files.wordpress.com/2013/01/8010.pdf

Saarni, C. (2011). Emotional development in childhood. In R. Tremblay, M. Boivin, & R. Peters. (Eds.), *Encyclopedia on early childhood development* (pp. 1–7). Montreal, QC: Centre of Excellence for Early Childhood Development and Strategic Knowledge Cluster on Early Child Development.

Sabella, R. (2009). Cyberbullying: Who, what, where, why, and what now? *Counseling and Human Development, 8*(41), 1–16.

Sabella, R. (n.d.). Home page. Retrieved from http://www.schoolcounselor.com/

Santrock, J. (2014). *Essentials of lifespan development* (3rd ed.). New York, NY: McGraw Hill.

Shen, Y., & Armstrong, S. A. (2008). Impact of group sandtray on the self-esteem of young adolescent girls. *Journal for Specialists in Group Work, 33*(2), 118–137.

Siegel, D. J., & Bryson, T. P. (2011). *The whole brain child: 12 Revolutionary strategies to nurture your child's developing mind*. New York, NY: Delacorte Press.

Sowell, E. R., Thompson, P. M., Leonard, C. M., Welcome, S. E., Kan, E., & Toga, A. W. (2004). Longitudinal mapping of cortical thickness and brain growth in normal children. *Journal of Neuroscience, 24*(38), 8223–8231.

Sowell, E. R., Thompson, P. M., Tessner, K. D., & Toga, A. W. (2001) Mapping continued brain growth and gray matter density reduction in dorsal frontal cortex: Inverse relationships during postadolescent brain maturation. *Journal of Neuroscience 21*(22), 8819–8829.

Strasburger, V., Jordan, A., & Donnerstein, E. (2010). Health effects of media on children and adolescents. *Pediatrics, 12*(4), 1–12.

Sweeney, D. S., Baggerly, J. N., & Ray, D. C. (2014) *Group play therapy: A dynamic approach*. New York: Routledge.

Taylor, J. (2012). *Raising generation tech: Preparing your children for a media-fueled world*. Naperville, IL: Sourcebooks.

Toga, A. W., Thompson, P. M., & Sowell, E. R. (2006). Mapping brain maturation. *Trends in Neurosciences, 29*(3), 148–159.

Wood, C. (2007). *Yardsticks: Children in the classroom ages 4–14* (3rd ed.). Turners Falls, MA: Northeast Foundation for Children.

12

THE EXTRAORDINARY 11-YEAR-OLD

Katie Purswell

Eleven is a difficult age for most children because they move from enthusiastically embracing the joys, challenges, and excitement of childhood, and begin to make their first forays into the world of adolescence, hormones, and acceptance of adult roles. In some school districts, sixth-graders are placed in elementary school; in others, they are placed in middle school. Both parents and teachers seem to be just as confused as 11-year-olds about where the children belong.

Jeremy is an outgoing 11-year-old. At the age of 10, he loved playing all sports and spent much of his spare time playing pickup games with the neighborhood kids or creating elaborate LEGO structures, such as models of cranes or airplanes, complete with moving pieces. He still enjoys these things, although he now prefers to focus more on baseball and soccer than other sports, and is increasingly able to implement the strategy and skill associated with these sports. He also still plays with LEGO, but instead of spending hours creating masterpieces in his room, he brings them out into the middle of the house, becoming upset when one of his younger siblings tampers with his creations. Mom tries to reason with him, explaining that if he were to keep his LEGO pieces in his room, they would be safer, but he angrily retorts that this is his house too and he has the right to play in the living room if he wants to do so: It is not fair that the only place his work can be safe is in his bedroom. Jeremy demands that his rights be respected.

Jeremy has never been much of a crier, but he is often tearful at this age. When he feels he is being treated unfairly, he often runs crying from the room and slams his bedroom door. Other than these episodes, Jeremy does not spend much time in his room. He seems constantly to want to be in the center of what the family is doing. Although his parents understand that he needs to feel a part of the family, they sometimes wish that he would spend more time taking a break from the family to cool down rather than spontaneously expressing whatever emotion he is feeling at the time, which tends to contribute to a rocky family environment.

Understanding the changes happening for Jeremy and other 11-year-olds across different aspects of development can help others in their lives respond to them in helpful ways.

BRAIN DEVELOPMENT

Although the amount of physical brain growth between childhood and adolescence is not particularly great, especially when compared with the rapid brain growth of the infant and toddler, important developmental processes are continuing to take place in the 11-year-old's brain (Siegel & Payne Bryson, 2011; Sowell, Thompson, Tessner, & Toga, 2001). The temporal cortex is one area that is still growing, and it is related to verbal and language abilities (Badenoch, 2008; Sowell et al., 2001). This growth is likely to be responsible for the 11-year-old's growing verbal reasoning skills and budding abstract reasoning skills, that will be discussed later (Sowell et al., 2001).

During late childhood and early adolescence, a thinning of gray matter occurs in the same areas in which growth is appearing, and neuroscientists hypothesize that this phenomenon is caused by an increase in myelination of the synaptic connections in the brain (Sowell et al., 2004). Myelination is an important aspect of brain development because it essentially streamlines the connections between the parts of the brain, increasing the 11-year-old's ability to process information and to respond to stimuli more quickly (Sowell et al., 2001). The left side of the brain is the part of the brain generally linked to logic, language, reasoning, and information (Badenoch, 2008; Siegel & Payne Bryson, 2011). It is part of the brain that likes sums to add up and lists to be checked off. The right side of the brain is responsible for emotions, for understanding nonverbal behavior, and for intuition. This side of the brain is more concerned with how things seem than how they really are. When both sides of the brain function in tandem, individuals are able to act on both logic and emotion. For an 11-year-old, this might mean deciding not to express anger by kicking something because, owing to greater myelination, she is able to access both the logical part of her brain ("I could get in trouble for this and kicking probably won't really get me what I want") and the emotional part ("I'm mad that he said something rude and I want to get even"), so that they can work in concert ("I'll go tell the teacher, so that I won't hurt him or get into trouble, but justice will be served"). As illustrated in this example, the increase in myelination means that, compared to younger children, preadolescents are becoming better at using reasoning rather than primarily using emotions to make decisions (Siegel & Payne Bryson, 2011).

> Although preadolescents are developing better reasoning skills, parents and caregivers cannot realistically expect them to be able to consistently operate from this newly developed part of the brain.

In Figure 12.1, myelination is illustrated by the larger arrows, indicating greater ease of transfer of information between the left and right hemispheres of the brain. The myelination process, as well as increasing neural pathways between these hemispheres (illustrated by the many thin arrows in Figure 12.1), allows preadolescents to begin using more strategies and planned approaches when it comes to academic work, as well as behavioral situations (Luna, Garger, Urban, Lazar, & Sweeney, 2004; Siegel & Payne Bryson, 2011). Parents and caregivers can encourage this increase in communication between hemispheres of the brain by engaging 11-year-olds in problem solving that involves both sides of the brain. For example, they might help a child to identify and acknowledge the feeling behind an impulsive behavior, and once the child has calmed down, work together with him or her to come up with a reasonable way of addressing the problem that caused the outburst (Siegel & Payne Bryson, 2011). In general, the development of the brain at age 11 is not the explosion of new growth that it was in early childhood, but is more of a specialization and *pruning* process that continues into adulthood.

PHYSICAL DEVELOPMENT

By the age of 11, children are noticeably better coordinated than they were in early childhood (Berk, 2013). They can jump, catch, dribble a ball, and perform other gross motor actions with far more skill and accuracy than ever before. Eleven-year-olds' increased processing speed,

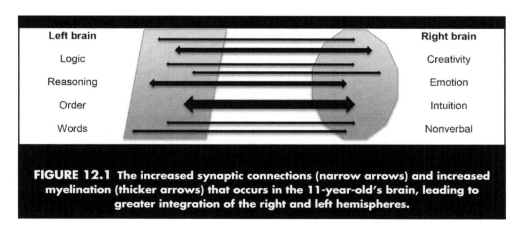

FIGURE 12.1 The increased synaptic connections (narrow arrows) and increased myelination (thicker arrows) that occurs in the 11-year-old's brain, leading to greater integration of the right and left hemispheres.

as noted above, contributes to better coordination (Sowell et al., 2001). Eleven-year-olds also experience an increase in fine motor skills, which is evidenced in their expanding ability to represent depth in their drawings (Berk, 2013). Eleven-year-olds make use of their improving motor coordination to be very active and they always want to be doing something (Ames, Ilg, & Baker, 1988). However, some 11-year-olds will drop out of competitive sports if they feel that their skills are not adequate, and girls, specifically, will sometimes discontinue participating in sports because of their changing bodies (Wood, 2007).

> Eleven-year-olds experience more minor illnesses, such as colds, flu, and ear infections (Wood, 2007).

At the age of 11, physical growth and development is very different for girls and boys (Ames et al., 1988; Scannapieco & Connell-Carrick, 2005). Most 11-year-old boys have not yet begun to experience the physical changes of puberty, although some may be in the early stages of their adolescent growth spurt. These boys may also be experiencing an increase in genital size and the emergence of some pubic hair (Malina, 2005). For almost all boys at this age, there may be a noticeable increase in bone size and a "padded" look, because of a greater percentage of fat tissue (Ames et al., 1988). Many boys at this age are also experiencing erections.

Although boys are a relatively homogeneous group in terms of size and body structure, the physical development among 11-year-old girls varies considerably (Ames et al., 1988). At this age, some girls still have the look of an elementary school student, while others could be confused with adolescents. Most girls fall in the middle range, and are experiencing some breast development and growth of pubic hair, while a few may begin menstruation (Malina, 2005). As a group, 11-year-old girls tend to be taller than 11-year-old boys. Girls, particularly those who are more fully developed, may feel self-conscious about their physical changes.

Most practitioners are familiar with Freud's psychosexual stages, but modern research does not support Freud's latency period (the ages of 6–11), during which period he posited that sexual exploration and erotic experiences disappeared for a time (Weis, 1998). However, the dearth of literature on the sexual development of children during middle childhood appears to be indicative of Freud's enduring legacy that the sexual development of school-age children is irrelevant, even though the existing research shows that his assumption is not accurate. What developmental theorists do know about the sexual development of 11-year-olds is that their changing cognitive capacities are allowing them to think about sex in different ways: They are becoming more curious about sexual acts and about the emotional side of sexual relationships (Ames et al., 1988). Not surprisingly, boys tend to be more interested in the act of sex, while girls spend time talking about romance and relationships (Weis, 1998). Girls and boys are both becoming more curious about their own bodies, and age-appropriate sex education is important at this age (Ames et al., 1988; NSVRC, 2013). Preadolescents who feel comfortable talking to their parents about sex and whose parents provide ample opportunities to address their children's questions are more likely to have safe sex and tend to wait longer before having sex (Koch, 1998; NSVRC, 2013). Some 11-year-olds may begin to realize that they are experiencing same-sex attraction and may feel confusion, guilt, or shame if they are receiving negative messages about homosexuality from others in their environment (Moe, Reicherzer, & Dupuy, 2011). It is important that these children have adults to whom they can turn for support.

It is important for adults in the lives of 11-year-olds to recognize that preadolescents' understanding of sexual behavior is on a different cognitive level than that of adults (Thanasiu, 2004). Therefore sexual knowledge and concepts need to be explained in concrete terms. Parents, teachers, and mental health professionals also need to be aware of the line between the developmentally appropriate sexual experimentation that comes from the child's growing intellectual curiosity and behaviors that may indicate that the child has been exposed to inappropriate sexual material or has experienced sexual abuse (NSVRC, 2013). Thanasiu (2004) offered some guidelines to differentiate normal sexual exploration from behavior that is cause for concern. A sense of anger, shame, or fear are all warning signs that the sexual behavior is not developmentally normal. In addition, experimentation with much older or younger children is cause for concern. Although arousal, and sometimes orgasm, may be normal for children, such experiences in typically developing children are usually marked by sensual curiosity and possibly embarrassment, but rarely shame or guilt. For example, if Avery is giggling with her friends on the way to school about kissing her movie star crush, parents probably do not need to be concerned – but if she is quickly closing the Internet browser window every time her parents come into the room, and is reticent and defensive when asked about it, her parents need to investigate further.

COGNITIVE DEVELOPMENT

At the age of 11, children are in the midst of a marked improvement in complex cognitive functioning (Luna et al., 2004). This improvement includes an increase in the child's ability to take in information quickly, manipulate it, and reproduce it in the same or a different form. By the age of 11, most children are putting their increased processing abilities to work as they transition between Piaget's (1969) "concrete operations" and "formal operations" stages (Broderick & Blewitt, 2010). Since the age of about 8, they have been in a process of decentering, or moving from a stage in which all of their experiences are focused on their own body and actions toward one in which they have a more objective view of how objects relate to one another and to themselves (Piaget, 1969). In the concrete operations period, conclusions drawn about objects and their relationships with the world "relate directly to those objects, and not yet to verbally stated hypotheses" (Piaget, 1969, p. 100). Some 11-year-olds may have cognitive processes that primarily represent concrete operations. Even so, at the age of 11, most children have become adept at the task of conservation, such as knowing that a ball of clay will still weigh the same even when it is rolled into a snake. Another operation mastered during this stage is reversal, or knowing that $4 - 1 = 3$ is the same operation as $3 + 1 = 4$.

Many 11-year-olds are moving into the formal operations stage (Piaget, 1969). They begin to use their abilities to classify, conserve, and reverse, to form hypotheses about the relationships between objects – but the difference is that these theories are separate from the objects themselves and exist in the abstract world. For example, rather than saying that a cat and a mouse are animals that chase each other, 11-year-olds are able to say that they are both mammals (Brigid, Wassell, & Gilligan, 2011). As the child transitions into formal operational thought, he or she is able to reason logically about things that he or she does not believe or see. Whereas the concrete operational child could use logic, the logic was tied to the object (Broderick & Blewitt, 2010). When children in the concrete operational stage were asked whether the statement "This [hidden object] is green or it is not green" was true or false, they responded that they did not know the answer, because they could not see the object: They could not separate reasoning from their experiences of the object. However, if children in the formal operations stage – that is, most 11-year-olds – were to be asked the same question, they would be able to reason that there are no other options: The object either is or is not green. Consequently, they could conclude that the statement was true without needing to see the object (Broderick & Blewitt, 2010). Eleven-year-olds are thus beginning to use inference rather than having to rely only on what they see (Brigid et al., 2011). With new reasoning skills, 11-year-olds prefer to learn new skills rather than review previous work, and they approach learning as a challenge (Wood, 2007).

Because 11-year-olds want to flex their growing logic and reasoning muscles, statements such as, "Because I said so," or "Because I'm the adult," are particularly frustrating to preadolescents (Siegel & Payne Bryson, 2011). Parents and caregivers can nurture 11-year-olds' brain development by respectfully explaining and discussing their rational for decisions. This discussion does not mean that the child will get his or her way, or that the adult is no longer the authority; nor does it mean that the child has permission to be disrespectful. The goal of such an explanation is to respect and nurture the 11-year-old's growing ability to think on his or her own.

> Eleven-year-olds learn well in collaborative groups and enjoy board games, brain teasers, and sometimes even tests (Wood, 2007).

WORLDVIEW/EGO DEVELOPMENT

Eleven-year-olds are between childhood and adolescence, and, because of biological changes, are beginning to experience new emotions and feelings, although not necessarily at the same rate as one another. Eleven-year-olds are reaching the height of Erikson's (1968) *industry vs. inferiority* stage, and if they are achieving a sense of industry, they are likely to feel competent and to have

155

a sense of satisfaction in their abilities to contribute to society in meaningful ways. Perhaps this shift in development is the reason for a general increase in self-esteem at this age (Berkm, 2013). However, for a child who has not yet worked through the earlier stages and developed trust, autonomy, or initiative, a satisfying sense of industry is not possible: If Tommy is afraid to try a new activity, such as snowshoeing (initiative), he will not have the opportunity to feel competent at that activity (Erikson, 1968).

Eleven-year-olds are in the midst of a shift from externally focused to internally driven rules (Greenspan, 1993). To make this shift, the 11-year-old must have successfully resolved the earlier stage, and be able to both win and lose while still feeling a sense of competence. Previously, the child's sense of self was defined by how peers and adults described him or her; now, the child's confidence in his or her own self-efficacy, or sense of industry, is beginning to allow him or her to make the shift from meeting the external expectations of others to creating his or her own expectations for himself or herself (Erikson, 1968; Greenspan, 1993). A child may still follow the rules of the group, but he or she is following the rule because he or she has internalized the rule into how he or she must be, rather than following the rule because others say that he or she should (Greenspan, 1993; Loevinger, 1976). As 11-year-olds are working to develop this internalized view of self, they may appear moody and deregulated, because in each moment they may still define themselves as who their parents or peers say they are, meanwhile having an emerging sense of self coming from within them without the tools to adequately express it.

Eleven-year-olds who are successfully navigating the shift from the external to the internal motivation stage are using their emerging abstract reasoning skills to focus less on specific behavior and more on concepts that define themselves in comparison with others (Brigid et al., 2011; Greenspan, 1993). For example, Jeremy can say, "I'm pretty good at math even though I got a C on my fractions quiz today. Fractions are just hard for me, but I know how to do the rest of it," rather than seeing himself as terrible in math because he did poorly on one quiz.

Loevinger (1976) calls this stage of the development of self the "conformist" stage. Although Loevinger determined that any human could be in any ego stage at any time during his or her lifespan, the conformist stage appears to fit with the ego development of most 11-year-olds in Western society. During this stage, children (or adults) "identify their own welfare with that of the group" (Loevinger, 1976, p. 17): a concept that aligns with Greenspan's (1993) idea that 11-year-olds internalize group rules. Loevinger emphasized that individuals at the conformist stage of development follow the rules out of respect for the rules rather than from fear of punishment, suggesting that they have internalized the rules. Conforming individuals are able to appreciate group differences, but have a more difficult time seeing differences within the group: Maria, for example, may see the children within her class in terms of racial lines and may assume that all of the people with light skin are different from her just because they look different from her, but that they are all the same as one another because their skin color is the same. This clearly has implications for racial and ethnic identity development, as well as for helping children to appreciate diversity.

Racial/Ethnic Identity Development

Little research exists on ethnic or racial identity development for children and preadolescents (French, Seidman, Allen, & Aber, 2006; Marks, Szalacha, Lamarre, Boyd, & Coll, 2007). Perhaps this is because most ethnic or racial identity models associate the development of abstract thought with all but the first stages of the model. Consider, for example, Sue and Sue's (2013) model. In the first stage, *conformity*, the individual believes that the values and members of the majority group are better than his or her own. In the second stage, *dissonance*, the individual must have an experience, or many experiences, that challenge(s) the previously held belief. However, progressing to the second stage requires a person to have the cognitive ability to draw conclusions about the world around him or her using abstract concepts, such as identification of group norms and oppression. Therefore children – even 11-year-olds – probably do not have the cognitive ability to move past the first stage of conformity. What consequently becomes important is helping them to feel good about themselves and their ethnicity or race in the conformity stage, so that they have the internal resources to move forward when their cognitive capacities are ready. It is also important to help children to build relationships with others who are different from them, so that they will have personal experiences with diversity and therefore will be able to challenge stereotypes as they develop more complex cognitive abilities.

Children are clearly aware of racial and ethnic lines (Marks et al., 2007). Research with American children whose parents originated from another country suggested that 11-year-old children seemed more aware of their own ethnic identity and could use more ethnic terms to describe themselves than could elementary-aged children. Other researchers found that group esteem – that is, an individual's positive feelings for his or her own ethnic or racial group – increased over time for 10- and 11-year-olds (French et al., 2006). However, they also found that children's exploration of their racial or ethnic identity (that is, their attempts to determine the meaning of racial/ethnic group membership for them personally) did not increase with age even for children in nondominant cultural groups. French and colleagues (2006) suggested that 10- and 11-year-olds did not have the cognitive abilities to think systematically about their racial or ethnic group, and that their increase in group esteem may be a result of increased socialization. Developmental theorists indicate that, cognitively, 11-year-olds tend to think "Anyone who looks like me is the same as me," so it makes sense that they would separate themselves into groups and then experience increased esteem for their identified group.

Taken together, the research presented seems to indicate that children are aware of racial differences, but that they are not yet cognitively ready to fully determine what those differences mean for them personally in their daily lives. However, these findings do not preclude parents and teachers from setting the groundwork for later, more cognitively complex, racial or ethnic exploration by providing positive experiences and role models of all races and ethnicities, and helping children to foster accepting, caring attitudes toward all people, including those who do not look like them (Brigid et al., 2011).

> Eleven-year-olds may not have the cognitive ability to fully understand the nuances of racial relations, but they do have the ability to understand and enact concepts such as respect and care toward all people.

EMOTIONAL DEVELOPMENT

Parents of 11-year-olds tend to see it as a difficult year because the child is trying to assert his or her independence commensurate with his or her developing sense of self (Ames et al., 1988). Parents may also be surprised and unprepared for the change in their happy, outgoing 10-year-old to a moody, unpredictable 11-year-old. However, the child may be just as surprised as the parent. In fact, 11-year-olds are often very aware of their changing moods, but do not understand where they are coming from or feel that they have much control over them: Tonia may sit on the front porch crying and complaining to her parents about how unfair she feels that they have been, all the while knowing, in the logical part of her brain, that what she was asking of them was unrealistic. However, she feels unable to control her angry feelings and to stop the torrent of unkind words.

The internalization of the 11-year-old's ego, or sense of self, may mean that the child no longer wants to be told what to do or be shown how to accomplish tasks; rather, he or she wants to exercise his or her newfound self-direction (Ames et al., 1988; Greenspan, 1993). This can be confusing for parents who know that their way of doing something is likely to be less complicated or emotionally difficult, but whose child does not want to listen. At this stage, it is important for parents to provide a supportive base for 11-year-olds who are exercising their own sense of self, but it is also important for parents to give children the freedom to explore: Without the freedom to try and fail or try and succeed, children will not be able to develop the sense of competency in their emotional lives that they have found in their physical lives (Erikson, 1968).

Although 11-year-olds may be outgoing and thoughtful away from home, they tend to take out their confusion with themselves on those closest to them (Ames et al., 1988). Eleven-year-olds may not be as physically aggressive toward siblings and parents, but their verbal aggression and aggression toward objects, such as slamming doors, is likely to increase. With regard to discipline and rules, 11-year-olds have a strong sense of fairness and may want to argue their point, but will be reluctant to hear their parents' counterarguments. Parents of 11-year-olds may find that bargaining is a useful tool for addressing 11-year-olds' need for fairness and logic. Parents might say, "I'll do my part in the family by cleaning the kitchen if you'll do your part by cleaning the bathroom." Such statements help the child to understand that his or her work will make a useful contribution (tapping into Erikson's concept of industry) and help the child to feel that he or she is being treated fairly ("Everyone is working on cleaning this morning").

SOCIAL DEVELOPMENT

Eleven-year-olds are becoming more interested in the world of their peers, although their family is still important to them (Ames et al., 1988; Piaget, 1969). With their friends, the focus of play is often on games with rules, but the rules are seen as more pliable and can be changed as the situation demands (Piaget, 1997). Because he or she has moved into the latter part of concrete operations or the early stages of formal operations, the 11-year-old is better able to adopt the perspective of others, but may still have difficulty separating his or her belief about the world from the "truth" (Berk, 2013; Broderick & Blewitt, 2010). Reagan, for example, may believe that drinking alcohol is bad, period, so for her that is the truth and she has difficulty seeing that her opinion is only one way of thinking among many.

Because of the child's growing sense of self and emphasis on individual rights, 11 can be a rocky age for friendships, especially among girls (Ames et al., 1988; Wood, 2007). Eleven-year-olds are also beginning to have a clear sense of who is good at what, rather than a general sense of everyone being equal: "John is good at school, but Robert is not," turns into "Eli is good at math, Jane is good at sports, and Francesca is good at making friends." This can lead to what Erikson (1968, p. 126) called the child's "first experience with division of labor". Erikson posited that this division of labor is directly correlated with the division of relationships that are so common among preadolescents.

> Boys tend to express anger through aggression, while girls tend to express it through relational means, such as exclusion or gossip (Scannapieco & Connell-Carrick, 2005).

RELATIONSHIP DEVELOPMENT

The family is still very important at this age, even though more and more time is being spent away from home, and a strong base from which to venture out into the world can positively impact on peer relationships (Brigid et al., 2011). Children in middle childhood, including 11-year-olds, engage with peers for more than 30 percent of their social interactions (Ross & Spielmacher, 2005), and are beginning to base their friendships more on shared characteristics and understanding than on proximity and shared activities (Brigid et al., 2011). By the age of 11, children can identify and define cliques in their social circles, and usually report their own clique membership (Ross & Spielmacher, 2005). Bullying may occur toward those who are not part of a particular group, and can include name calling, physical harm, and cyberbullying through text messaging and social media (Brigid et al., 2011).

Eleven-year-olds are in the process of moving out of the more sheltered, structured world of elementary school, in which friends are primarily found in extracurricular activities and most children report having an array of "close" friends (Ross & Spielmacher, 2005). Eleven-year-olds have moved, or will soon move, into the world of middle school, and have a greater volume and probably a wider variety of friends from among whom to choose. Although many 11-year-olds may find this an exciting time, others may find the changes in themselves and their friends difficult, and can benefit from a caring, supportive environment at home with caregivers who are able to listen patiently to preteen dramas about who is angry with whom for what obscure or unknown reason. More than someone to fix their problems, preteens need adults who care about them and who are willing to support them through their struggles. When preteens feel comfortable and valued talking with their parents about the little problems, they are more likely to come to them with the big problems.

> Eleven-year-olds need lots of time to talk with peers, including face-to-face, text messaging, and social media interactions.

Eleven-year-olds' ways of being with adults may sometimes negatively affect their relationships. Eleven-year-olds frequently challenge parents, teachers, and other adults with questions and doubts about adults' actions and rules. These challenges are inspired by newfound cognitive abilities and a focus on social-emotional growth. Eleven-year-olds are often confused when adults become frustrated or angry about being challenged, because, in the child's eyes, he or she was just trying to learn (Wood, 2007). Adults who provide patience, explanations, and openness to challenges help 11-year-olds to learn to manage their worlds more effectively and develop supportive relationships.

DEVELOPMENT IN THE AGE OF TECHNOLOGY

The use of technology is a given in today's society, and 11-year-olds have never known a world without computers, tablets, smartphones, and social media. The abundance of information at their fingertips is a relatively new phenomenon, and scientists are still unsure of the impact that the digital world is having on children's learning, behavior, and attitudes – a question for which parents are eager to know an answer. "Technology" is a broad term that encompasses many different modalities. It is therefore less helpful to ask whether technology is "good" or "bad," and more helpful to ask how specific technologies or media impact on children (Bavelier, Green, & Dye, 2010). One of the challenges is that the potential merits or deficits of a particular media may not be obvious: Most parents would not be surprised to learn that frequent video game play has been associated with a lower grade point average among children and adolescents (Jackson, von Eye, Fitzgerald, Witt, & Zhou, 2011), but they might be surprised to learn that playing certain video games has also been associated with increased visual spatial skills, concentration, and visual short-term memory (Bavelier et al., 2010). Other, more ostensibly learning-based, technology, such as some television shows or language acquisition computer games, may be ineffective or even have a deleterious effect – so how are parents to know what games, shows, or computer programs are beneficial for their children? Researching the technology online is one option; another is to assess the extent of active participation in the technology, because that was one factor common among many of the television shows that had positive learning outcomes (Bavelier et al., 2010).

> Many 11-year-olds may be more technologically savvy than their parents.

Regardless of opinion on children's use of technology, the technology appears to be here to stay. Thus parents and other caregivers must work to find the balance that maximizes the benefits of technology while counteracting the negatives. One reason to provide children access to technology is that success in today's workforce almost certainly requires proficiency with computers and often with other types of technology (Bavelier et al., 2010). Further, children who used the Internet more were found to have better reading skills than did those children who used it less (Jackson et al., 2011). Despite many practical benefits to Internet and technology usage, there are also dangers, and parents and other caregivers need to educate themselves, so that they can help their children to make wise choices. Preteens may often be unaware of the impact that their posts on social media may have on their futures and are not likely to be thinking about potential employers or colleges down the road. "Sexting" is another risky behavior that teens, and even preteens, may not see as unusual or problematic (McBride, 2011). However, sexting among minors is a felony in some states, because it can technically be considered child pornography. Eleven-year-olds are likely to vary in terms of their use of social media, but they will probably have some kind of online access, and parents need to be in the habit of having open, nonpunitive conversations with their children about Internet use and the sites that the children visit. If 11-year-olds feel that their parents are on their "team" when it comes to Internet use, they will be more likely to keep their parents informed of their Internet activity as they progress into adolescence when the stakes are even higher. Regarding social media, parents need to weigh the child's ability to manage interactions and the child's social needs. Frequent monitoring, discussion, and interaction of social media between parent and child can help a child to learn to face the challenges of meeting social needs through technology.

BEST PRACTICES FOR COUNSELING/THERAPY

When Counseling/Therapy Is Indicated

As discussed throughout this chapter, 11 is a difficult age for children and parents alike. What might have been indicative of concerning psychosocial problems at the age of 10 may now be considered normal development. Whenever possible, counselors need a thorough understanding of the child's family environment and developmental history before they can assess whether concerns such as arguing with parents, emotional lability, and difficulty getting along with peers warrant clinical intervention or are simply an expected reaction to normal developmental processes.

Any extreme behaviors, such as a serious attempt to run away from home, suicidal ideation, or extreme aggression, are all cause for concern. Age-normed assessments, such as the Child Behavior Checklist (CBCL), can be useful tools for providing one piece of the puzzle in understanding how a child's behavior compares to that of same-aged peers (Achenbach & Rescorla, 2001). Eleven-year-olds typically want to be a part of whatever is going on in their families, even if their participation may appear to have the purpose of creating disequilibrium (Ames et al., 1988). Therefore, if the 11-year-old is constantly secluding himself or herself in his or her room, this is cause for concern. In addition, an 11-year-old who is picking at food that he or she liked in the past, or a child who is skipping meals, is also cause for further investigation, because neither of these behaviors are normal for the voraciously hungry 11-year-old.

Developmentally Appropriate Approaches

Before describing interventions at length, a word needs to be said about counseling rooms, often called "activity rooms," for this age. An activity room for an 11-year-old should reflect the child's sometimes unsteady movement from the world of childhood into that of adolescence. Although play is becoming less important for children of this age, some may still revert to it as a means of communication. Therefore a few toys of wide variety from the categories mentioned in Landreth (2012) should be provided. A wide variety of art supplies is also important. These need not be expensive and can even be free, such as squares of cloth cut from old clothing or a stack of egg cartons.

Child-centered activity play therapy (CCAPT) Child-centered activity play therapy (CCAPT) can be an effective intervention for 11-year-olds, because the child-directed nature of the sessions provides an opportunity for the child to explore his or her growing sense of self in a safe, accepting environment, free from the pressures and constraints of adult expectations: a situation that is certain to be unique for the unpredictably emotional 11-year-old. In addition, a person-centered environment allows for the development of self-direction and self-efficacy within the child. The accepting environment and limits placed on unsafe or harmful behavior can facilitate the growth of an internal locus of control within the child: something that will serve him or her well as her or she prepares to navigate the world of adolescence. The many craft supplies and art projects available in activity therapy give the 11-year-old the opportunity to gain a sense of industry and competence.

Adlerian play therapy (AdPT) Adlerian play therapy (AdPT) is another intervention that can be useful for 11-year-old children and can be implemented in an activity room (Kottman, 2003). Kottman's concept of sharing power with the child ("Sometimes I decide what we do in here. Sometimes you decide.") is appropriate for this age, because 11-year-olds are experiencing this dynamic in their daily lives. Experiencing power sharing in a supportive, caring environment can consequently help them to work through similar challenges outside of counseling. Kottman also provides a variety of structured activities, such as puppet shows, and describes how to create interventions that focus on helping the child to understand his or her experience of the world. For practitioners preferring a more directive approach, AdPT or Adlerian activity therapy can allow for some directed activities while still focusing on the relationship and the child's experience of the world.

Gestalt play therapy One of the primary goals of Gestalt play therapy is integration of the self, a task that is well suited to the developmental challenges faced by 11-year-olds (Blom, 2006). Gestalt play therapists use play, art, and other expressive media to help children to develop awareness of discomfort caused by imbalance with the self, so that the cause of the discomfort can be addressed and integrated (Carroll, 2009). Gestalt play therapists make use of projections through art activities and other means, but rarely attempt to interpret the projections for the child (Oaklander, 1978). Rather, they prefer to describe what they are seeing or sensing, and allow the child to provide feedback as to whether the therapist's sight or sense is accurate or not. Because of the use of art activities, as well as the making of connections between abstract art and the child's life, Gestalt play therapy can be a useful intervention for 11-year-olds.

Cognitive-behavioral play therapy (CBPT)   Cognitive-behavioral play therapy (CBPT) "incorporates cognitive and behavioral interventions within a play therapy paradigm" (Knell, 2009, p. 203). One key goal of cognitive-behavioral therapy (CBT) is to pinpoint and modify maladaptive thoughts. However, the abstract thinking necessary for this process is too advanced for 11-year-olds, even with their increasingly abstract thinking. Further, talk therapy does not address preadolescents' need for movement and self-expression. Cognitive-behavioral play therapists address these developmental concerns by using activities, movement, roleplaying, and other play media to help children to identify and modify maladaptive thoughts, whether verbally or indirectly through play scenarios (Cavett, 2015; Knell, 2009). The intervention may be helpful for 11-year-olds because they are able to use their growing cognitive abilities, as well as to express playfulness and movement. For example, one technique, behavioral rehearsal, involves roleplaying a social situation in different ways to help the child to explore and identify the most helpful ways of responding in the situation (Scannapieco & Connell-Carrick, 2005). This technique could be helpful for 11-year-olds dealing with social anxiety or struggling with specific behavioral concerns.

Although CBPT has some behavioral components, strict behavioral therapy is not indicated for 11-year-olds because of their internalized sense of fairness that extends to the group. They may feel poorly treated or frustrated when everyone does not receive the same consequences for behavior. Further, 11-year-olds are developing a stronger internal sense of right and wrong versus an external orientation to morality. Behavioral interventions are likely to be less effective because 11-year-olds are beginning to care less about what others say should be done and more about their personal values. At its worst, behavioral interventions could serve to threaten this growing sense of internal values.

Group activity therapy   Group activity therapy is one intervention that can target 11-year-olds with difficulty in interpersonal relationships, whether with siblings or peers. In group activity therapy, children are placed in a context in which they must learn to work through interpersonal problems without the option to avoid conflict and with firm limits set in place regarding harm to others. The children are provided an opportunity to work through their relationships with the support of a caring adult, who is able to help the preadolescent to give voice to feelings and desires that he or she may not yet be able to express himself or herself. Group activity therapy (that is, group play therapy with preadolescents) usually consists of two to three preadolescents and follows a person-centered or other humanistic approach in which there may be some activities, but the focus is on the here and now. Eleven-year-olds have the primary ingredient needed for effective group activity therapy: social hunger. "Social hunger" refers to the child's desire to be in relationship with others and caring about how his or her behavior is impacting on others (Ginott, 1961). This social hunger means that children are constantly seeking out relationships and, for children who do so in inappropriate ways, group activity therapy is a place in which they can have new experiences that reinforce positive ways of relating.

Family activity therapy   For 11-year-olds in families in which challenging dynamics seem to be a large part of the presenting concern, family activity therapy is one option. The 11-year-old's growing abstract reasoning skills make him or her more adept at identifying and discussing patterns within the family system, with a little help from the counselor. Any interventions with families need to be developmentally appropriate for all members of the family and, for the 11-year-old, engaging in activities rather than simply talk therapy will be more meaningful. Activities in which the entire family must work together or interact to perform some task can be helpful in bringing out family dynamics. Most 11-year-olds then have the ability to sit and talk with the family about how the dynamics occurring in session also take place at home: Activities help to bridge the gap between concrete and formal operational thinking.

Sandtray therapy Similar to family activity therapy, sandtray therapy, whether individual, family, or group, allows for the concrete representation of abstract thought (Armstrong, 2008; Homeyer & Sweeney, 2010). Sandtray therapy is appropriate for individuals over the age of 10 or 11, and, with 11-year-olds, it can help to bridge the developmental gap between play and talk therapy. Sandtray therapy provides the child something to do with his or her hands, as well as a concrete way in which to represent abstract ideas and feelings.

Working with Teachers, Parents, and Caretakers

Teachers and parents can benefit from more knowledge about child development and what to expect or not to expect from the children in their care. For example, teachers and parents can be educated on the child's experience to try to help them see from the child's perspective. The emotional lability of an 11-year-old can be challenging for teachers and parents, and many parent consultations may be spent helping them to see that a child is responding to changes within himself or herself, and does not have as his or her primary goal the wreaking of havoc on the family environment.

Parents can also be involved in filial therapy geared toward older children, also referred to as child–parent relationship therapy (CPRT) (Landreth & Bratton, 2006). Instead of having special playtimes with their child (although this may be appropriate for some 11-year-olds), the parent might allow the child to pick a craft or something to bake and then practice using reflective listening while engaging in the activity with the child. Craft activities can foster the child's feelings of competence, while active listening from a parent can help the parent to understand the child better and the child to feel understood. Such a dynamic in the parent–child relationship can facilitate the child being open with the parent about difficulties at school or with friends: something that will become increasingly valuable as the child approaches adolescence. Going on special outings with the child can also be beneficial.

> Parenting 11-year-olds requires a substantial amount of patience and understanding.

Parents and caregivers of preadolescents who are able to build caring relationships with their 11-year-olds set the foundation for higher levels of open communication and trust during the teen years. Thus parents of 11-year-olds do well to continually ask themselves how their parenting strategies are impacting on the parent–child relationship. One way in which parents and other adults can respect 11-year-old's sense of fairness and sense of belonging in the family is to emphasize that tasks that might seem menial to an 11-year-old, such as cleaning the bathroom or taking out the trash, are part of belonging to the family and that the parent completes such tasks as well. An attitude of "we're all working together" versus "do that because I told you so" can help to strengthen the parent–child relationship. Another way in which parents can strengthen the parent–child relationship is to help children to label their emotions. Eleven-year-olds may often feel confused and overwhelmed by their emotions, and a parent who is able to label emotions in a calm, accepting way demonstrates care and helps the preadolescent to sort through his or her own feelings.

It is also important for parents and caregivers of 11-year-olds to feel comfortable talking about sex and sexuality with their children. Because of the prevalence of sexual imagery in social media, children will certainly be exposed to sexual content beyond their developmental level, and parents need to be prepared to answer questions about sex and sexuality in a calm and unembarrassed manner. This may be difficult for parents for whom sex was a taboo subject growing up. However, if children feel that they cannot approach their parents for honest conversations about sex, they will turn to friends, social media, and the Internet for answers – and these answers may not be healthy or developmentally appropriate. Child counselors can work with parents to determine the ways in which they might best talk with their children about sexual issues.

Eleven-year-olds who have experienced trauma may benefit from some age-appropriate education about how their traumatic experiences impact on how their brain works, for example counselors might introduce Siegel's hand model of the brain to parents, so that they and their children can use it to discuss the child's emotions and behaviors (Siegel & Payne Bryson, 2011). With some support, 11-year-olds are cognitively ready to apply an abstract concept such as brain functioning to their own experience, and are likely to feel empowered when adults respect them enough to acknowledge their ability to process and use such information.

CONCLUSION

Eleven can be a trying age, both for children and parents. Eleven-year-olds are beginning to encounter many physical and emotional changes. Their bodies are changing, as is their social environment, and many 11-year-olds may feel confused or betrayed by both themselves and their peers. Meanwhile, their brains are developing new ways of thinking and processing information. It can be a challenging time for children because they feel like a child one moment and like an adolescent the next. They want the independence and excitement of adolescence, yet they want the safety of depending on their families. Eleven can also be a challenging time for parents, who struggle to keep up with their child's changing emotions, thoughts, and opinions. What is most important during this time is that parents provide a stable environment in which the child can feel safe to explore his or her growing identity. Parents who are able to find ways in which to support their 11-year-old through these difficult changes will have set a solid foundation for moving into adolescence.

REFERENCES

Achenbach, T. M., & Rescorla, L. A. (2001). *Manual for the ASEBA school-age forms & profiles*. Burlington, VT: University of Vermont, Research Center for Children, Youth, & Families.

Ames, L. B., Ilg, F. L., & Baker, S. M. (1988). *Your ten- to fourteen-year-old*. New York, NY: Dell.

Armstrong, S. A. (2008). *Sandtray therapy: A humanistic approach*. Dallas, TX: Ludic.

Badenoch, B. (2008). *Being a brain-wise therapist: A practical guide to interpersonal neurobiology*. New York, NY: W. W. Norton.

Bavelier, D., Green, C. S., & Dye, M. W. G. (2010). Children, wired: For better and for worse. *Neuron, 67*(5), 692–701.

Berk, L. E. (2013). *Development through the lifespan* (9th ed). Upper Saddle River, NJ: Pearson.

Blom, R. (2006). *The handbook of Gestalt play therapy*. Philadelphia, PA; Jessica Kingsley.

Brigid, D., Wassell, S., & Gilligan, R. (2011). *Child development for child care and protection workers* (2nd ed). Philadelphia, PA: Jessica Kingsley.

Broderick, P. C., & Blewitt, P. (2010). *The life span: Human development for helping professionals*. Boston, MA: Pearson.

Carroll, F. (2009). Gestalt play therapy. In K. J. O'Connor & L. D. Braverman. (Eds.), *Play therapy theory and practice: Comparing theories and techniques* (2nd ed., pp. 283–314). Hoboken, NJ: John Wiley & Sons.

Cavett, A. (2015). Cognitive behavioral play therapy. In D. A. Crenshaw & A. L. Stewart. (Eds.), *Play therapy: A comprehensive guide to theory and practice* (pp. 83–98). New York, NY: Guilford.

Erikson, E. H. (1968). *Identity: Youth and crisis*. New York, NY: W. W. Norton.

French, S. E., Seidman, E., Allen, L., & Aber, L. (2006). The development of ethnic identity during adolescence. *Developmental Psychology, 42*(1), 1–10.

Ginott, H. G. (1961). *Group psychotherapy with children: The theory and practice of play therapy*. Northvale, NJ: McGraw-Hill.

Greenspan, S. I. (1993). *Playground politics: Understanding the emotional life of your school-aged child*. New York, NY: Addison-Wesley.

Homeyer, L. E., & Sweeney, D. S. (2010). *Sandtray: A practical manual* (2nd ed.). New York, NY: Routledge.

Jackson, L. A., von Eye, A., Fitzgerald, H. E., Witt, E. A., & Zhou, Y. (2011). Internet use, video game playing, and cellphone use as predictors of children's body mass index. (BMI), body weight, academic performance, and social and overall self-esteem. *Computers in Human Behavior, 27*(1), 599–604.

Knell, S. (2009). Cognitive behavioral play therapy. In K. J. O'Connor & L. D. Braverman. (Eds.), *Play therapy theory and practice: Comparing theories and techniques*.(2nd ed., pp. 203–236). Hoboken, NJ: John Wiley & Sons.

Koch, P. B. (1998). Sexual knowledge and education. In R. T. Francoeur, P. B. Koch, & D. L. Weis (Eds.), *Sexuality in America* (pp. 70–87). New York, NY: Continuum.

Kottman, T. (2003). *Partners in play: An Adlerian approach to play therapy* (2nd ed.). Alexandria, VA: American Counseling Association.

Landreth, G. L. (2012). *Play therapy: The art of the relationship* (3rd ed.). New York, NY: Routledge.

Landreth, G. L., & Bratton, S. C. (2006). *Child-parent relationship therapy*. New York, NY: Routledge.

Loevinger, J. (1976). *Ego development*. San Francisco, CA: Jossey-Bass.

Luna, B., Garger, K. E., Urban, T. A., Lazar, N. A., & Sweeney, J. A. (2004). Maturation of cognitive processes from late childhood to adulthood. *Child Development, 75*(5), 1357–1372.

Malina, R. M. (2005). Milestones of motor development and indicators of biological maturity. In B. Hopkins (Ed.), *Cambridge encyclopedia of child development* (Appendix 2). Cambridge: Cambridge University Press.

Marks, A. K., Szalacha, L. A., Lamarre, M., Boyd, M., & Coll, C. G. (2007). Emerging ethnic identity and interethnic group social preferences in middle childhood: Findings from the Children of Immigrants Development in Context (CIDC) study. *International Journal of Behavioral Development, 31*(5), 501–513.

McBride, D. L. (2011). Risks and benefits of social media for children and adolescents. *Journal of Pediatric Nursing, 26*(5), 498–499.

Moe, J. L., Reicherzer, S., & Dupuy, P. J. (2011). Models of sexual and relational orientation: A critical review and synthesis. *Journal of Counseling and Development, 89*, 227–223.

National Sexual Violence Resource Center (NSVRC). (2013). An overview of healthy childhood sexual development. Retrieved from http://www.nsvrc.org/sites/default/files/saam_2013_an-overview-of-healthy-childhood-sexual-development.pdf

Oaklander, V. (1978). *Windows to our children*. Gouldsboro, ME: Gestalt Journal Press.

Piaget, J. (1969). *The psychology of the child*. New York, NY: Basic Books.

Piaget, J. (1997). *The moral judgment of the child*. New York, NY: Simon & Schuster.

Ross, H. S., & Spielmacher, K. E. (2005). Social development. In B. Hopkins (Ed.), *Cambridge encyclopedia of child development* (pp. 227–233). Cambridge: Cambridge University Press.

Scannapieco, M., & Connell-Carrick, K. (2005). *Understanding child maltreatment*. New York, NY: Oxford University Press.

Siegel, D. J., & Payne Bryson, T. (2011). *The whole-brain child*. New York, NY: Delacort.

Sowell, E. R., Thompson, P. M., Leonard, C. M., Welcome, S. E., Kan, E., & Toga, A. W. (2004). Longitudinal mapping of cortical thickness and brain growth in normal children. *Journal of Neuroscience, 22*(38), 8223–8231.

Sowell, E. R., Thompson, P. M., Tessner, K. D., & Toga, A. W. (2001) Mapping continued brain growth and gray matter density reduction in dorsal frontal cortex: Inverse relationships during postadolescent brain maturation. *Journal of Neuroscience, 21*(22), 8819–8829.

Sue, D. W., & Sue, D. (2013). *Counseling the culturally diverse: Theory and practice* (6th ed). Hoboken, NJ: John Wiley & Sons.

Thanasiu, P. L. (2004). Childhood sexuality: Discerning healthy from abnormal sexual behaviors. *Journal of Mental Health Counseling, 26*(4), 309–319.

Weis, D. L. (1998). Interpersonal heterosexual behaviors. In R. T. Francoeur, P. B. Koch, & D. L. Weis. (Eds.), *Sexuality in America* (pp. 70–87). New York, NY: Continuum.

Wood, C. (2007). *Yardsticks: Children in the classroom ages 4–14* (3rd ed.). Turners Falls, MA: Northeast Foundation for Children.

13

THE EXTRAORDINARY 12-YEAR-OLD

Julia E. Smith and Emily Michero

The age of 12 is marked by significant development and change in myriad aspects of life. On the cusp of adolescence, a typical 12-year-old will experience major cognitive, interpersonal, emotional, and physical changes, and will begin to undertake the work of the teen years: cultivating peer relationships, testing boundaries, exploring things that are unknown and exciting, and striving for independence (Siegel, 2013). Cognitively, 12-year-olds begin to emerge from the simplicity and refuge of childhood into the world of complex, sometimes troubling, ideas. Emotionally, 12-year-olds experience feelings more intensely owing to changes in the brain. Interpersonally, they expand their social contexts to include family and, now, connections with peers. Physically, they often grow taller, enter puberty, and feel a pull to find sexual connection (Badenoch, 2008). Whereas many 12-year-olds encounter significant change across these and other aspects of life, the exact nature, timing, and degree of change in each child is unique.

Twelve-year-olds tend to emerge from the age of 11 with a greater sense of comfort, achievement, and security with self and in relationships with others, which typically flow more smoothly than in the past. In school, the 12-year-old's newly developed sense of security allows him or her to adapt to the often tumultuous experience of middle school, with its changing classes and branching out of friend groups. Old friendships dissipate and new ones form, as new interests develop and preferences change. Among peer groups, 12-year-olds often begin to notice others in a new way, often romantically or sexually, and to evaluate their own and others' behavior more critically. At varying rates, boys and girls become involved and begin to date, or, at the very least, express a desire to do so (Ames, Baker, & Ilg, 1988).

Many 12-year-olds are moody and temperamental, alternating between the emotionally intense behavior of a young child and the more regulated behavior of an older adolescent in mere seconds. Along with the fluctuations in mood and behavior within each 12-year-old, there is great variance in maturity: Some 12-year-olds have clearly moved on to adolescence, whereas others resemble much younger children in one or more aspect of being.

Lauren, a typical 12-year-old girl, is eager to convince her parents to let her have a smartphone. In a mature fashion, she presents a strong rationale, building a case in support of her need for a smartphone. She offers a persuasive argument about the safety that a cellphone offers and the intricate ways in which her social world will be enhanced. She voices fear about being excluded socially in the absence of a smartphone. Her presentation is thoughtful and well planned, and Lauren's parents listen patiently as she talks – but they inform her that they have not changed their minds and she will not be getting a smartphone. In a matter of seconds, Lauren explodes into anger and tears, storming out of the room. She cries and sulks in her room, refusing to speak to her parents for the rest of the evening. The mature adult-like creature who made the intelligent and coherent case seemed to have disappeared and been replaced by a child in the throes of a temper tantrum.

In 12-year-olds, significant brain changes typically begin to take place that contribute to certain hallmark qualities of this preadolescent period, including emotional intensity, novelty seeking, social engagement with peers, and creative exploration (Siegel, 2013). These brain changes result in a potential for increased risk, greater rewards, and an often tumultuous time with parents.

Many 12-year-olds are described as friendly, expressive, cooperative, and exuberant. At the age of 12, the child's adult personality often begins to emerge, which can be an exciting development for parents and other adults in the child's life. For many 12-year-olds, cognitive development shifts from concrete operations to formal operations, and they begin to reason abstractly and consider the viewpoints and feelings of others (Piaget & Inhelder, 1969).

A 12-year-old's new understanding of broader issues, such as prejudice and justice, begin to rouse idealism (Badenoch, 2008). Twelve-year-olds strive for independence from parents and teachers, and begin to think and make decisions more autonomously, often with peer influence. Together, these qualities culminate in a more mature, cooperative, thoughtful, and happy child.

Whereas 12-year-olds may be friendly and accommodating individually, they are often difficult to manage in groups, causing problems for teachers in classrooms. The more restrictive they perceive their environment to be, the more 12-year-olds will likely feel the need to control their space. Twelve-year-olds are fearful of being seen as a "goody goody," so may act out and take risks in order to be perceived as tough (Ames et al., 1988).

The ability of 12-year-olds to reason abstractly often leads to a new awareness of more complex ideas. Significant brain changes impact on a 12-year-old's mood and temperament, often leading to rapid and extreme mood shifts. Because 12-year-olds experience emotions so intensely, negative emotions can be overwhelming for child and parents alike (Siegel, 2013).

BRAIN DEVELOPMENT

The brain of a 12-year-old is changing at a rapid rate. Structural changes in both gray and white matter continue through this age. These changes coincide with alterations in functional organization, which, in turn, are reflected in behavior (Stiles & Jernigan, 2010). The brains of 12-year-olds experience a burst of neuronal production at the onset of puberty, known as "exuberance," which is an overgrowth of new dendrites and synapses in the brain (Badenoch, 2008). This process creates the potential for billions of new connections and contributes to a period of increased neuroplasticity, or experience-based structural changes in the brain. For 12-year-olds, exuberance manifests as a cycle of rapid, widespread learning, as well as differentiation of all areas of the brain (Diamond & Hopson, 1998). In this period, 12-year-olds are primed to seek novelty and take in as much about the world as is possible. They crave stimulation and are often overwhelmed with new experiences (Siegel, 2013).

The period of exuberance is marked by generalized learning, whereas later in adolescence a dendritic *pruning* process takes place, involving the loss of many of these newly formed connections, followed by integration of differentiated parts (Siegel, 2013). This pruning process primes the brain for specialization, allowing individuals to concentrate learning in specific areas such that skills and competence in those areas are refined. At the age of 12, this entire process is just beginning, and a child's brain is highly active in creating new connections and taking in an overabundance of information. As a result, some mental and emotional disorganization, or lack of neural integration, may be outwardly apparent.

The neuronal exuberance process affects many areas of the brain as they become differentiated, but not yet integrated, which leads to slow or out-of-synch communication between parts. For example, as the frontal lobes continue to develop in 12-year-olds, many aspects of intelligence, including judgment, rationality, mental organization, perseverance, planning, working memory, and impulse control, are enhanced (Diamond & Hopson, 1998; Sowell, 1999). However, neither the frontal lobes nor their connections with other brain areas are fully developed in 12-year-olds (Sabbagh, 2006). Because of this lack of integration, 12-year-olds have less access to executive functioning and therefore process information at a much slower rate than adults. The impulsive decision making of many 12-year-olds may not paint a clear picture of their intelligence or reasoning abilities. In reality, their impulsive actions are likely to result from their inability to fully access frontal lobe functioning.

Lack of integration in the middle prefrontal cortex may explain why a 12-year-old will, at times, struggle to make sound judgments, have difficulty communicating in an attuned fashion, fail to understand and empathize with others, be emotionally unstable at times, or inaccurately read social cues. Struggle in any one of these areas is especially pronounced during times of stress (Badenoch, 2008). Prefrontal regions in a 12-year-old's brain are far less efficient and must work harder than the same regions in an adult brain to process the same information. As a result, 12-year-olds may become easily overwhelmed or appear to shut down altogether when given complicated tasks or in stressful situations (Sabbagh, 2006).

> Because the prefrontal cortex is not always online and accessible, 12-year-olds may commit impulsive or risky behaviors before they are able to reflect on the outcome.

The corpus callosum, which connects the right and left hemispheres of the brain, is not fully integrated in the 12-year-old brain; as a result, communication between newly differentiated areas in the right and left hemispheres is inhibited. Therefore, in this growth period, 12-year-olds lose about 20 percent of their ability to name or to regulate emotions (Strauch, 2003).

Because this differentiation–integration process is experience-based, the significant brain changes experienced by the 12-year-old will undoubtedly be affected by the quality of his or her relationships, home life, and school environment. Each experience promotes or inhibits neural integration; thus the quality and nature of a 12-year-old's experiences are critical (Badenoch, 2008). Parental and other important relationships marked by presence, attunement, empathy, and trust will provide a context for healthy brain development (Siegel, 2013). School and home environments in which children feel safe and secure, and in which there is attention to interpersonal dynamics and engagement between individuals, will enhance development in 12-year-olds (Cozolino, 2013). But it is apt to sound a note of caution: Any structural or functional deficits in the brain originating from childhood trauma, ranging from mild to severe, can become more pronounced in the rewiring process of brain that begins around the age of 12. Healthy interpersonal and environmental experiences can be beneficial for those who have experienced early trauma (Badenoch, 2008).

PHYSICAL DEVELOPMENT

In a group of 12-year-olds, one will notice a variety of body types and sizes, some looking like older children and others like fully mature adolescents. Twelve-year-olds have heights ranging from 4 to 6 feet tall and have experienced varying degrees of sexual maturation; all are within normal limits of development (Diamond & Hopson, 1998). One noticeable difference between 12-year-old girls and boys is that, by the end of the year, many girls are close to their mature height, whereas boys are usually only beginning a growth spurt. Compared to other body parts, both boys' and girls' legs grow the fastest, although their arms and torsos catch up during later adolescence. Twelve-year-old boys and girls may experience pain in various parts of the body – commonly referred to as "growing pains" – which often signal the onset of puberty.

During puberty, a 12-year-old may tend to go to bed later and want to sleep later than in previous years. This change results because melatonin, a hormone associated with sleep, is produced about two hours later and remains in the system longer in the morning in children who have begun puberty. Too little sleep can result in daytime sleepiness, depressive mood, and sleep/wake behavior problems (Wolfson & Carskadon, 1998). Because of their growing bodies, 12-year-olds need substantial amounts of sleep, food, and exercise. Wood (2007) noted that a mid-morning school snack for a 12-year-old is just as important as it was when he or she was 5 years old (Wood, 2007).

> Parents may believe that their 12-year-old is sleeping the day away, particularly on weekends. In fact, many 12-year-olds are actually sleep-deprived and need about ten hours of sleep a night.

Sexual Development/Puberty

The onset of pubertal development occurs at different times for different children. On average, girls enter puberty 18 months earlier than boys. Factors that influence the onset of puberty include heredity, nutrition, exercise, and physical health. The entire pubertal process lasts four or five years and most 12-year-olds will be somewhere in the process, but at different stages and rates. Some 12-year-olds experience an early or late onset of puberty, and, because they are often unaware that the onset and rate of puberty vary immensely, they need reassurance from parents that their growth and development are normal.

Increasing levels of estrogen released by the ovaries trigger the onset of puberty in girls around the age of 12. As they enter puberty, girls grow taller, their hips begin to widen, and their breasts begin to develop. In addition, girls begin to grow hair on the legs, under the arms, and in the pubic region. On average, girls begin menstruating around the age of 12 or 13, with the age of onset ranging from 10½ to 15½ years of age (Berk, 2007; Chumlea, 2003). The first menstrual cycle is termed "menarche," after which girls can become pregnant. Another pubertal change that occurs in girls is the accumulation of body fat, which can be unsettling for many 12-year-olds, who are often self-conscious about their bodies (Berk, 2007).

Increasing levels of the hormone testosterone trigger the onset of puberty in boys between the ages of 12 and 14. With puberty, boys become taller, heavier, and stronger. Their shoulders broaden, and their voices deepen and crack, causing a change in voice that many boys find

> Friends who were the same size and body type at the age of 11 may look years apart at 12. Depending on gender and culture, early development may be a source of shame or pride for a 12-year-old.

embarrassing. In addition, boys begin to grow hair under the arms, on the face, and in the pubic region. At this time, the testes grow and begin to produce sperm, and the penis and other reproductive organs enlarge. On average, a boy's first ejaculation, or "spermarche," takes place around the age of 12. After this time, boys can impregnate girls who have reached menarche. Many 12-year-old boys will experience nocturnal emissions, or "wet dreams," which are a release of semen during sleep. Pubescent boys often gain weight, but will thin out during adolescence. Whereas most girls are approximately halfway through pubertal development at the age of 12, most boys are only beginning their pubertal development.

Motor Skills

A 12-year-old who has entered puberty develops increased muscular strength and coordination. The enthusiasm of 12-year-olds can lead to all-out immersion in play or sports followed by collapse from overexhaustion. The fingers of 12-year-olds, which are growing longer, can help them to grasp objects better. Both boys and girls may be clumsy because of the accelerated growth in their legs, hands, and feet. Gross motor skills are significantly improved during adolescence, although girls' improvement is gradual, while boys' gains are more dramatic (Berk, 2007). Because motor development and physical activity improvements emerge more quickly and dramatically for boys, some 12-year-old boys will be significantly more advanced than others based on their developmental rate.

COGNITIVE DEVELOPMENT

> The cognitive development of a 12-year-old can be deceiving. Removed from social stressors, 12-year-olds can appear thoughtful and logical, but social pressure and stress can quickly cause 12-year-olds to revert back to concrete thinking.

As a result of drastic changes in the brain, a major hallmark in 12-year-old cognitive development is a shift from concrete to formal operational thinking. Many 12-year-olds are on the brink of the "formal operational" stage, which was described by Piaget and Inhelder (1969) as a time at which the individual develops the ability to form abstract thoughts. Formal operational thinking typically begins around the age of 11, but is not fully reached until the ages of 15–20. Whereas most 12-year-olds possess some access to formal operational thought, this is not likely to be their primary mode of thinking. A 12-year-old's newly acquired formal operational thought may regress during times of stress.

As they begin to utilize formal operational thinking, 12-year-olds develop an ability to think about the past and future. They are less confined to the here and now, and are more able to focus on future possibilities and goals. Children utilizing formal operational thinking can solve problems and draw conclusions by means of hypodeductive thought, and they can assimilate reality by means of imagined or deduced events (Piaget & Inhelder, 1969). With the ability to hypothesize and imagine scenarios without concrete evidence, a 12-year-old no longer relies on trial-and-error learning, but rather can imagine the possible consequences before taking action. However, 12-year-olds may struggle to make connections between events, feelings, and situations. Although they are beginning to develop the capacity to create links, they still may miss important connections. Their newfound capacity to think about possibilities often leads to idealistic thinking, which is in conflict with reality. As a result, 12-year-olds may be critical.

A 12-year-old beginning to use formal operational thinking shifts from a polarized "black and white," "right or wrong" way of thinking and is able to see a gray area. This shift may provide a 12-year-old with clarity and assurance about some issues, but it may also lead to confusion about long-held dichotomous beliefs and ideas about the world. At the same time, a 12-year-old is beginning to see others' viewpoints, often creating additional confusion in the absence of the familiar concrete right-or-wrong categories.

Twelve-year-olds begin to develop the ability for metacognition and to reflect on their own thoughts. As a result, they think more about themselves and become increasingly self-conscious. Many 12-year-olds come to believe that they are the focus of everyone else's attention or concern, imagining that they always have an audience. They may feel awkward, work hard to keep up appearances, and avoid embarrassment. In addition, they may develop a personal fable, or a sense of self-importance or a belief that the world revolves around them (Elkind, 2007). This apparent egocentrism is actually newly developed perspective taking, which can cause 12-year-olds to be more concerned about what others think about them. This experience sometimes has a negative effect, because some 12-year-olds become self-deprecating or place blame upon themselves.

WORLDVIEW/EGO DEVELOPMENT

Some 12-year-olds have a need to gain a sense of competence in certain activities. They may seek activities in which they are already capable or they may strive to develop skills that they perceive as important for acceptance. If children are successful in these skills, they will gain a sense of industry and ability, whereas they may develop a sense of inferiority and lack confidence if they are unable to complete these tasks (Erikson, 1968). Twelve-year-olds are able to identify their strengths, but may not remember them during times of stress.

Many 12-year-olds begin to ask the question "who am I?" as they begin to solidify a personal identity. As children develop a stronger sense of self, they will strive to find a balance between this sense of self and societal expectations, and to create a perceived role in society (Erikson, 1968; Lerner, 2002). During this period of identity exploration, 12-year-olds will experiment with different ways of being to see what fits them personally and may even change their friends, music, or style of dress. This is a normal "trying on" of identities for many preadolescents. Parental consistency and acceptance are critical for children navigating this period of identity development (Berk, 2007).

Some 12-year-olds will identify with rules and roles of their peer group and attempt to rigidly conform. As a result of rigid conformity, some 12-year-olds become increasingly self-conscious and develop a mode of self-evaluation (Loevinger, 1966). Twelve-year-olds are often overly sensitive about appearance and performance. Many will become irrationally overwhelmed with a bad haircut, uncool clothing, or a pimple. Most 12-year-olds avoid being different from their peers, although they do want to be unique. This polarity presents a difficult challenge for 12-year-olds, who strive for exceptionality, yet fear being seen as different or unacceptable.

About 2–3 percent of young people identify as lesbian, gay, or bisexual. Twelve-year-olds are just beginning to develop their sexual identity. Biological factors, including genetics and prenatal hormone levels, play a significant role in homosexuality. Many adults who identify as gay or lesbian report that they were aware of same-sex attractions by the age of 12. Lesbian, gay, and bisexual teenagers face special problems in developing a positive sexual identity (Berk, 2007).

Racial/Ethnic Identity Development

Twelve-year-olds tend to develop a greater understanding of cultural and race differences, and to be more aware of the attitudes and behaviors of persons in positions of power. They may also begin to understand various perspectives of historic events. Twelve-year-olds can see individual and family struggles against bias, and are often willing to openly discuss culture, race, and other differences. As they develop, 12-year-olds will gain a more in-depth understanding of individual, family, and community identity based on cultural values (Batiste, 2001).

Most 12-year-olds are able to grasp racial and cultural stereotypes and to speak from multiple perspectives. Many 12-year-olds are aware of the valuing/devaluing of culture and race by peers, media, and society, and they are also aware of the advantages and disadvantages of membership of some groups (Batiste, 2001). Twelve-year-olds may develop a sense of unfairness and be willing to speak out with passion about what they perceive as wrong.

Whereas many 12-year-olds are able to see the injustice of oppression, others may cling to group or family norms of prejudice. Driven by an intense desire to be accepted, 12-year-olds may fear or be hurtful to those who are different, including those from different ethnic backgrounds (Rutland & Killen, 2015). Familial influence plays a role in the development of racial/ethnic prejudice, although 12-year-olds value the norms of their peers more than those of their families, which may lead to a shift in beliefs, for better or for worse.

EMOTIONAL DEVELOPMENT

Twelve-year-olds commonly experience mood swings and irritability, especially in the family setting. This elevated emotionality may result from increased school and peer pressure, and concern about puberty. Twelve-year-olds may begin to talk back to parents as they explore their identity and seek autonomy. Lack of sleep may also augment mood swings in 12-year-olds.

Years away from toddlerhood, 12-year-olds may exhibit a new type of temper tantrum. They are often just as surprised by the overwhelming emotional outburst as their parents!

When 12-year-olds express emotions, they display much passion and very little middle ground, and may feel overwhelmed by the intensity of their feelings. Twelve-year-olds may mask emotions such as fear, guilt, shame, and sadness by expressing anger, which is often confusing for 12-year-olds and their parents alike. Although anger is a frequent emotional response for 12-year-olds, many are able to contain their anger because they have developed a greater degree of self-control; however, outward expression of anger in the form of yelling and throwing things is more common than withdrawing.

Whereas 12-year-olds cry, they are more likely to cry at home than in public because they may be hesitant to express emotions in front of peers for fear of social rejection. Twelve-year-olds worry about many things including school, friends, and physical appearance. They are concerned not only for themselves, but for others as well – especially friends. However, at home, they may hesitate to verbally communicate their feelings as they sort them out internally (Wood, 2007). Twelve-year-olds show interest in others, and have the capacity for empathy and understanding.

SOCIAL DEVELOPMENT

Twelve-year-olds spend more time socializing with peers and less with parents. Twelve-year-olds may visit each other's houses and hold sleepovers. Twelve-year-old boys and girls differ in how they spend time with their friends, but for both this time is invaluable. Boys may be uncomfortable and refrain from sharing feelings, but bond with others over the shared experiences such as sports, games, or activities. Girls tend to be more comfortable with feelings and strive to connect emotionally with friends. Around the age of 12, both boys and girls begin to gossip, discussing those whom they admire and critically evaluating others. Although girls are more intimate in their social relationships, at the age of 12 girls also have more discord within their social relationships. Girl's friendships are less stable during this period as a result of the greater emotional intensity (Collins & Steinberg, 2006). Girls invest significant emotional energy in their friendships and may feel betrayed, hurt, or ignored easily.

With increased competence and confidence, some 12-year-olds seek greater independence, which may lead to new friction within the family, particularly if parents are unprepared or unaware of this developmentally appropriate shift. Some 12-year-olds will be less likely to agree with parents and may even appear to disagree just for the sake of disagreeing. Twelve-year-olds are now fully immersed in their peer groups and are often more influenced by their peers than their parents. In spite of their wishes for independence, however, 12-year-olds will, at times, be dependent on parents for support in the midst of confusion and vulnerability associated with their expanded world.

> Most 12-year-olds desire parental affection in the safety of their own homes, but may cringe at a parent's attempt at a public hug.

Because of 12-year-olds' enthusiasm and peer-oriented focus, groups of 12-year-olds may give teachers difficulty in the classroom, whereas individual 12-year-olds typically do not. Because 12-year-olds desperately want to be accepted by the group, for many children this desire supersedes following a teacher's rules. Twelve-year-olds who perceive themselves as having freedom in the classroom may be less disruptive. When relating to teachers, 12-year-olds are less dependent on them than in previous years and possess more self-direction in their studies. For many 12-year-olds, homework is a primary struggle because it requires discipline, motivation, and organization, which are often underdeveloped qualities in 12-year-olds.

RELATIONSHIP DEVELOPMENT

At the age of 12, children begin to develop increasing independence from parents and shift the focus of relationships from home to peers. This shift allows 12-year-olds to explore interests within a greater community of influence. Twelve-year-olds seek out peers as their primary source of support and go to parents less often in times of need. Because of their reliance on peers for acceptance, peer influence is very powerful. Often, 12-year-olds will follow unspoken or explicit social rules about how to dress and behave, and are vulnerable to criticism or evaluation by others – especially same-sex peers. They may alter behavior to fit in, including intentionally decreasing academic performance or participating in acting-out behavior. Twelve-year-olds want balance in their social relationships and strive to be equal to, rather than better or worse than, their peers (Ames et al., 1988).

> Some 12-year-olds may focus on the quantity, rather than quality, of friendships.

Twelve-year-olds' interest in romantic relationships varies. Some interest in a romantic other is almost assured for most 12-year-olds, even though the interest may be short-lived. Generally, girls are more interested in boys than boys are in girls. Boys are often annoyed and irritated by unwanted attention from girls. Twelve-year-olds are likely fond of attending school social functions and enjoy coed group activities. Boys and girls show a change in their concern about grooming and appearance, and dress for various occasions.

> Most 12-year-olds relate to peers of both the same and opposite genders, and may develop sexual feelings for others as a new dimension of relationships.

Many 12-year-olds would not attempt to kiss a romantic other, with the exception of ritual kissing games. Most 12-year-olds are just beginning to realize more fully that sexual activity occurs outside of the conception of babies. Boys and girls of 12 will focus on sexual body parts, be curious about sexual behavior, and have increased interest in sexual stimulation (Campbell, Mallappa, Wisniewski, & Silovsky, 2013). They will often engage in same-sex and opposite-sex sexual experimentation, which is considered normal and does not cause or predict sexual orientation (Ames et al., 1988). Most 12-year-olds are aware of same-sex attraction, although many do not understand the dynamics, particularly sexual, of same-sex relationships. Lesbian, gay, bisexual, and transgender (LGBT) children are at great risk of confusion and discrimination (Savin-Williams & Ream, 2003).

DEVELOPMENT IN THE AGE OF TECHNOLOGY

As they are transitioning into adolescence, the technology and media use of 12-year-olds increases exponentially. Whereas only 8 percent of 12-year-olds own a smartphone, most 12-year-olds engage in a range of computer activities and spend the most time on social networking sites, watching online videos, and playing online games (Lenhart, 2012; Rideout, Foehr, & Roberts, 2010). When 12-year-olds are doing their homework at the computer, a large part of the time they are also instant messaging, listening to music, texting, surfing the Internet, or updating/viewing Facebook pages (Rideout et al., 2010).

The advent of technology has changed the way in which 12-year-olds interact with each other socially. In fact, social networks can cultivate emotional intimacy, strengthen interpersonal relationships, and give 12-year-olds access to friends with privacy from their parents. However, the increase in social media interactions brings with it concerns for 12-year-olds, such as cyberstalking and cyberbullying (Giedd, 2012).

When parents set limits, 12-year-olds spend less time with media, and are subject to less exposure to violent, sexual, and other developmentally inappropriate content. Parents will do well to understand what their 12-year-olds are doing online, what kinds of content they are consuming, and with whom they are communicating. When parents monitor these things, they can ensure that children are engaging with safe online content and digital interactions. Parents' interactions with 12-year-olds online and through texting can enhance the parent–child relationship; yet parents should allow 12-year-olds limited privacy to interact with friends.

BEST PRACTICES FOR COUNSELING/THERAPY

For counselors, seeing 12-year-olds can be rewarding and challenging. An important factor for counselors to consider is a 12-year-old's unique degree of development across multiple domains, because this will guide counseling plans and goals. In addition, counselors will benefit from understanding the common therapeutic needs of 12-year-olds, such as warmth and affection, respect, empathy, and someone who can hear and understand them – especially in troubling times (Badenoch, 2008).

When Counseling/Therapy Is Indicated

A healthy and well-adjusted 12-year-old may struggle with emotion regulation, making it hard to determine what is "normal" and what warrants outside assistance from a counseling professional. Drastic developmental changes in 12-year-olds often lead to sensitivity in peer and family relationships. Internal and external pressure may cause 12-year-olds to worry about performance, acceptance, and appearance. In addition to seeking support for stressful transition to adolescence, some 12-year-olds need counseling for specific issues, such as depression and suicidal ideation, self-harm, body image issues, and drug/alcohol abuse.

Depression may be masked by the mood swings and increasing need for autonomy expressed by 12-year-olds. Isolation is a warning sign of depression. Whereas 12-year-olds are usually exuberant and enthusiastic, a 12-year-old who does not want to engage socially or who withdraws from the family may well be depressed. A lack of attention to appearance and hygiene may indicate depression in 12-year-olds, who are usually very concerned with image, although unconcerned with clean rooms and homes. In early adolescence, girls are more likely to experience depression than boys. There may be a link between early pubertal development and depression among preadolescent girls (Ge, Conger, & Elder, 2001).

Related to depression, suicidal ideation is cause for concern, regardless of age. Suicide is the third leading cause of death for young people after homicide and automobile accidents. Boys are more successful in completing suicide, although girls make more suicide attempts. Risk factors for suicidal ideation among 12-year-olds are exposure to suicide by friends or family, social isolation, substance abuse, and guns in the home (Bearman & Moody, 2004).

Nonsuicidal self-harm consists of cutting, scratching, burning, or any other self-destructive behavior in the absence of a desire to die. In 12-year-olds, self-harm often appears as an outward sign of internal pain and a warning sign of distress. "Emo" culture has somewhat popularized teenage angst and self-injurious behavior. The elevation of depression and angst through music, poems, movies, and fashion has both normalized and promoted these phenomena. A 12-year-old's identification with emo culture does not, however, automatically mean that he or she participates in self-harm; the prevalence is higher among older adolescents.

Twelve-year-olds, especially girls and some boys, may feel dissatisfaction with their bodies and thus may be at risk of developing an eating disorder. The media, peers, and family can impact on a 12-year-old's body image, especially when conversations focus on appearance, weight, body fat, or diet. When 12-year-olds comment on body dissatisfaction and express intense shame, embarrassment, or insecurity about their bodies, body image problems may be suspected. In addition to body image disturbances, warning signs of eating disorders may include restriction of food intake, skipping meals, significant weight loss, preoccupation with calories, vomiting after meals, or obsessive exercise.

Most 12-year-olds do not experiment with drugs or alcohol beyond the occasional sip of a parent's drink. Although common in later adolescence, most 12-year-olds do not seek out opportunities to drink or use drugs. Alcohol or drug use in 12-year-olds can be a warning sign of larger issues, and therefore warrants exploration.

Developmentally Appropriate Approaches

A 12-year-old's unique place in his or her developmental journey will signify which mode of counseling is appropriate. Because of the cognitive shift to formal operational thinking and the capacity of many 12-year-olds to engage in conversation, use abstract thinking, and to be insightful, therapists may opt for cognitive-based techniques and talk therapy with this age group. However, for many 12-year-olds, activity and expressive arts therapies may be more appropriate. Cognitive-based therapies can be limiting for several reasons. Twelve-year-olds may be able to process content, but not verbalize their experiences (Kottman, 2011). As they transition into formal operational thinking, they may still struggle to answer questions, to see multiple sides of an issue, or to use abstract thinking and logic, all of which are necessary for cognitive-based therapies. Specific cues, such as a 12-year-old's affinity for conversation, capacity to remain seated, or observable desire to play or create in session, can be helpful in determining the most appropriate intervention (Shokouhi, Limberg, & Armstrong, 2014). Depending on the developmental stage, many potentially appropriate interventions can be used with 12-year-olds.

Activity therapies   Activity therapy may be appropriate for 12-year-olds who are less conversational, have trouble remaining seated, or gravitate toward objects or activities in the room (Shokouhi et al., 2014). Child-centered activity play therapy (CCAPT) is a modification of child-centered play therapy (CCPT) whereby materials and play are adapted to fit a mature 12-year-old. In CCAPT, children have the opportunity to participate in various activities, such as woodworking, baking, arts and crafts, theater, and music, with or without engaging in conversation. Another form of activity therapy, Adlerian play therapy (AdPT), may be appropriate for a 12-year-old struggling with family or peer relationships, because it uses play or activity to focus on family and social interactions, roles, and encouragement (Kottman, 2003).

Expressive arts therapy   Many 12-year-olds enjoy expressive arts, such as painting, sandtray work, clay, music, or acting. Expressive arts allow children to communicate without words and to tap into creative expression (Bratton & Ferebee, 1999). Expressive arts therapy may be fitting for 12-year-olds who are less talkative, but are able to describe their own creation, to receive insight, and to use and understand metaphors, or who are more closed or rigid (Shokouhi et al., 2014). Expressive arts provide an outlet through which some 12-year-olds can express themselves nonverbally and, perhaps, more freely. Using imagination and creativity, they are often able to gain insight into emotions and behaviors (Flahive & Ray, 2007).

Cognitive-based therapies   Cognitive-based therapies may be useful for 12-year-olds who are comfortable with silence and can see multiple aspects of an issue, think abstractly, and answer questions (Shokouhi et al., 2014). Cognitive-behavioral therapy (CBT) is an intervention that emphasizes problem solving and skill building in which therapists aim to reduce clients' symptoms through challenging and changing dysfunctional thought patterns (Beck & Beck, 2011). Cognitive-behavioral therapy may be effective for 12-year-olds who are able to identify their own thoughts and use metacognition in order to challenge maladaptive thought patterns.

Another cognitive-based therapy, brief counseling is often used with 12-year-olds in school settings where time is limited (Littrell & Linck, 2004). Brief counseling offers 12-year-olds an opportunity to focus on exceptions to problems, untapped resources, and goals. Brief therapy counselors can help 12-year-olds to focus on strengths and to determine what works rather than what does not. Solution-focused brief counselors ask questions that are future-focused, and aim to elicit hope and healing from the client (Berg & Stiner, 2003). Because of the focus on forethought and hypothetical situations, brief counseling requires formal operational thinking.

Group therapies   Relevant to the peer and social focus of 12-year-olds is group work. Because 12-year-olds are more likely to accept feedback from peers than from authority figures, group interventions may be appropriate (Sonstegard, 1998). Groups are helpful because they allow for real-time reactions from others (Shechtman & Yanov, 2001). Twelve-year-olds in a child-centered or activity group help one another assume responsibility for their relationships (Landreth, 2002). In adventure-based groups, 12-year-olds can form cohesive relationships with others in order to solve problems, often using ropes courses and group dynamic activities.

Filial therapy/child–parent relationship therapy (CPRT)   Parents of 12-year-olds may be confused about the changing emotional, social, and parental needs of their child, and may lose confidence in their parenting skills, leading to a possible disconnect between parent and child. Child–parent relationship therapy (CPRT), a form of filial therapy, was designed to enhance the child–parent relationship (Landreth & Bratton, 2006). It may be a fitting addition to counseling in that it can help parents and children to renegotiate their changing relationships and to remain firmly connected. Adaptations can be made to CPRT to meet the developmental needs of 12-year-olds (Packman & Solt, 2004). Whereas CPRT typically involves play with toys, a 12-year-old participating in CPRT may prefer to engage in activities such as baking or arts and crafts. Regardless of the activity, the relationship between 12-year-old and parent is the focus, and parents strive to communicate acceptance and understanding.

Working with Parents, Teachers, and Caregivers

Twelve-year-olds want to be heard and feel important. Group acceptance and approval is paramount, and often parents and teachers feel devalued by a 12-year-old's focus on peer relations. Parents can best support a 12-year-old by being consistent, caring, and available. Whereas 12-year-olds may have new reasoning abilities with which to argue against rules and boundaries, parents can support this transition by remaining consistent with developmentally appropriate rules. Family meetings, in which a 12-year-old can participate in household decision making, help children to feel that they are significant members of the family who are taken seriously. In response to a 12-year-old's heightened emotions, parents can offer support by acknowledging and empathizing with a child's feelings, whether or not they agree with them.

Parents are often quick to give advice, dismiss feelings, or good-naturedly laugh off a child's problems. Instead, parents can offer support by listening and attempting to understand a child before responding. It is also important for parents to show love and acceptance, even when a 12 year-old may not reciprocate. Parents are also encouraged to be available and present, but not probing. Children may not acknowledge a parent's presence, but 12-year-olds need parents to be emotionally and physically available.

Teachers can enhance the learning process of 12-year-olds by activating the social interest of their students through attention to interpersonal dynamics and by engaging students with one another in order to build classroom communities (Cozolino, 2013). Teachers may choose to allow flexibility within the classroom, giving the more independent 12-year-old a chance to self-regulate and feel less-controlled (Ames et al., 1988). Teachers can support the development of autonomy by allowing students to have space for self-direction. Additionally, 12-year-olds enjoy rituals and ceremonies, especially those that confirm that they are moving toward becoming responsible adult members of society (Wood, 2007). Finally, teachers may choose to cultivate student discipline, motivation, and organization within the classroom, so that students can eventually apply them to self-directed learning and homework.

CONCLUSION

The age of 12 is a time of great change across multiple domains of development. Twelve-year-olds are in the midst of a transition period between childhood and adolescence, and must navigate significant cognitive, interpersonal, emotional, and physical changes. Twelve-year-olds begin to cultivate peer relationships, test boundaries, explore new things and ideas, and strive for autonomy. Twelve-year-olds enter the world of complex ideas and find themselves feeling much more intensely as a result of changes in the brain; they expand their social world to include peers, who become very important and influential; and they experience many physical changes, including puberty, and begin to be curious about sex. Most 12-year-olds experience significant change across all aspects of life – but the change in each 12-year-old is unique.

Counselors who work with 12-year-olds must be aware of the unique development of each individual. Some 12-year-old clients will enthusiastically engage in traditional introspective counseling, whereas others are unprepared to express themselves verbally through formal thought. Flexibility is key in working with this diverse age group.

REFERENCES

Ames, L. B., Baker, S. M., & Ilg, F. L. (1988). *Your ten- to fourteen-year-old*. New York, NY: Delacort.

Badenoch, B. (2008). *Being a brain-wise therapist: A guide to interpersonal neurobiology*. New York, NY: W. W. Norton.

Batiste, D. (2001). *A world of difference institute anti-bias study guide (elementary/intermediate level)*. New York, NY: Anti-Defamation League.

Bearman, P., & Moody, P. (2004). Adolescent suicidality. *American Journal of Public Health, 94*(1), 89–95.

Beck, J., & Beck, A. (2011). *Cognitive behavior therapy: Basics and beyond* (2nd ed.). New York, NY: Guildford.

Berg, I. K., & Stiener, T. (2003). *Children's solution work*. New York, NY: Norton.

Berk, L. E. (2007) *Development through the lifespan* (4th ed.). Boston, MA: Allyn & Bacon.

Bratton, S. C., & Ferebee, K. W. (1999). The use of structured expressive art activities in group activity therapy with preadolescents. In D. S. Sweeney & L. E. Homeye. (Eds.), *The handbook of group play therapy: How to do it, how it works, whom its best for* (pp. 192–214). San Francisco, CA: Jossey-Bass.

Campbell, C., Mallappa, A., Wisniewski, A. B., & Silovsky, J. F. (2013). Sexual behavior of prepubertal children. In D. S. Bromberg & W. T. O'Donohue (Eds.), *Handbook of child and adolescent sexuality: Developmental and forensic psychology* (pp. 145–170). San Diego, CA: Elsevier.

Chumlea, W. H. (2003). Age at menarche and racial comparisons in US girls. *Pediatrics, 111*(1), 110–113.

Collins, W. A., & Steinberg, L. (2006). Adolescent development in interpersonal context. In W. Damon & N. Eisenberg (Eds.), *Handbook of child psychology, vol. 4: Socioemotional processes* (pp. 1003–1067). New York, NY: Wiley.

Cozolino, L. (2013). *The social neuroscience of education: Optimizing attachment and learning in the classroom*. New York, NY: W. W. Norton.

Diamond, M., & Hopson, J. (1998). *Magic trees of the mind: How to nurture your child's intelligence, creativity, and healthy emotions from birth through adolescence*. New York, NY: Plume/Penguin.

Elkind, D. (2007). *The hurried child: Growing up too fast too soon* (3rd ed.). Cambridge, MA: Perseus.

Erikson, E. (1968). *Identity, youth, and crisis*. New York, NY: Norton.

Flahive, M. W., & Ray, D. (2007). The effect of group sandtray therapy with preadolescents. *Journal for Specialists in Group Work, 32*(4), 362–382.

Ge, X., Conger, R. D., & Elder, G. J. (2001). The relation between puberty and psychological distress in adolescent boys. *Journal of Research on Adolescence, 11*(1), 49–70.

Giedd, J. N. (2012). The digital revolution and adolescent brain evolution. *Journal of Adolescent Health, 51*(2), 101–105.

Kottman, T. (2003). *Partners in play: An Adlerian approach to play therapy* (2nd ed.). Alexandria, VA: American Counseling Association.

Kottman, T. (2011). *Play therapy basics and beyond*. Alexandria, VA: American Counseling Association.

Landreth, G. (2002). *Play therapy: The art of the relationship*. New York, NY: Routledge.

Landreth, G., & Bratton, S. (2006). *Child parent relationship training (CPRT)*. New York, NY: Routledge.

Lenhart, A. (2012). *Teens, smartphones, and texting*. Washington, DC: Pew Research Center.

Lerner, R. M. (2002). *Concepts and theories of human development*. Malwah, NY: Lawrence Erlbaum.

Littrell, J. M., & Linck, K. (2004). Brief counseling with children and adolescents: Interactive, culturally responsive, and action-based. In A. Vernon. (Ed.), *Counseling children and adolescents* (3rd ed., pp. 137–159). Denver, CO: Love.

Loevinger, J. (1966). The meaning and measurement of ego development. *American Psychologist*, *21*(3), 195–206.

Packman, J., & Solt, M. D. (2004). Filial therapy modifications for preadolescents. *International Journal of Play Therapy*, *13*(1), 57–77.

Piaget, J., & Inhelder, B. (1969). *The psychology of the child*. New York, NY: Basic Books.

Rideout, V. J., Foehr, U. G., & Roberts, D. F. (2010). *Generation M²: Media in the lives of 8- to 18-year-olds*. Menlo Park, CA: Kaiser Family Foundation.

Rutland, A., & Killen, M. (2015). A developmental science approach to reducing prejudice and social exclusion: Intergroup processes, social-cognitive development, and moral reasoning. *Social Issues & Policy Review*, *9*(1), 121–154.

Sabbagh, L. (2006). The teen brain, hard at work. *Scientific American*, *17*(2), 54–59.

Savin-Williams, R. C., & Ream, G. L. (2003). Suicide attempts among sexual-minority male youth. *Journal of Clinical Child & Adolescent Psychology*, *32*(4), 509–522.

Shechtman, Z., & Yanov, H. (2001). Interpretives (confrontation, interpretation, and feedback) in preadolescent counseling groups. *Group Dynamics: Theory, Research, and Practice*, *5*(2), 124–135.

Shokouhi, A. M., Limberg, D., & Armstrong, S. A. (2014). Counseling preadolescents: Utilizing developmental cues to guide therapeutic approaches. *International Journal of Play Therapy*, *23*(4), 217–230.

Siegel, D. J. (2013). *Brainstorm: The power and purpose of the teenage brain*. New York, NY: Jeremy P. Tarcher/Penguin.

Sonstegard, M. (1998). Counseling children in groups. *Journal of Individual Psychology*, *54*(2), 251–267.

Sowell, E. W. (1999). In vivo evidence for postadolescent brain maturation in frontal and striatal regions. *Nature Neuroscience*, *2*(10), 859–861.

Stiles, J., & Jernigan, T. L. (2010). The basics of brain development. *Neuropsychology Review*, *20*(4), 327–348.

Strauch, B. (2003). *The primal teen: What the new discoveries about the teenage brain tell us about our kids*. New York, NY: Anchor Books.

Wolfson, A. R., & Carskadon, M. A. (1998). Sleep schedules and daytime functioning in adolescents. *Child Development*, *69*(4), 875–887.

Wood, C. (2007). *Yardsticks: Children in the classroom ages 4–14* (3rd ed.). Turners Falls, MA: Northeast Foundation for Children.

Part V

THERAPIST RESOURCES

14

AGE-TO-AGE SERIES

Dee C. Ray and Kimberly M. Jayne

The Age-to-Age Series is a handout series intended for therapists to use as resources for parents, caregivers, teachers, or other systemic partners. Each handout provides a description of typical characteristics for the age group, along with expected challenges, tips for caregivers, and indicators of when caregivers should seek support. For ages 3–6, each handout is divided into half-years to emphasize the differences that occur during that year of maturation; for ages 7–12, the handouts characterize the year as a whole. Our intention is that the reader will copy and distribute these handouts as needed to clients. However, the handouts should not be altered or digitally posted/distributed without permission from the publisher.

3

Brain & Cognitive Development

- Has a brain that is two-and-a-half times more active than the adult brain
- Learns and uses many new vocabulary words
- Speaks in sentences of between three and six words
- Masters basic grammar rules and pronouns
- Understands numbers and basic counting
- Follows simple directions with no more than three steps
- Struggles with problem-solving skills
- Names colors and recalls parts of familiar stories
- Enjoys repetition, rhymes, sounds, and new words
- Plays make-believe with dolls, animals, and playmates
- Has a vivid fantasy life and sometimes struggles to distinguish fantasy from reality

Physical Development

- Appears taller and thinner – less toddler-like
- Sleeps through the night for 10–12 hours
- Feeds, dresses, washes hands, and brushes own teeth, with some help from adults
- Has greater coordination, and is able to walk, run, jump, climb, and swing with ease
- Walks on tiptoes, and stands and hops on one foot
- Is able to ride a tricycle, throw a ball overarm, and kick a ball
- Is active and plays until exhausted
- Holds crayons and markers with fingers instead of fists
- Completes large-piece puzzles
- Is able to master toilet training, with some accidents

Emotional Development

- Is often silly and enjoys laughing
- Experiences a wide range of emotions with intensity

- Identifies own and others' feelings
- Shows concern by offering hugs or comfort
- Struggles to regulate emotions when tired, stressed, or experiences changes in routine
- Throws fewer tantrums than at 2½

Relationship & Social Development

- Begins to identify peers as friends
- Loves playing with other children
- Understands taking turns, but struggles to put other's needs before his or her own
- Has difficulty sharing and engaging in cooperative play
- May prefer to play alone to avoid social conflicts
- Often pushes, hits, yells, cries, or displays physical aggression during playtime
- Observes other's behavior and play, and imitates that behavior
- Desires to please his or her parents
- Prefers to be with one parent than the other
- Imitates the actions of parents and other adults
- Displays more independence from parents and caregivers

Normal Challenges at 3

Three-year-olds often have behaviors that parents find challenging or concerning, but which are a normal part of development, such as:

- Frequent potty training accidents when engaged in play, or withholding to avoid missing out on activities
- Masturbating in private or in public
- Enjoying being naked and frequently taking off their clothes
- Asking questions about genitalia and where babies come from or being fascinated with body parts
- Wanting to wear costumes or pretending to be a fictional character or animal

3^{1/2}

Brain & Cognitive Development

- Is imaginative, playful, and prone to fantasy
- Often stutters
- May report difficulty seeing because of growth of depth perception
- May appear to have difficulty hearing because of self-focus/concentration

Physical Development

- Is clumsier and falls more frequently
- Is hesitant to approach tasks
- Finds drawing and building with blocks more difficult because of decreased muscle control
- Has fewer toilet training accidents and is able to sleep through the night without wetting the bed

Emotional Development

- Expresses emotions more intensely
- Cries, whines, or has more difficulty separating from parents
- Is very determined and strong-willed
- May have imaginary friends
- Seems sensitive and becomes upset easily
- Can be inflexible; responds negatively to changes in schedule

Relationship & Social Development

- May try to control others through language
- Likes to play with friends
- Can be argumentative
- Becomes more aggressive and defiant in relationships

Normal Challenges at 3½

- Biting nails, picking nose, sucking thumb, or chewing on clothes to self-soothe
- Excessively blinking or developing facial tics
- Refusing to be cooperative or flexible
- Whining and complaining

Tips for Parents & Caregivers

- Maintain a consistent and predictable daily routine
- Expect your child to be willful, playful, and sometimes silly
- Be patient with toilet training and accidents
- Ask your child to help with simple tasks such as setting the table
- Encourage his or her efforts and don't expect perfection
- Provide appropriate and consistent limits to promote the child's sense of safety and security
- Follow through with consequences
- Avoid using physical punishments, threats, or yelling to prevent unwanted behaviors
- Encourage your child's awareness of others' feelings and needs
- Make time to play with your child at least a few minutes every day

When to Seek Help

- Your child's behavior or abilities seem significantly different from those of other children his or her age
- Your child demonstrates extreme separation anxiety, or withdraws from friends or play
- You need parenting support to address concerns or issues related to discipline
- Your child experiences a significant change or traumatic experience, including loss, disruption in the home or family environment, abuse, or a medical emergency
- You frequently feel disconnected and stressed in your relationship with your child
- Your child has extreme temper tantrums or lacks self-control
- Your child has significant difficulties sleeping or toilet training

4

Brain & Cognitive Development

- Is experiencing a peak period of brain development
- Is experiencing increased integration and communication across right and left brain hemispheres
- Has a short attention span
- Learns new words each day and has an expanding vocabulary
- Asks lots of questions
- Learns best by doing
- Engages in imaginative, dramatic play and enjoys make-believe
- Needs to play and explore; loves dressing up and drama
- Often has rigid and illogical thinking
- Struggles to take other's perspectives
- Enjoys singing, dancing, rhyming, and being read to
- Needs many hands-on experiences, such as with puzzles, sand, and paint
- Moves quickly from one thing to another
- Talks in complete sentences
- Can count between three and six objects
- Tells fantastical lies; has trouble distinguishing between fact and fiction

Physical Development

- Maintains a high energy level without tiring easily
- Is constantly moving; needs lots of room to move
- Is clumsy and accident-prone
- Is able to eat and get dressed independently
- Is able to throw and catch a ball, kick, jump, and climb
- Is able to string beads, stack blocks, and use scissors
- Grows 3–4 inches taller
- Likes to explore his or her body (both boys and girls may masturbate as they discover themselves)

Emotional Development

- Often reacts strongly, with intense feelings of happiness, silliness, anger, and sadness
- Needs adult help to find words to express needs, instead of reacting physically
- Can be aggressive and bossy
- Loves and hates many things
- Has a growing sense of humor, and enjoys laughter and silliness
- Learns from modeling; needs chances to practice new behavior
- May throw temper tantrums

Relationship & Social Development

- Wants to please others
- Likes to talk, but not to listen
- Needs to explore and take the initiative
- Is increasingly concerned about "right" and "wrong"
- Is able to share and take turns with others
- Has increased awareness of differences between self and others
- Develops stronger friendships with other children
- Enjoys pretending and has an active imagination in play
- Is interested in differences between boys and girls
- Can be aggressive with siblings at times
- Plays in groups of mixed sex/gender

Normal Challenges at 4

Four-year-olds often have behaviors that parents find challenging or concerning, but which are a normal part of development. Knowing what to expect from your 4-year-old can reassure you that even when lying, crying, or kicking, he or she is doing exactly what 4-year-olds are supposed to do – and will grow out of these behaviors.

- Aggressive behavior including hitting, kicking, and throwing temper tantrums when angry
- Lying when in trouble
- Frequent nightmares stemming from new feelings and experiences
- Imaginary friends
- Fascination with their own bodies and masturbation
- Fascination with going to the bathroom and using "potty" words or name-calling
- Constant motion and noise

4 1/2

Brain & Cognitive Development

- Starts to tell the difference between fantasy and reality with more ease
- Starts to see that letters and numbers have meaning, but probably is not yet ready to read
- Shows more competency in skills
- Loves to learn new information

Physical Development

- Holds pencil tightly and writes more firmly
- Still active, but a little calmer than earlier in the year

Emotional Development

- Is often fearful or anxious
- May have frequent nightmares
- May develop phobias
- Can stay on-task for a longer period of time, yet still not long
- Is dramatic

Relationship & Social Development

- Having friends becomes important
- Will cooperate more if not pressured
- Initiates interactions and learning
- Plays collaboratively with others

Normal Challenges at 4½

- Seeming "at odds" with environment
- Frequent fears
- Fears developing into phobias (typical for this age)
- Fears regarding what is real and what is not
- Inconsistency, making them hard to predict

Tips for Parents & Caregivers

- Spend one-on-one time with your child, doing things you both enjoy
- Give your child encouragement and support as he or she learns new skills
- Provide consistent routines for your child, including morning and bedtime
- Provide consistent limits and consequences for problem behaviors
- Don't worry too much if your child lies, swears, or exaggerates; model appropriate behavior and he or she will grow out of it
- Read to your child, and honor his or her natural curiosity and questions, but avoid putting pressure on your child or yourself to learn to read, write, etc.
- Reassure your child with your presence when worries/fears are prevalent, rather than trying to reason with them, which is not helpful
- Spend at least a few minutes a day playing with your child
- Many children wet the bed until the age of 5 or 6; use bed pads or pullups to minimize cleanup

When to Seek Help

- Your child's behaviors or abilities seem significantly different from those of other children his or her age
- Your child experiences severe or prolonged anxiety or sadness
- Your child experiences excessive phobias that interfere with daily functioning
- You need parenting support to address concerns or issues related to discipline
- Your child experiences a significant change or traumatic experience, including loss, disruption in the home or family environment, abuse, or a medical emergency
- You frequently feel disconnected and stressed in your relationship with your child
- Your child demonstrates highly aggressive behavior toward you or others
- Your child shows little interest in play or playing with others

5

Brain & Cognitive Development

- Gains in short-term memory
- Is able to connect emotional and factual aspects of memories
- Masters simple planning and organization
- Is talkative and enjoys learning new words
- Learns best through repetition
- Often sees only one way in which to do things
- Ascribes life and movement to inanimate objects, such as stuffed animals
- Learns through active play and hands-on activities such as cutting and gluing
- Thinks intuitively rather than logically
- Loves to be read to by adults and to look at books on his or her own
- Enjoys storytelling, imaginative play, and being creative
- Knows the days of the week, and understands the difference between the past and the future
- Has some difficulty distinguishing between fantasy and reality
- May draw false conclusions about cause and effect

Physical Development

- Boys and girls are similar height and weight
- Gains more control over body movements
- Colors inside the lines and writes letters
- Tiptoes, rides a bicycle, and skips
- Folds paper in half and cuts interior shapes from large pieces of paper
- Is able to trace hands and holds a pencil

Emotional Development

- Is calm and confident in his or her own abilities
- Feels safe with consistent guidelines and routine
- Is positive and optimistic about self and life
- Is quieter and at times more withdrawn
- Avoids overstimulation
- Is able to express feelings verbally
- Demonstrates more self-control and less impulsivity
- Becomes more independent and gains sense of competence

Relationship & Social Development

- Likes to help, cooperate, follow rules, and be "good"
- Seeks approval from adults
- Is kind and accepting toward others
- Is eager to please others and compliant
- Is adoring and affectionate toward parents
- Is polite and friendly toward new people
- Plays well with older siblings, and is kind and protective toward younger siblings
- Engages other children in play and conversation
- Gets along well with peers and plays well with others
- Enjoys spending time at home or in familiar environments

Normal Challenges at 5

Five-year-olds often have behaviors that parents find challenging or concerning, but which are a normal part of development, such as:

- Frequent nightmares, and often waking up screaming and crying
- Enjoying watching television and playing on the computer and needing limits on screen time
- Sometimes *too* obedient and should be protected from overly dominating or aggressive playmates
- Lying to avoid punishment
- Stealing items from other people

Readiness for kindergarten can also be difficult to determine, but not all children are ready to start when they are 5. It is important to consider your child's overall development, in addition to his or her chronological age, birthday, and cognitive abilities, when deciding the best time for your child to start kindergarten.

5 1/2

Brain & Cognitive Development

- Frequently reverses numbers and letters, even if he or she did not do so earlier in the year
- Questions and desires explanations
- Has growing cognitive abilities with which to determine right and wrong
- Gives more elaborate answers to questions

Physical Development

- Appears clumsier and more awkward
- Struggles to keep his or balance
- Is more restless and disorganized
- Has difficulty sitting still for long periods of time
- Tires easily

Emotional Development

- Is still eager to do activities, but less motivated to please than earlier in the year
- Displays extremes in behaviors, both positive and negative
- May seem overly demanding and disobedient
- Experiences intense range and fluctuations in emotions
- May bite nails, pull hair, or cry to relieve anxiety
- Is indecisive
- Is hesitant and insecure

Relationship & Social Development

- Can disobedient with adults, especially parents, which is markedly different from earlier in the year
- Can be oppositional when playing with others
- Is increasingly attuned to others and developing a sense of empathy toward others

Normal Challenges at 5½

- Opposition to adults and peers
- Complaining frequently
- Becoming easily overwhelmed with choices
- Tattling

Tips for Parents & Caregivers

- Spend one-on-one time with your child doing things you both enjoy
- Limit his or her exposure to emotionally intense or violent shows or media
- Model socially appropriate behaviors when your child lies or steals, but avoid harsh punishment
- Provide consistent and structured schedules for daily routines
- Provide opportunities for unstructured, creative play alone, with friends, and with parents
- Give limited choices to avoid overwhelming your child
- Read to him or her, and possibly with him or her, frequently
- Maintain regular bedtime routines
- Be patient with oppositional behavior, and reflect the child's need to exert his or her will
- Provide consistent limits and consequences

When to Seek Help

- Your child's behavior or abilities seem significantly different from those of other children his or her age
- Your child experiences severe or prolonged anxiety or sadness
- Your child does not show interest in developing friendships or playing with friends
- Your child has problems in school or another academic environment
- Your child displays extreme disobedience or defiance
- Your child has frequent accidents or difficulties toileting during the day
- You need parenting support to address concerns or issues related to discipline
- Your child experiences a significant change or traumatic experience, including loss, disruption in the home or family environment, abuse, or a medical emergency
- You frequently feel disconnected and stressed in your relationship with your child
- Your child demonstrates highly aggressive behavior toward you or others
- You are having a difficult time deciding whether your child is ready for kindergarten

Brain & Cognitive Development

- Has an increased ability to focus, concentrate, plan, and set goals
- Is able to complete multistep projects and to follow more complicated directions
- Applies "rules" for behavior in appropriate social contexts, such as saying "thank you" and "you're welcome," or understanding "knock knock" jokes
- Is able to differentiate between fantasy and reality
- Loves to ask questions and learns best through discovery
- Has a 20–30-minute attention span
- Enjoys reading and looking at books
- Understands seasons and holidays, but cannot tell time
- Is intensely curious, and enjoys learning and completing assignments
- Expands his or her vocabulary and verbal communication, with better understanding of grammar
- Enjoys telling and hearing stories
- Learns in an environment of noise and movement

Physical Development

- Gets sick more frequently, and complains about aches and pains
- Moves with speed and high energy, but tires easily
- Starts losing baby teeth and permanent teeth come in; chews objects to relieve teething pain
- Is able to dress, bathe, and tie his or her own shoes,
- Can print the alphabet and write his or her own first and last names
- Is able to bounce and catch a ball, and to ride a bicycle without training wheels

Emotional Development

- Is highly sensitive to criticism and correction
- Is more emotionally volatile under stress, or when hungry and tired
- Is gaining a greater sense of competence and mastery
- Is more aware of other's needs and feelings
- Is proud of accomplishments

Relationship & Social Development

- Wants to be the best and first at everything
- May lie to avoid punishment and has difficulty admitting when he or she is wrong
- Values friendships and selects friends who are similar to himself or herself
- Creates new rules or cheats to win at games; is a poor sport
- Often wrestles, chases, and screams when playing with friends
- Is affectionate and friendly with, and eager to please, teachers
- May express fears about parents becoming sick or dying
- Is becoming more independent from parents and may be more defiant
- May be competitive with siblings

Normal Challenges at 6

Six-year-olds often have behaviors that parents find challenging or concerning, but which are a normal part of development, such as:

- Fear at bedtime and needing a nightlight or security object
- Bedwetting or accidents during times of high stress
- Lying, which is quite normal for this age, but stressful for parents and other adults
- Poor sportsmanship in games
- Defiance of and arguments with parents as the child tries to gain more independence
- More anxiety and fears at bedtime, and needing extra reassurance and comfort
- High sensitivity to criticism and correction, to which perceived judgment or failure they may respond with intense emotion

6 1/2

Brain & Cognitive Development

- Enjoys learning new ideas, facts, and skills
- Likes sharing new knowledge and demonstrating skills for others
- Can count to 100
- Is able to read stories out loud and to use context clues to decode new words
- Writes using capitals and lower case letters
- Can identify familiar forms of money

Physical Development

- Slows down from the high speed of earlier in the year
- Displays greater balance

Emotional Development

- Is calmer and more easygoing
- Is likeable and affectionate
- Has a good sense of humor
- Likes to try new things

Relationship & Social Development

- Gets along well with parents and teachers
- Is talkative
- Is calmer and more easygoing

Normal Challenges at 6½

There are fewer challenges with a 6½-year-old than there were earlier in the year. Among them are:

- Extreme sensitivity to criticism
- High levels of activity
- Performance anxiety
- A tendency to lie to win or to get out of trouble

Tips for Parents & Caregivers

- Avoid criticism or harsh punishment and use encouragement to support your child's developing independence and sense of competence
- Provide consistent daily routines and establish a nightly bedtime routine
- Allow your child to try new skills and work independently, providing support when he or she gets stuck or frustrated
- Provide time for unstructured activities, free play, and physical activity after school
- Provide your child with spacious environments in which he or she can move freely and quickly
- Avoid asking questions that your child will respond to with a lie to avoid getting in trouble or losing
- Respond with patience when your child lies or cheats
- Use logical consequences for problem behaviors, such as cleaning up when your child has broken something or drawing a picture to apologize when he or she cheats
- Play games with your child and model good sportsmanship
- Limit screen time and exposure to scary or violent media

When to Seek Help

- Your child's behavior or abilities seem significantly different from other children his or her age
- You need parenting support to address concerns or issues related to discipline
- Your child experiences a significant change or traumatic experience, including loss, disruption in the home or family environment, abuse, or a medical emergency
- You frequently feel disconnected and stressed in your relationship with your child
- Your child demonstrates highly aggressive behavior toward you or others
- Your child becomes highly discouraged when, or avoids, learning new skills or knowledge
- Your child shows little interest in interacting with others or making friends
- Your child shows little interest in play or physical activities
- Your child is struggling to read or has significant difficulty in school

7

Brain & Cognitive Development

- Is highly observant and aware of the world around him or her
- Has better impulse control and self-control, planning abilities, and problem-solving skills
- Understands irony and sarcasm
- Enjoys reading and being read to by others
- Enjoys challenges at school and is often perfectionistic in his or her work
- Has more logical and stronger reasoning abilities
- Is learning to spell words correctly
- Shows gains in reading comprehension
- Uses more adult-like speech and phrases

Physical Development

- Boys are typically larger in size than girls
- Growth slows, with only small increases in height and weight
- Has stronger hand–eye coordination
- Is able to jump rope, swim, ride scooters
- Enjoys physical activities and is better at organized sports, gymnastics, dance, or martial arts
- Writes clearly and is able to use fine motor skills accurately for cutting, drawing, and stringing beads
- Demonstrates hyperfocus and likes to be visually close to work

Emotional Development

- Is often more withdrawn and quieter
- Experiences large shifts in mood, and is more sensitive and serious in general
- May seem moody and sad without cause
- Tends to worry about serious things, such as wars, illness, natural disasters, and money
- Is more introspective and self-reflective
- May blame others for wrongdoing and has difficulty admitting failure
- Cries easily, but often hides his or her tears to avoid embarrassment

- Is easily disappointed and clings to his or her own plans
- Works hard to control his or her temper, voice, thoughts, and body, and often feels fatigued
- Likes to observe others
- Develops great empathy for others and is highly sensitive to others' feelings

Relationship & Social Development

- Enjoys playing with friends and tends to be more cooperative in play
- Frequently compares himself or herself to others and want others to like him or her
- Wants to follow the rules and is a good listener
- Enjoys spending time with parents and teachers
- Often believes that everyone is out to get him or her, or that the world is unfair
- Tends to make friends with children who are similar to himself or herself
- Is more aware of and concerned about acceptance from peers
- Is less argumentative with parents and siblings
- Is protective of younger siblings and admires older siblings
- May fight for his or her desired seat at the table or in the car

Normal Challenges at 7

Seven-year-olds often have behaviors that parents find challenging or concerning, but which are a normal part of development, such as:

- Seeming more withdrawn, quieter, and sadder in general (but this does not necessarily mean that they are depressed or struggling)
- Worrying more about death, the loss of loved ones, natural disasters, getting good grades, making friends, and other concerns
- Perfectionistic tendencies and repeating a task or assignment multiple times to meet their own high standards
- Sensitivity to rejection and failure, and interpreting bad experiences or mishaps as rejection and responding dramatically

Tips for Parents & Caregivers

- Spend one-on-one time with your child doing things you both enjoy
- Provide consistency and predictability in routines, discipline, and home environments
- Be patient and empathic toward child's complaints and whining
- Give your child tasks and chores to help him or her to feel included and to develop a sense of personal responsibility
- Allow extra time for completion of tasks and encourage breaks when needed
- Provide simple directions with no more than three steps
- Allow your child to have privacy or spend time alone when needed
- Arrange game nights, with developmentally appropriate board and card games
- Ensure your child has a regular bedtime routine and gets enough sleep
- Encourage your child's collections or interests

When to Seek Help

- Your child's behavior or abilities seem significantly different from those of other children his or her age
- You become discouraged by your child's attitudes or behaviors
- Your child appears excessively withdrawn
- Your child is aggressive and engages or welcomes conflict with you or others.
- Your child cries excessively or displays extreme agitation
- Your child has no or few friends or does not socialize with peers
- You need parenting support to address concerns or issues related to discipline
- Your child experiences a significant change or traumatic experience, including loss, disruption in the home or family environment, abuse, or a medical emergency
- You frequently feel disconnected and stressed in your relationship with your child

Brain & Cognitive Development

- Experiences gains in long-term memory and selective attention
- Has an attention span of th30irty minutes
- Learns best through interactive and hands-on experiences
- Enjoys humor and loves to play jokes on others
- Converses on an adult level and adjusts language for different social contexts
- Expresses feelings and emotions verbally
- Uses slang and abbreviated language in conversation and writing
- Understands cause and effect
- Uses repetition and patterns to remember and retrieve information
- Builds and takes things apart to see how they work

Physical Development

- Tends to be physically healthy
- Growth slows overall, but children vary widely in height and weight
- Peaks in activity levels, has high energy, and is often in a hurry
- Draws detailed pictures and shows good fine motor coordination
- Throws at targets with accuracy
- Has improved fine motor skills, is able to sew and play musical instruments, and to hold a pencil in an adult way
- Enjoys high-energy activities such as soccer, basketball, swimming, and karate
- Hormonal activity begins and may result in mood swings
- Has increased awareness of and curiosity about sex and reproduction

Emotional Development

- Is outgoing and sociable, with bouts of rudeness and being demanding

- Is sensitive and tends to be dramatic
- Is able to understand and interpret other's emotions
- Is able to regulate his or her own emotions
- Is self-critical and self-competitive
- Experiences more fear and anxiety, but refrains from sharing those fears with adults

Relationship & Social Development

- Likes to talk
- Prefers group over solitary play, and outdoor over indoor
- Spends increased time with friends
- Enjoys clubs, teams, board games, music, art, and academics
- Is influenced by peer pressure and desires to be accepted by peers
- Focuses on gaining attributes or skills that will garner acceptance from peers
- Likes to play with same-sex peers
- Uses technology to connect with and relate to peers
- Seeks approval from teachers and parents
- Is affectionate and enjoys interactions with adults
- Is competitive with siblings
- Is interested in what others think of him or her
- Is sensitive to criticism and correction

Normal Challenges at 8

Eight-year-olds often have behaviors that parents find challenging or concerning, but which are a normal part of development, such as:

- High levels of activity and energy, and a need for physical activity that adults may find surprising
- Increased focus and concern about peer relationships and acceptance
- Testing rules and limits as they become more independent
- Excessive self-criticism

Tips for Parents & Caregivers

- Provide opportunities for physical activity, and positive ways for your child to focus and expend his or her natural energy

---

- Provide opportunities for group activities and social interaction with friends
- Discuss use of technology, and provide guidance and supervision of child's Internet and media access, limiting his or her access to digital social interaction
- If your child enjoys video games, become familiar with the games and play along
- Provide age-appropriate education and conversation about puberty, healthy relationships, and sex
- When your child becomes self-critical, listen to his or her concerns and offer encouragement
- Spend one-on-one time with your child for at least 30 minutes each week, allow your child to choose the activity

When to Seek Help

- Your child's behavior or abilities seem significantly different from those of other children his or her age
- Your child wets the bed or has difficulty sleeping
- Your child behaves impulsively, lies, or steals frequently
- Your child experiences intense anxiety regarding his or her performance
- Your child experiences intense anxiety when separated from you (his or her parents)
- Your child has difficulty making friends, withdraws from peers, or is overly sensitive to peer pressure
- You need parenting support to address concerns or issues related to discipline
- Your child experiences a significant change or traumatic experience, including loss, disruption in the home or family environment, abuse, or a medical emergency
- You frequently feel disconnected and stressed in your relationship with your child
- Your child is struggling in school or failing subjects

9

Brain & Cognitive Development

- Enjoys mastering new tasks and skills independently
- Is focused and independent in schoolwork and projects
- Is able to be interrupted and return to task successfully
- Thinks logically and rationally, and is able to follow the scientific method
- Has decreased interest in fairy tales, fables, and magic
- Enjoys reading silently and is able to master chaptered books
- Is able to solve mathematical word problems and multiplication tables
- Is more detail-focused and self-sufficient

Physical Development

- Moves at a slower and more purposeful pace
- Complains frequently about somatic discomfort, pains, stomach aches, and headaches
- Tends to push physical limits and tires easily
- Frequently twists hair, bites nails, or bites lips when anxious
- Is able to master cursive handwriting and print neatly
- Enjoy wrestling and rough-and-tumble play (usually boys)
- Enjoys physical activity and organized sports
- Holds objects close to his or her eyes to read or sits too close to the television
- May show early signs of puberty and experience hormonal changes
- Desires more privacy and is more conscious of his or her physical appearance

Emotional Development

- Tends to worry or become anxious
- Gets feelings hurt easily
- Is determined, motivated, and independent
- Is more mature and generally calmer
- Is persistent and sometimes impatient
- Is able to take the perspective of others and understand others' thoughts and feelings
- Follows rules and is eager to gain approval from teachers, parents, or peers
- Is generally self-confident and dependable
- Is able to communicate and express his or her feelings with others
- Has strong and intense internal world and emotional experiences
- Tends to be perfectionistic

Relationship & Social Development

- May seem detached and disinterested in parents
- Is less argumentative with adults, but may become more so with peers
- Understands romantic relationships and has an increased knowledge of sex
- Displays little interest in the opposite sex or romantic partnerships
- Is more acutely aware of differences and similarities between himself or herself and peers
- Is more concerned with social groups and peer acceptance
- Prefers same-sex friends
- Is competitive with peers
- Tends to be overly self-critical and critical of others

Normal Challenges at 9

Nine-year-olds often have behaviors that parents find challenging or concerning, but which are a normal part of development, such as:

- Struggling with taking tests and becoming more anxious about academic performance
- Excessive perfectionism

- Excessive worries
- Competitiveness with others
- Self-criticism
- Sensitivity and avoidance of situations in which they believe they will fail

Tips for Parents & Caregivers

- Allow your child to have spaces and times for privacy
- Support your child's growing independence and provide opportunities for your child to help to make family decisions
- Listen to your child's worries without becoming overly anxious and offer encouragement
- Provide opportunities for group activities and social interaction with friends
- Support your child's competitive interests
- Offer encouragement when your child fails or withdraws because of fear of failure
- Spend one-on-one time with your child for at least 30 minutes each week, and allow your child to choose the activity
- Limit and monitor social interaction over digital sources given the 9-year-old's high level of sensitivity
- Engage as a participant in video games that your child enjoys and also allow your child time with friends without your involvement

When to Seek Help

- Your child's behavior or abilities seem significantly different from those of other children his or her age
- Your child's worries interfere with his or her daily functioning
- Your child withdraws from interaction or competition because of fear of failure
- Your child is overwhelmed by social interactions or has difficulty developing friendships
- Your child experiences severe or prolonged anxiety or sadness
- You need parenting support to address concerns or issues related to discipline
- Your child experiences a significant change or traumatic experience, including loss, disruption in the home or family environment, abuse, or a medical emergency
- You frequently feel disconnected and stressed in your relationship with your child
- Your child demonstrates highly aggressive behavior toward you or others

10

Brain & Cognitive Development

- Tends to think concretely and logically
- Is good at memorization and problem-solving
- Has difficulty solving problems unrelated to his or her previous experiences
- Has increased processing speed
- Likes to classify and organize
- Has increased concentration and an improved attention span
- Likes to learn
- Learns by doing; likes active learning approaches

Physical Development

- Has increased balance, agility, and flexibility for running, climbing, and kicking
- Enjoys organized sports activities
- Has increased power, speed, and accuracy
- Can make quick movements and changes in direction
- Has less upper body strength
- Commonly injures himself or herself because of frequent physical activity
- Has strong hand–eye coordination; drawing and writing improves
- Tends to have sloppy penmanship
- Is beginning a period of speedy physical growth (girls); has yet to start the intense growth period (boys)

Emotional Development

- Is relatively calm
- Is typically flexible and easygoing
- Is comfortable in his or her environment
- Needs to be perceived as "good"
- Has a strong sense of right and wrong
- Demonstrates self-confidence
- Is drawn to activities in which he or she feels competent
- Uses cognitive skills to regulate emotions
- Can become angry quickly, but will calm equally quickly

- Prefers his or her environment to be organized and predictable

Relationship & Social Development

- Is cooperative and pleasant
- Understands and accept rules of social interaction
- Seeks out friends and emotional support through friendships
- Is highly concerned with belonging to a peer group
- Takes on the values and norms of the identified group
- Identifies himself or herself in terms of the peer group
- Experiences a growing sense of racial identity
- Commonly has peers of the same racial/ethnic/cultural background
- Largely determines sex identity by conformity to social roles
- May be becoming aware of same-sex attractions
- Enjoys being part of organizations, teams, or clubs

Normal Challenges at 10

Ten-year-olds often have few behaviors that parents find challenging or concerning, but the following are a normal part of development:

- Excessive concern with belonging to the group
- Choosing peer values over family values
- Desire to spend substantial time with peers
- Spending time and energy on maneuvering through social interactions

Tips for Parents & Caregivers

- Provide opportunities for group activities and social interaction with friends
- Offer advice on how to interact socially or build friendships; at this age, your child is more open to adult feedback than he or she was in the previous year or will be years to come
- Spend one-on-one time with your child for at least 30 minutes each week, allowing your child to choose the activity

- Organize consistent family times, such as game nights or weekend outings
- Engage as a participant in video games that your child enjoys, but also allow your child time with friends without your involvement
- Monitor social media, making sure that you are "friends" with your child on each social media outlet
- Encourage your child's desires to organize and classify, and talk with him or her about his or her interests
- Encourage your child to interact with people who are culturally different from him or her

When to Seek Help

- Your child's behavior or abilities seem significantly different from those of other children his or her age
- Your child shows disinterest in social communication or interaction with peers
- Your child is moody and sullen
- Your child demonstrates a lack of appropriate social skills
- Your child becomes overwhelmed with social pressures or interactions
- Your child experiences severe or prolonged anxiety or sadness
- You need parenting support to address concerns or issues related to discipline
- Your child experiences a significant change or traumatic experience, including loss, disruption in the home or family environment, abuse, or a medical emergency
- You frequently feel disconnected and stressed in your relationship with your child
- Your child demonstrates highly aggressive behavior toward you or others

11

Brain & Cognitive Development

- Has increased processing speed
- Has increased deductive reasoning skills
- May have the ability to manipulate information mentally, but still largely has concrete and logical thinking
- Starts to reason logically about things that he or she cannot see or touch
- Prefers to learn new skills rather than practice old ones
- Likes to discuss ideas logically and practice reasoning
- Begins to take others' perspectives
- Takes on increasingly challenging academic work

Physical Development

- Gross motor skills continue to improve with precision and accuracy
- Experiences more frequent illnesses; may complain of headaches
- Is restless and likes to move
- Prefers team sports, but may discontinue sports at this age if he or she does not feel competent
- Has yet to hit a growth spurt (boys); varies widely in terms of physical growth (girls)
- Tends to be self-conscious about body changes (girls)

Emotional Development

- Is moody and unpredictable
- Is more internally focused and self-involved
- Has a growing sense of self that is based on internal evaluation
- Is at odds with himself and herself and his or her environment
- Has a strong sense of fairness
- Is overly sensitive
- Is prideful and sensitive to public correction
- Is easily frustrated
- Challenges or questions rules

Relationship & Social Development

- Is concerned with social belonging
- Defines his or her identity and values mostly by peer group
- Has a wider variety of potential friends
- Enjoys working in collaborative groups
- Is argumentative and can be cruel to peers
- Can be verbally and physically aggressive (mostly limited to the home environment)
- Tends to challenge parents, teachers, and other adults
- Is aware of racial/ethnic identity and uses racial/ethnic terms to define himself or herself
- Commonly has peers of the same gender/racial/ethnic/cultural background
- Is interested in sexual acts and sexual relationships
- May experience same-sex attractions

Normal Challenges at 11

Eleven-year-olds often have behaviors that parents find challenging or concerning, but which are a normal part of development, such as:

- Arguing with and opposing adults
- Unpredictable moods
- Social problems with belonging, cliques, and bullying
- Less interest in skill-based activities if they do not feel competent; dropping out of activities
- High sensitivity to being corrected in front of peers or in public

Tips for Parents & Caregivers

- Spend one-on-one time with your child for at least 30 minutes each week, allowing your child to choose the activity
- Organize consistent family times, such as game nights or weekend outings
- Provide opportunities for group activities and social interaction with friends
- Keep in touch with what is happening with peer relationships through listening and observing
- Engage as a participant in video games that your child enjoys, but also allow your child time with friends without your involvement

- Monitor social media and make sure you are "friends" with your child on each social media outlet
- Listen and respond openly if your child wants to discuss difficult topics such as prejudice, sex, or peer relationships – and don't try to fix the problem if not asked to do so
- Respect your child's growing opinions and views of the world
- Encourage your child to interact with people who are culturally different from him or her
- If your child has a cellphone, text him or her throughout the week with fun texts
- Allow your child to participate in family decision making
- Set limits and consistent consequences when your child is disrespectful, but ensure you have given him or her the opportunity to express his or her discontent with your decisions

When to Seek Help

- Your child's behavior or abilities seem significantly different from those of other children his or her age
- Your child is bullying other children or is having difficulty responding to a bully
- Your child's mood and opposition are interfering with his or her daily functioning
- You are having difficulty knowing how to support your child's growing independence and autonomy, while helping him or her to stay within appropriate bounds
- Your child experiences severe or prolonged anxiety or sadness
- You need parenting support to address concerns or issues related to discipline
- Your child experiences a significant change or traumatic experience, including loss, disruption in the home or family environment, abuse, or a medical emergency
- You frequently feel disconnected and stressed in your relationship with your child
- Your child demonstrates highly aggressive behavior toward you or others

12

Brain & Cognitive Development

- Onset of puberty brings vigorous brain activity
- Craves brain stimulation and novelty, but can easily become overwhelmed
- Limited executive functioning leads to impulsive actions
- Has a developing ability for abstract thinking; is able to focus on patterns and possibilities
- Thinks with less dualism; sees "gray" areas
- Tends to be unmotivated to spend time on homework

Physical Development

- Has almost completed physical maturation (girls); is just starting to manifest physical maturation (boys)
- Is sensitive to body changes and differences among peers
- Commonly experiences "growing pains" caused by physical maturation
- May change sleep patterns, staying up later at night and rising later in morning
- Needs substantial amounts of food, sleep, and exercise
- Needs approximately 10 hours of sleep a night
- By this age, most boys and girls have the physical maturity to sexually reproduce
- Because of variation in growth, some boys will be significantly more advanced and powerful in physical activity than others

Emotional Development

- Is enthusiastic
- Is unpredictable and hard to read
- Desires to make meaningful contributions
- Is developing a stronger sense of self; presents as more secure
- May experiment with different ways of being or acting

- May not verbally share his or her emotions with family members, but try to work through strong feelings himself or herself
- Is overly sensitive about appearance and performance

Relationship & Social Development

- Spends more time socializing with peers and less with family
- Seeks out peers as primary source of support
- Values norms of peers rather than family
- Will alter behavior to fit in with group
- Strives to be equal to, rather than better than, peers
- Is less likely to agree with parents or teachers
- Desires to discuss rules and influence decision making
- May begin to engage in gossiping
- Show more intimacy, as well as discord, in his or her peer relationships (girls)
- Is aware of racial/ethnic identity and uses racial/ethnic terms to define himself or herself
- May cling to group norms of prejudice
- May be curious about sex and engage in experimental sexual behavior with opposite- and same-sex partners
- May become aware of being attracted to members of the same sex

Normal Challenges at 12

Twelve-year-olds often have behaviors that parents find challenging or concerning, but which are a normal part of development, such as:

- Lacking motivation to do schoolwork if not interested in subject
- Challenging rules and authority figures
- A growing interest in sex and romantic relationships
- Seeking out peers instead of parents for advice
- Changing personal characteristics or interests to fit in with peers
- Excessive focus on social matters
- Excluding some peers to fit in with others
- Demands to be treated and respected like an adult

Tips for Parents & Caregivers

- Spend one-on-one time with your child doing things that you both enjoy
- Organize consistent family times, such as game nights or weekend outings
- Provide opportunities for group activities and social interaction with friends
- Keep in touch with what is happening with peer relationships through listening and observing
- Engage as a participant in video games that your child enjoys, but also allow your child time with friends without your involvement
- Monitor social media and make sure you are "friends" with your child on each social media outlet
- Listen and respond openly if your child wants to discuss difficult topics such as prejudice, sex, or peer relationships – and don't try to fix a problem if not asked to do so
- Talk openly, yet appropriately, about sex and relationships to send the message that your child can talk with you whenever he or she has questions
- Respect your child's growing opinions and views of the world
- Encourage your child to interact with people who are culturally different from him or her
- If your child has a cellphone, text him or her throughout the week with fun texts
- Allow your child to participate in family decision making
- Set limits and consistent consequences when your child is disrespectful, but ensure that you have given him or her the opportunity to provide feedback about your decisions
- Ensure that your child is getting enough sleep, food, and exercise

When to Seek Help

- Your child's behavior or abilities seem significantly different from those of other children his or her age
- Your child is bullying other children or is having difficulty responding to a bully
- Your child shows disinterest in developing friendships
- Your child becomes overwhelmed with social pressures, expectations, and skills
- You are having difficulty knowing how to support your child's growing independence and autonomy, while helping him or her to stay within appropriate bounds
- Your child experiences severe or prolonged anxiety or sadness
- You need parenting support to address concerns or issues related to discipline
- Your child experiences a significant change or traumatic experience, including loss, disruption in the home or family environment, abuse, or a medical emergency
- You frequently feel disconnected and stressed in your relationship with your child
- Your child demonstrates highly aggressive behavior toward you or others

Index

Made in the USA
Las Vegas, NV
07 December 2022